THE GOD EXPERIENCE

THE CARDINAL BEA LECTURES

VOLUME II

THE GOD EXPERIENCE

Essays in Hope

Edited by
Joseph P. Whelan, S.J.

NEWMAN PRESS
New York / Paramus / Toronto

CONTENTS

PART TWO

FAITH AND HOPE IN THE FUTURE

For Christopher

PREFACE

This volume collects the third and fourth series of lectures delivered during the years 1968-1970 in the Cardinal Bea Institute of Spirituality, formerly of Fordham University and now at Woodstock College in New York. The Bea Lectures, now in their fifth year, represent a continuing exploration of the larger theme which in part served to inaugurate the Institute itself six years ago and which still occupies and even vexes both theological thought and pastoral practice: the problem of atheism, of belief and unbelief as experienced at once without and within the Christian community.

In 1966 this general theme was specified as "The Phenomenon of Unbelief," while in 1967 inquiry centered on "The Contemporary Problem of God." These two series were edited for publication by Christopher F. Mooney, S.J., former director of the Bea Institute, as *The Presence and Absence of God* (New York: Fordham University Press, 1969). Former Bea lecturers have included Robert O. Johann, James M. Gustafson, Christopher F. Mooney, Langdon B. Gilkey, John Courtney Murray, Leslie Dewart, Robert McAfee Brown, Henri Bouillard, John Coleman Bennett, and Bernard Lonergan.

In keeping with the general problematic which the Bea Institute seeks to address, the lectures show a consistent interest in probing the immediate content, context and structure of both biblical and contemporary religious experience where this experience takes flesh as personal and corporate commitment and as doctrine in the lives of confessedly religious individuals and of ecclesial communities. Nevertheless, there is an equally urgent curiosity about secular man and about the larger political society which significantly shapes the sensibilities of non-believer and believer alike.

The present collection initially asks about man's awareness of transcendence. It does so through a progressive inquiry into those secular and religious challenges and opportunities afforded to an authentic God experience by such phenomena as our present social-political situation, the death-of-God movement, recent interest in Buddhism, man's historical consciousness, etc. Contributors to this theme include: Michael Novak, Julian Hartt, Gabriel Vahanian, Raymond Panikkar, E. L. Mascall, Gregory Baum.

A second section of the present volume strives to articulate and to evaluate modern man's religious and secular hope—his *hope* rather more than his hopes—as this gets enlightened, criticized or threatened by the evidence of the New Testament theologies, Marxist and more recent revolutionary philosophy, the phenomenon of prophecy, etc. Writing on this theme of hope are: Piet Fransen, S.J., Daniel Day Williams, David Stanley, S.J., Louis Dupré, George Lindbeck, Avery Dulles, S.J.

As was the case with the first volume of Bea Lectures (*The Presence and Absence of God,* p. x), the effort once again is to keep the *complexity* of man's adventure in focus: "At times the primary concern of the lecturer is for the religious experience itself, at times for the mode by which this experience is conceptualized. In each case too there is an effort to take seriously the outlook of the unbeliever, for there is general agreement that unbelief is itself a witness that the meaning of God is a problem for the atheist as well, and that his testimony must challenge the Christian to a fuller articulation of his own commitment."

It remains for me here to thank the lecturers themselves for the honor they do the Bea Institute. My gratitude also goes to Mrs. Helen Zeccola, secretary of the Institute, for so many kindnesses, and to Mrs. Lewis Watters, former secretary to the President of Woodstock College. Further, I wish to acknowledge Mr. John Polk, S.J., who assisted me in preparing the manuscript. I want to thank too President John H. Fischer, Teachers College, Columbia University, for the hospitable home he has given to the Bea Lectures in the Horace Mann Auditorium. Finally, I wish to offer grateful and affectionate thanks to Rev. Christopher F. Mooney, S.J., founder and former director of the Institute, who conceived and planned these lectures which I now have the pleasure of offering to a larger public.

Joseph P. Whelan, S.J.
Woodstock College

Part One

The Awareness of God

Michael Novak

The Unawareness of God

M ost of the people I live among every day are unaware of God. It is not so much that they are repulsed by the notion of God (although many are); it is, rather, that they can think of no single way in which belief in God might enrich their lives. "Our hearts are restless, Lord," St. Augustine prayed, "until they rest in thee." His view is not verified in many of the people I work with. The empirical fact of their unawareness and difference has obliged me, over the past decade, to account for my own attitude toward God carefully, apart from conventional ways of expressing it.

A note on method may not be amiss. Bernard Lonergan has recently written: "Just as in religious living 'a man who is unspiritual refuses what belongs to the Spirit of God; it is folly to him; he cannot grasp it' (1 Cor 2:14), so in theological reflection on religious living there have to be distinguished the horizons within which religious doctrines can or cannot be apprehended; and this distinction is foundational." [1] For some time now, I have been methodically engaged in those new fields of specialization which Lonergan has designated dialectics, foundations, and communications. [2] These are areas in which, because of their concreteness and because of the attention to the imagination, to the sensibilities, and to unspoken assumptions which they require, the laborers are few. The present essay is chiefly foundational, although insofar as it contrasts the standpoint of the believer and the atheist it is dialectical. Finally, here as elsewhere, I work in the theological phase which Lonergan calls *in oratione recta*, aimed directly at the horizon of our own time, rather than in the phase which he calls *in oratione obliqua*, directed to recounting what other theologians and the giants of the past have said.

I

Recently in a law-abiding neighborhood several high school youths placed a NO PARKING sign along a residential street. The sign posed a dilemma for car owners as they returned from work. Who put the sign there? Was its authority legitimate? Many of the traditional signs of God's presence invite similar doubts today. The authority of the generations, of traditional experience and customary interpretation, has been shaken. Granted that I sometimes feel as though I am in the presence of God, or that there might be a God, are such feelings to be trusted? Or are they a sign that I am turning to God as a crutch in my emptiness, a *deus ex machina* in my confusion of feelings, an illusory strength in my weakness? Is my lifelong awareness of God merely an arbitrary sentiment to which my family acculturated me?

Many persons, even among those in the churches, find it impossible to believe in God. The customary experiences and ways of perceiving which in the past led to belief in God have been altered, or have lost their direct and spontaneous power. Many men, consequently, no longer have access to God. They are, simply, unaware of God. Their unawareness does not mean that God does not exist; *only that he does not exist effectively for them*. But that meaning is sufficiently powerful for each person it affects.

This unawareness is of three kinds: an unawareness of experience, an unawareness of interpretation, an unawareness of decision.

II

The key experiences through which God becomes real to people are, in our society, systematically blocked; many do not have them. Since, then, such persons are not aware of God in their concrete experience, they must fall back upon authority, or habit, or social conformity. In their experience there is no analog for God at all. The experiences in question are those of freedom, honesty, community, courage. Let us call these experiences "t" experiences; they are the chief experiences of transcendence in our daily lives. Each of them leads us beyond any identifiable part of our selves, and beyond our present state of development. Each pushes our horizon and our identity into fresh territory. It is in this sense that the word "transcendent" applies to them. In each such experience more than our self, or any part of our self, seems to be operative. People who lack such experiences cannot understand the bearing of talk about God. People who have such experiences often feel inclined to express themselves in religious language, even if they are uncertain what they think about God.

1. Despite the rhetoric of freedom in the United States, it does not appear that many Americans frequently make significant acts of freedom. We are, by and large, a very highly socialized people, sentimental, gregarious, taking our signals from groups of peers. Young people commonly find their lives, by tacit and gentle channelling, mapped out in advance: "Work hard, compete, keep your nose clean, establish yourself." Faced with unwanted service in the army in a war of which they do not approve, many find it tolerable to live in bad faith.[3] "I disapprove of the war and the military life, but I have no alternative." But there are alternatives: jail, exile. If Americans are not taught to accept the risks and terrors of freedom, how can they come to know the mystery in which God dwells?

Freedom in the United States too often reduces to a consumer's freedom: to use Crest rather than Ipana, to take Social Science 108 instead of Political Science 202, to work for J & L instead of for LTV, to drive a Maribou rather than a Mustang, to live in Rosewood rather than in Rosemont. Americans have external freedoms, but these are not the freedoms of self-transcendence. The freedom which makes men wonder about their own identity is that which shakes their identity to its core, terrifies them, makes demands on them, draws them into the pit of nothingness in order to confront them: "Now choose." For many, the first philosophical problem is that of suicide. Why do anything at all? Why live? Freedom is creation out of nothingness: an act of self-affirmation, for no particular reason, out of no necessity, "because I *want* to." It is in exercising such freedom, brooding over an inner chaos, that man acts in the image of the God spoken of in the myth of Genesis.

Most of our young people, however, grow up in a totally man-made environment, designed to be as secure for them as possible, and to eliminate hunger, passion, chaos, ignorance, disease, conflict, despair. They are given to imagine that as Americans and children of God, they have a constitutional duty to be happy. It is un-American to feel despair. They try, for as long as they can, to repress the sickness, rage, and bitterness hidden in their hearts; they try to smile often and be affable in the normal American way. What would mass-produced patriots know about the annihilating mysteries of God? Their God is as American as cherry pie; he smiles on crew cut hair, moccasins, and lots of personality.

2. Sincerity, Sartre tells us, is ontologically impossible.[4] Whatever it is in myself that I am trying to be sincere *to* lies in the past and at the moment of sincerity no longer is my present. Each second is fresh, a new opportunity for freedom. To be honest is to create oneself anew. In monastic life, too, one learns to live "from moment to moment," totally abandoned into the hands of God (i.e., into darkness and obscurity, for one feels, especially in moments of darkest trial, no support from anything at all). In America, by contrast, countless networks of distraction con-

stantly give one roles, cues, purposes, lines to speak. The American way of life (not unlike other ways of life) is a systematic contrivance designed to cover over our nothingness. Think of how many persons in the United States are paid to cover over our terror with distraction and smooth assurance: radio announcers, television personalities, public relations personnel, stewardesses on airlines, receptionists, teachers (speaking objectively, not for themselves but for their fields), preachers (speaking impersonally, not for themselves but for God, church, tradition), salesmen, hucksters, reporters (as Daniel Boorstin shows, reporting not events but news they themselves have created through telephone calls, interviews, press conferences, mimeographed handouts, planned "leaks," demonstrations for their benefit [5]), and the rest. We live in a land of images not of experiences. Nearly everything we see, handle, touch, hear is artificial, fake, pretend. Even our personalities, we find, have been shaped by social images, propaganda, reinforcement, inhibition.

Who am I? What shall I become? What identity has been handed me? Which identity do I wish to invent for myself, having discovered what resources I can call my own? These are questions for honesty. They arise only when one has ceased living by a borrowed identity. How many Americans (human beings) are like children placed on roller skates and given a push down the corridor of their life: Their life chosen by others? A great many Americans have feelings of anger, rage, fear, vulnerability, weakness, which they do not dare allow themselves to utter: such feelings do not fit the self-image they wish to maintain. Since such a self-image is not true to themselves but imposed upon themselves, like an idol of clay, how—so long as they are content with an idol—can they stand before the darkness in which the true God resides? Those who know the darkness concerning themselves which arises from a commitment to unceasing honesty begin to understand what is meant by speaking of a God whom no man has seen. For when one is being honest, to what in oneself is one being honest? There is no feeling, sound, sight, image, perception, concept in oneself which is not subject to questioning. There is no part of oneself which escapes the scrutiny of honesty. Thus honesty leads us to suspect that, in being honest, we do not belong only to ourselves but are participating in some other. Honesty is a peculiar experience. However we are to conceptualize it, it leaves us wondering about ourselves, voyageurs of the night. The language of the mystics gains in plausibility, even if one decides to remain an atheist.

3. Many Americans (human beings) hardly dare to voice all the stray fantasies, feelings, impulses, instincts that course through them, sometimes just below the limina of consciousness, sometimes in bursts of emotion or daydreaming, sometimes in the dreams of the night. For if a young person told his parents of his murderous, sexual, insane impulses wouldn't they think something was wrong with him? If a young girl voiced every instinct, fantasy, rage she dimly felt, wouldn't people be ashamed of her? If a person let everything buried within come to light, wouldn't that person himself (herself) think he (she) was going mad? The underground life of each person is forced by social convention and private fear to remain underground. The result is that in their interpersonal dealings persons are not wholly present to one another. They do not present their underground life along with their handshake and affable smile; they do not look beneath the handshake and affable smile of the other. Masks.

It is as if Americans thought of themselves as minds, psyches imprisoned within skins, in such a way that others should deal with the external mask, and they with the other's mask, and that "communication" would be limited to occasional "breakthroughs." Entering a room for a cocktail party or a mixer, the American seems to imagine himself as an atomic individual, living and breathing in secret behind his mask, hoping that in one way or another his psyche will be able to come up from "inside" and cross the no-man's-land of silence "outside" and then manage to break "inside" some other isolated psyche. The problem is "community." The starting place is imagined to be individual isolation. (For most people in human history, the images appear to be reversed: men imagine themselves to be inextricably communal, and must struggle to attain individuality. Karl Jaspers suggests that Socrates was the first man in human history to distinguish himself from the community; and yet even Socrates imagined that the city had every right to command his exile and death.)

In Christian theology God, the Really Real, is spoken of as Trinity. God is community. What is most like God is community. What is most *real* about our experience is community. What is most like God in our experience is community. The American is likely to find this Christian affirmation foreign to his own ¬?ontaneous experience. What seems most real to Americans is the experience of the Marlboro man, the cowboy, the loner. Even American gregariousness is lonely. (Loneliness is an Anglo-Saxon trait, not solely American. "All the lonely people!" the Beatles sing. They include "Father MacKenzie.")

Consequently, many Americans first find language about God plausible when, for the first time, the power of the experience of community finally reaches their consciousness and re-orients their attitude to the world. I have found, in a study of some one thousand papers written for me at Stanford, Carleton, and Old Westbury, that students who have not broken out of their feeling of isolation tend to react to language about God as if it described an alien, threatening other. Students who had had a powerful (often recent, occasionally habitual) experience of community tended to be sympathetic to language about God, even though they might still consider themselves atheists. I attribute this to the fact that those who had experienced community could no longer interpret reality chiefly in pragmatic, functional terms. Reality began for them to demand a new standpoint, a new method, a new way of perceiving and understanding. According to this new standpoint, they no longer merely "looked at" the world, as more or less objective and objectifying observers. Now they "felt their way into" it and into others. "Do you *hear* me?" "A *taste* of joy and beauty." The metaphors for their relationship to the world, to others, and to themselves moved from metaphors of the eye, to those of touch, taste and hearing. These latter metaphors are pre-eminently personal; those of the eye are distancing, objectifying, scientific.

The point is not that one approaches God through touch, taste, hearing. It is that one approaches him through community. The experience of community disrupts a habit of mind that is pragmatic, functional, objective, isolated, atomic. It forces one to adopt a fresh sense of reality. The tyranny of the eye over our metaphors for knowing is broken.

It should be added that it is, not infrequently, sexual inter-course, licit or illicit, which such students pointed to as their teacher of a new way of perceiving others. Many proved incapa-ble of merely using the other as a means, even when that had been their first, spontaneous motivation. To treat others as ends in themselves, with reverence and honesty, is to learn what a becoming human attitude toward God might be like. If one takes such community as the most precious part of one's experi-ence, as one's token of what is really real in the "blooming, buzzing confusion" of human experience, one has a tangible, vivid, powerful analog for speech about God. The ancient anti-phon runs often through one's ears: "Where there is charity and love there Christ is." (Not all those among sexually "liberated" young people reverence the other as an end; in young love there is also conformity, vulnerability, deception, betrayal, and despair.)

Finally, community brings into human experience the sense of mutual creation. One person's praise, approval, love makes the other break forth in abilities he (she) did not know he (she) had—perhaps did not have, would not ever have had. One person's relentless criticism, honesty, different sense of reality calls another's attention to self-deceptions, fraudulence, inauthenticity he (she) might never have noticed in himself (herself). Human beings bring one another to and through the aesthetic, moral, religious stages (Kierkegaard). They mutually create each other's humanity. We are a community first, and our maturity lies in expanding our connectedness to the human community. It does not lie (as in the dominant Anglo-American myth) in never needing others, never showing hurt, in being a rugged and unique and stoical individual: cool, unflappable, independent. The counter-paradox is that unless one knows solitude, independence, and terror, and can survive these alone, one's quest for community tends to be instrumentalist and false. Those who *need* community, who want it as a solution to their anguish, commonly render themselves incapable of it. Sensitivity sessions may lead only to self-indulgence, not to conversion and new life. Solitude and community are not opposites, but correlatives, like left foot and right. To ascend Mt. Carmel one takes one step, then the other, again and again.

4. Without courage, neither freedom, nor honesty, nor community can be pursued. Men fear nothing so much as liberty, for liberty includes the risk of being wrong, of hurting oneself or others, of bearing responsibility for destroying one's whole life. It is easier to be safe, to follow rules, to do what others expect, than to risk striking out on one's own—and perhaps being wrong. Each man loves certain illusions, has favorite evasions, projects a beloved self-image, which even his friends soon learn to be sensitive to, not to crush, occasionally to flatter, often to lament. Friends do not usually demand of us too much reality; they "take us as we are" rather than insist on rigorous, painful honesty. In a word, men are not noteworthy for courage sufficient to be entirely honest. There are not, Pascal said, three honest men in a century. There are none. And without the courage to risk rejection, misunderstanding, and deep vulnerability, one can scarcely enjoy community. It is safer behind our barriers. That is why we keep barriers.

When does courage come? How does it happen that sometimes we are willing to risk everything we have and are? Sometimes it is plain that the courage which moves us does not come from ourselves; at least, we can identify no source in ourselves whence it comes. Tillich: "The courage to accept despair." At one moment it is not there, when suddenly, as required, it appears. In advance we rack our minds looking for ways to strengthen ourselves; we seem to lack the required will. And yet it comes. The old self, so beloved, dies. Courage is an often renewed evidence of our capacity to transcend what we just were, what we are. It seems to suggest that, in some way, our true identity (what we *will be*) lies up ahead, calling to us, drawing us. We do not know what it is, what it will demand. It is no projection of ours. Characteristically, it calls us in directions we would never have chosen for ourselves, had never imagined—quite the opposite: often it leads us in precisely the direction we are certain we would never have to go. (A young man, in love with his nation, finds himself convicted by that nation, incarcerated in a federal prison for five precious years, a felon.)

III

The experiences of freedom, honesty, community, courage—which are not as frequent as the occurrence of the words upon our lips, and yet are daily experiences, ordinary experiences, precious and rare among the day's demands—are of a more-than-I. They are the symbolic forms (Cassirer) in which the transcendent is immanent in our experience. They are as close to the life of God as human beings get. They are the experiential ground of all language about God. Each of them places the I under a total judgment, exempting no aspect, moment, or part of the I. The one who experiences them recognizes them both as his own experiences, belonging to him, and yet leading him beyond himself, attributable to no part of himself. At the very least, these experiences lead even the atheist to feel at moments *as if* he might be participating in the life of an other than he. Because of social, political, and personal uses of the word, concept, and institutions of "God," the atheist may choose not to interpret these experiences by means of religious language. But they also require more than a pragmatic, functional, mechanistic language. They involve man in wonderment about himself. They lead him to reverence, to silence, to quiet fidelity, to joy, often to compassion and gentleness with others. They are the supremely humanizing experiences. Without them, language about God has nothing to illuminate in human experience; it has no experiential base. If attachment to God—in language, interpretation, ritual, aspiration, struggle—does not mean an increase in experiences of freedom, honesty, community, courage, why should any man desire such attachment? If there were no such experiences, language about God would not arise, would not attract, would have no worthy meaning. (Freud: *Future of an Illusion*.)

It is open to the atheist, of course, to notice that these experiences are strictly human experiences, nothing more. But what does it mean to be "human"? These experiences indicate that man is not wholly in conscious possession of himself; he is not master of his own depths. He is drawn beyond everything he knows about himself. Moreover, sensitive reflection on these experiences often suggests—never compels—the recognition that human life is a participation (Plato's word) in some other life, in some Other's life. There sometimes arises a strange presentiment, an oblique perception, that one is being lived in, dwelt in, by Another. It arises in those modalities we have here called freedom, honesty, community, courage. It arises often in connection with nature: a feeling of community not only with others but with one's own body, with mountains, trees, ocean, a wooded path, even a city street at twilight, a throughway as streams of red tail-lights flow into the distance. Consciousness plays its own tricks, has its own mysteries, eludes our hardest, most exact theories.

I would not like to push the evidence further than it goes. I am sufficiently diffident about my own interpretation not to wish to force it upon any atheist. But, unless I am seriously mistaken, he knows already what I speak of, is sometimes tempted by it, but has his own strong reasons for not contributing to the harm, as he sees it, brought into the world by religious language and the uses to which it is put. I am content to receive from him a recognition of the plausibility of the interpretation which I give to these experiences, a concession that these experiences bring him, too, to wonderment about the meaning of man.

For what shall we say about man—what strange animal is he in this silent, absurd world—if he can be free, honest, mutually creative, courageous? A man stands alone, in solitude, and is one with others. He finds the beauty of understanding, loving, acting, powerfully attractive; to that beauty, many commit themselves. The theist wishes to interpret these experiences by saying: When men live in freedom, honesty, community, courage, they are living the life of God, participating in "the Really Real," in touch with the source and center of all things, one with everything. The atheist replies: "Why bring God into it at all? Above all, do not bring the church into it! The oceanic feeling you speak of is childlike and immature, a regression.[6] It is adult to distinguish and to perceive the separateness of things." The theist replies that the experiences of freedom, honesty, community and courage are not experiences of separateness. That is the trouble. Without these experiences, the analytic, functional, mechanical interpretations make sense. But once one has had these experiences, such theories are flat, thin, incredible. The world is one, textured, interrelated. To sense that, with reverence, is surely not counter to science but supportive of it. To say "Thou" to the universe is not to take it out of the domain of science, but to support the domain of science with another, fuller one. It is also to bring all one's experiences, not only one's science, into intelligent consciousness.

In this way, God is not imagined as another object, or even as a person (on the model of human persons). Rather, a man's own experiences of freedom, honesty, community, and courage lead him to imagine that a man who places the weight of his life behind such experiences places his weight truly: i.e., does what is most real, central, creative, productive, evolutionary in this

world. The world is the sort of place in which such a commitment is an act of beauty and integrity. It is its own fruit, not to be
judged instrumentally but in and for itself, like a work of art. To
live in such a way is to be real, is beautiful. Being and beauty
are convertible.

In such an act we do not "see" God. But following the line of
intentionality which propels acts of freedom, honesty, community
and courage, our reflections are led like arrows pointing in the
direction of what we now take God to be. The arrows fall short.
But we take God to be more like human freedom, honesty, community, and courage than like anything else in our experience.
We do not have to have the category of object or person in our
minds when we think of God. We can shatter such categories,
recognizing their inadequacy. We do not see God, do not have
a satisfactory category. We can only look in a direction; get a certain feel; taste and see; listen in the silence. Negatively, we have
protection enough to turn aside from fanaticism and to reject
idols. Positively, we do not penetrate the mystery and stand,
seeing, before God. Meanwhile, we remain faithful to our humanity; we do not falsify freedom, honesty, community, courage. What keeps these streams strong and pure is of God; what
sullies them is not. We wait.

In this interpretation, there is sufficient guidance both to live
by and to reflect by—although the reflection, following a defined direction, comes at last to "a place where no one appears"
(St. John of the Cross), an empty spot, a darkness. The darkness encountered by the serious believer is identical with that
encountered by the serious non-believer. But the former does
not fear to fall upon his knees. The latter has his own, other
forms of reverence.

John Dewey has generously suggested, from his point of view,
that if what we mean by God is a projection of human ideals,
then such a God is the object of our common faith. What I
intend, however, is significantly stronger than that. It is true
that what we know experientially about God we know from our
own best operations, as described above. (It is true, inciden-

tally, even for those conservative theologians who derive their sense that God is truth, love, beauty, Father, etc., from other than experiential sources. How do they know what such names mean apart from their own human experience? "He who loves poorly knows God poorly." Knowledge of self and knowledge of God advance in tandem.)

Our reflections about the life of God are led by our experience of what we value most in our own life. But I do not think of God merely as a fiction projected to serve as symbol for the fulfill-ment of our own ideals, or even as an otherworldly model of what we would be like if we could. Quite the contrary. God is experienced, I wish to say, as a life within which our lives draw nourishment for the operations we most value. He is the source of the values that move us, and of our movement toward those values. He is far more than a name pinned onto those values. Dewey wishes to celebrate man and man alone. My experience compels me to celebrate man and God (in whom man lives) as well.

The issue between Dewey and myself is not easy to settle by appeal to one fact or other. It is, rather, chiefly a question of standpoint, horizon, and sense of reality. According to Dewey's sense of things, we fix our eyes upon the concrete, vivid, ex-periential things that man does, and upon that dynamism that propels man's agency toward the future. To fix one's gaze upon God would result in the image of an alienating, heteronomous, falsifying other; and it would distract our attention, fruitlessly, from those operations that man can and should perform, if he is to satisfy his own idealistic, dynamic nature. I wish to go with Dewey a long way down that road. I begin with human experi-ence, and with those same dynamic, ideal-fulfilling operations he mentions. The human operations to which he draws attention, I only wish to add, are richer, more wonder-provoking, more meaningful than he notes.

It is not only the case that t-experiences draw us toward the future, toward our own ideals. It is also the case that we experi-ence them as enveloping us, as not belonging entirely to us, as arising from sources within us which can be identified with no single part of ourselves, as putting every part of ourselves under judgment. To this, the atheist (imagine Dewey, or Freud, or Anthony Flew) may reply: "Well *I* don't experience them so." To which the rejoinder is: "Alter your expectations and your way of approaching your own experience. Open yourself to the possibility. The fruitfulness of so doing—for the richer exercise of the very operations in question—will become apparent to you." The empirical test lies in doing. Taste and see.

But the test can also be, though less adequately, stated in words. To imagine that my own freedom is a participation in God's freedom, my honesty a participation in his, my community and courage the same, is to shift the character of my image of myself, my relationship to the world, my relationship to others. To imagine my life as a participation in the life of God is to see it as participating in all life. It is to have a sense of oneness, of stillness, of vitality, of quiet, humble charity (such as Dostoevski wrote of). It is to recognize that I am not obliged to imagine the universe in functional, objectifying, more or less mechanistic terms, such that I imagine myself to be merely a part of the world contiguous to other parts and at best a functional part in a dynamic mechanism. It is to give my experience of the world a more *internal* cast than that: The same life courses through me as through all else, the differentiated and various life of the source of freedom, honesty, community, courage, in respect to whom all things are closer or further in similarity.

Critiques of mechanism, I should here add, are often poorly aimed. As a theory, mechanism holds that all psychic events have a physiological base, and that if we follow the rigorous methods employed so far in the natural sciences we will have a more powerful tool for understanding and directing psychic events than any available tool. It is a mistake to try to fault mechanistic theory on the score of inconsistency, by posing counter examples which it does not yet explain. E.g., "If John is depressed, why don't you send him to a physiologist? Why to a psychoanalyst?" At the present state of our knowledge, psychoanalysis, although it is clearly an inefficient and fallible tool, provides more immediate help than physiology. But mechanism as a theory—or, perhaps, as a project—is not thereby impugned. Slow, quiet work, the theory holds, will inexorably diminish the gap between promise and performance.

A more telling criticism of mechanism follows the lines laid down by Alfred Schutz.[7] The key difference between the use of mechanism in the natural sciences and in the human sciences is that, in the latter, scientific theory must also account for the ways in which human action has meaning for its human participants. Physical laws "mean" nothing to atoms, neutrons, molecules. Laws concerning the behavior of men must account for the "meanings" they bring to their actions. For such "meanings" affect the nature, scope, intensity, and direction of action. In this respect, mechanism may be true but insufficient. Every psychic event may have a physiological basis; but it is not certain that that basis has only one psychic expression.

A second line of criticism, also enunciated by Schutz, is that mechanism is itself a social phenomenon. The relevant and even urgent methodological question is *not,* "Is any science of human behavior possible apart from the rigorous prosecution of the mechanistic hypothesis?" but rather: "How is any human science possible?" That is, what is it about the way we have of experiencing, perceiving, thinking about, and inquiring into the *Lebenswelt* in which we find ourselves that makes possible the construction of those abstract models and principles of verification which constitute the language and power of science? The language of science is clearly not the language of common sense. How, then, does one grow from the other? Is science dependent on, parasitic on, or self-contained and totally independent of ordinary social experience?

The predictive power of common sense is impressive. When I drop a letter into the mail box I am entitled to a rather high degree of certainty that it will reach its addressee. The theory of mechanism, in a word, appears to be but one among many species of social knowledge. It is a peculiarly neat and powerful

tool. One need not deny its extraordinary power in accomplishing its chosen task in order to want to attempt other tasks, including the task of accounting in a rigorous, testable way for
the various ways in which action has "meaning" to the participants in the action. To account for the way human behavior
appears to an objective observer, and even for the way in which
it is physiologically based is highly useful. To account, as well,
for the ways such behavior has "meaning" for various participants is also useful, and may be done with equal (but different)
objectivity.

Should mechanism turn out to be true, it would verify the
extent to which man's body and psyche are one; it would ground
a sort of religious mysticism. "You are what you eat." "Mind is
rooted in earth." Religious people need not be afraid of the
mechanistic theory. But even when the work of that theory
has been accomplished, many will still be more interested in the
way experience appears to its subject than in the way it appears
to a physiologist. And many are prepared to argue,[8] even now,
that, although mechanism may be true on one level, still, the
human being is so complex that a series of higher viewpoints—
each emergent from, subsuming, and integrating its predecessor
from above—is required for a complete and satisfactory interpretation of man. In this view, mechanism takes up a true, important, but partial standpoint by which to account for human action. There no doubt is a physiological base for every psychic
event. But the differentiations in psychic events must also be
accounted for from successive other viewpoints as well.

Insofar as science is commensurate with a sense of reverence,
a feeling of unity, even a penetrating love, the image of self of
which I speak does not run counter to science. It forms a context within which science plays a powerful, instrumentalist role.
One need not deny instrumentalism, any more than one needs to
deny mechanism, in order to recognize that to think of man
merely in terms of instruments and purposes does not do justice
to his experience of freedom, honesty, community or courage.
The metaphors "instrument," and even "ends," "goals," and "pur-

poses," are finally too alienating. They too mechanically separate things from one another, subordinate things to one another,
and feed the lust for domination, control, manipulation.

The metaphor "participation," by contrast, induces reverence
without demanding that one close one's eyes. It requires a reverence which is a ceaseless questioning, a reverence which rein-
forces and is reinforced by the exercise of relentless honesty.
It demands a reverence whose sole task is to remind a man that
whatever he studies in the world is united to himself, and that
when he is acting in freedom, honesty, community, courage he
acts in accord with what is central, vital, propelling not only in
himself but in the universe. It is a reverence which unmasks
mechanism as an alienating image of the world, which unmasks
scientism as a short circuit in reflection, which unmasks func-
tionalism as manipulative. It is a reverence which promises a
reconciliation between (to speak too simply) Eastern spirituality
and Western technology. It is a reverence which offers our new
concern for ecology deep, silent, rich rootage.

IV

To survive in America, it is necessary for most people to hang
loose, to play it cool, to drift, to avoid premature commitment.
Life in a technological society is so specialized that it picks
young people up and, as it were, places them on iron rails from
which it is difficult to escape. One is pushed hard in grammar
school in order to get into a good high school in order to get
into a good college in order to get into a good graduate school
in order to get into a good corporation in order to get into a
good suburb in order to get into a good casket. To defend themselves against the competitive narrowing down, against the iron
rungs of success, many commit themselves only piecemeal.
They do not live by a life project but by the absence of projects.
They hold themselves in reserve. They wait. There is a form of
other-directedness which is constituted, not by picking up signals

for one's own behavior from the behavior of others,[9] but by waiting for things to happen, waiting for things to break, waiting for excitement from outside.

This American instinct is a mechanism of survival; there is a certain health in it. But there is also a human failure involved. Those who do not define their lives for themselves find their lives, nevertheless, defined. Their hanging loose easily slides into alienation and bad faith: something else, someone else, makes the key decisions of their life for them. They are channelled. They absent themselves spiritually from the driving forces of direction in our society. They have abandoned their own inmost citadel and inwardly they are empty; alien winds sweep the place where soul ought to be. There is no freedom, community, courage, and only an ineffectual honesty, because there is no action. The American way of life breaks men into two classes: The boosters, the movers, the competitors, the actors—and the shiftless, the silent, the drifting, the unwilling. Those who do not define themselves by the competition and rewards of "the system" fall by the wayside. Action is defined by the others. Until and unless there is a revolutionary possibility, a possibility of defining action in a new way, the rules of the game in a new way, those who drift experience themselves as less than men or less than women. For what makes a man a man (a woman a woman) is decision. Deciding is a passing over from observing to acting. Deciding makes acting one's own, personal, self-committing, self-inventing.

When people talk about commitment, however, they usually think of commitment to a cause, program, movement. That is, I think, an all-too-American error. One does not need to find "a cause." One does not need to belong to "a movement." One does not need "to join" an organization, or to establish a committee. (A lecturer to American audiences can tangibly feel rising from the floor at the end of his remarks a profound ritual need: "Yes, but what can we *do* about it? You can't just leave us here." As if one *could* do things about life. As if to the human situation action, almost any action, were a fitting response).

The commitment to freedom, honesty, community and courage is not a commitment to a cause, program, or movement outside oneself, although these are not precluded. It is a commitment to a line of action demanding that one steadily, quietly, constantly transcend what one now is. It is a commitment to discovering the bad faith of one's present ("Do not trust anyone over thirty, under thirty, or Thyself"), and to taking yet one more step of liberation, honesty, community, courage. It is a concrete, practical commitment, for this moment, in this place, among these people—not forever, everywhere, for humanity. It is a commitment to a way of directing one's attention, a line of intentionality, a way of life, a style of living. It draws in its train all the supporting values without which freedom, honesty, community, and courage cannot be exercised. It involves a quite powerful ethic.

It also involves a powerful, critical politics. Action always takes place in a social, economic, political context. Who we think we are is taught to us, not so much by words, as by the roles society asks us to assume: consumer, competitor, opinion sample. Often those roles leave little room for genuine action; our resources of feeling and energy are taken for granted rather than drawn upon. The ordinary Christian in America has a self-image fashioned more by his present political, economic and social roles than by Christian images from the past. And that self-image, propaganda aside, is emphatically not one that calls forth a man's resources of freedom, honesty, community, courage. The system of relationships is well defined. If a man calmly takes his place in them he will be rewarded. The degree to which selling himself to others alienates him from himself corresponds to the degree of quiet rage, resentment, and unhappiness among the people of America: a people immensely restless, confused, torn. Suburban life is established to diminish the amount of risk, chaos, disorder in the human situation. The environment is

as thoroughly man-made and controlled as possible. No wonder
the ad-men appeal so often to a yearning for escape.

It is not that suburban American life is evil (although in its
economic dependence on lower standards of living among the poor
of the world it is), or even philistine (although given its imita-
tive tastes and expensive pretensions what else can one say?). It
is rather that the social pressures of suburban life thoroughly
control, and often repress, the instincts, impulses, anarchic in-
clinations, mad risks, sensibilities, bodies and feelings of those
who live in them. There have probably never been human environments as rational and organized as suburbs. The individual
has seldom, on the one hand, been so well educated, so well
travelled, and, on the other hand, felt so unimportant and so
disciplined. Young people brought up in such environments
crave unprocessed experience, are starving for a taste of freedom, honesty, community, courage.[10] If they are to have that
taste, our nation requires a new politics, a new economic order,
a new social arrangement. Theology, in any case, can no longer
be politically unaware. For what people think of themselves is
decided, in the first place, by the political system under which
they live.

To act—to decide—is implicitly to launch a life project, and
to have a view of the world, within which such action makes
sense. To act is to have a theology. Theology, in the foundational
sense, is a horizon which gives meaning to one's personal and
communal identity.

Let me say, then: "I willingly commit myself to expand the
freedom, honesty, community, and courage effectively operative
in my life." In some sense the transcendence of these values is
not only a transcendence which draws me ever beyond myself;
they also lead me to imagine a transcendence by which I
participate in a source of life not merely my own, and not merely
alien. The suggestion is a dark one. No one appears. In that
darkness, does God live? Should I dare to pronounce the word
"God" as a name for that in which I seem to participate?

Each man answers that question for himself. His answer defines his identity and, quite possibly, defines it erroneously. The definition is not merely arbitrary. It is not true that "anything goes." At issue is who interprets human life most truly.[11]

The test is in living. Do I live more like a man if I live as an atheist? Or if I say "Thou" to that in which I participate? Which interpretation more truly unlocks the secret of human identity?

That test is ambiguous. And thus we reach the final unawareness. No one sees God. No one sees the secret of human life, in itself, apart from the struggle and the night. What signs we detect of God are mediated by our own experience. The will to believe might be a will-o'-the-wisp. God may be, as Dewey avers, merely a projection of our own best selves. Such possibilities do not dissuade me. The atheists I live among seem to me to live *as if* there were a God: as if they participated in a source of freedom, honesty, community, and courage to whose non-alienating judgment they willingly exposed every part of themselves, and as if their actions in fulfillment of these values made sense out of the chaos of our experience.

The general point remains that man is a mystery to himself. In the darkness of that mystery, he does not know for certain whether to be cautious or to adore. Either way, he falls short of seeing God. We cannot directly make ourselves experience God. If we "experience" him at all, it is by a sort of indirection, by a quietness and unity and complacence (overlooking creation and seeing: "It is good") that steals over us, by a dark communion.

We cannot eliminate suffering from this world, Camus wrote, but we can diminish at least by a little the number of those who suffer. What seems most to matter, in this age of unawareness in which we live, is that through respecting that fundamental mystery in themselves men try to diminish the number of those who suffer. It is far more important that men join together in doing such a work, than that they join together in having a correct theory about what they are doing. For, in the end, religion is a matter of doing, even if it falls to theology to thematize that doing reflectively.

It is of the utmost importance, however, that foundational theology be brought to political consciousness as, over the past three generations, it has been brought to historical consciousness. For the unawareness of God is a consequence of our political, social, and economic system. It will be cured by political action before it will be cured by dialectics. It is not a mental mistake but the texture of a way of life which has destroyed our conscious participation in the "Love that moves the sun and all the stars." And that way of life is rapidly destroying the religious texture of other cultures, other peoples, in the name of scientific, democratic progress: rapidly generating a world of cities, slums, and impoverished peasant areas, dominated by military men and police.

The experiences whence language about God springs—freedom, honesty, community and courage—abut on politics. They will not be contained.

NOTES

1. "Functional Specialities in Theology," *Gregorianum,* 50 (1969), p. 491.
2. *Ibid.,* pp. 488-492.
3. Cf. Jean-Paul Sartre: "If I am mobilized in a war, this war is *my* war; it is in my image and I deserve it. I deserve it first because I could always get out of it by suicide or by desertion; these ultimate possibles are those which must always be present for us when there is a question of envisaging a situation. For lack of getting out of it, I have *chosen* it. This can be due to inertia, to cowardice in the face of public opinion, or because I prefer certain other values to the value of the refusal to join in the war (the good opinion of my relatives, the honor of my family, etc.). Anyway you look at it, it is a matter of a choice." *Existentialism and Human Emotions,* New York, 1957, pp. 54-55.
4. *Being and Nothingness,* New York, 1956, pp. 47-70.
5. *The Image,* New York, 1964, esp. pp. 3-44.
6. Cf. Freud, *Civilization and Its Discontents,* New York, 1964. The quote in my text is not from Freud; it represents a type of response.

7. Alfred Schutz, "Concept and Theory Formation in the Social Sciences," Journal of Philosophy, Vol. LI, no. 9 (1954). Reprinted in N. Lawrence and D. O'Connor (eds.), *Readings in Existential Phenomenology,* Englewood Cliffs, N.J., 1967, pp. 377-389.
8. Cf. Bernard Lonergan, *Insight,* New York, 1957, pp. 203-206, 254-255, 424-425, 480ff.
9. Cf. David Riesman on "other-directed behavior," *The Lonely Crowd,* New York, 1953, pp. 34ff.
10. See Kathy Mulherin, "Memoirs of a (Later Day) Catholic Girlhood," *The Commonweal* (February 28, 1970).
11. See my *A Time To Build,* New York, 1967, Part I.

Julian N. Hartt

Encounter and Inference in Our Awareness of God

T he topic of this essay may have confirmed a widely held conviction that some theologians manage to miss the existential flavors of their times by a small margin and the rest by a large margin. "Encounter and inference" indeed! Surely the times cry out for candid confession that the collapse of the traditional structure of belief has brought down the traditional *problematic* as well. Standing honestly in the middle of this scene we might then assay the incantations and imprecations of new pieties that fill the air. Instead of that I seem to be proposing an exercise in logic. The religiously concerned will hardly find comfort in the fact that the exercise is a very primitive one; for why bother with that sort of thing at all when the crisis of church and culture is so severe? Logic never lifted a soul to God nor brought heaven to earth. Why then wander on the cold, arid and infertile plateaus of logic while here below the multitudes hunger desperately and thrash about frantically for a meaningful existence?

What is worse, I am not a logician of high technical competence. Thus to the melancholy generalization that theologians past 30 have a habit of getting to the scene after the action has shifted elsewhere, it may be necessary to add the judgment that the one arrived with a gun one end of which he couldn't tell from the other. Need I add that self-destruction has a 50% probability in that case?

I must, accordingly, now make one thing clear: this is not an exercise in logic. My purpose in this essay is to offer an account of the way a certain vivid religious experience can be related to certain elements in the structure of Christian belief. What I have in mind by "vivid religious experience" is the prophetic encounter with the living God in the maelstrom of social revolution. What I have in mind by "the structure of Christian belief" is a body of teachings in which God is the capital item, the beginning and the end.

The central thesis of this essay could, then, be expressed in a somewhat more argumentative way. The prophetic encounter with God makes arbitrary demands upon the structure of Christian belief; and making the most of this encounter requires the development and employment of routes of inference (or inference patterns). The fact—as I take it to be—that prophets are impatient with inferences and preoccupied with encounters— serves to remind us that there is and must be more to Christianity than prophecy. The prophet, in fact, does not add to our knowledge of God. He may bring to us a fresh recognition of our actual situation in the sight of God. That is a great, dangerous and painful thing to accomplish: painful for us, dangerous for him, great with the possibilities for the reconstruction of the service of God.

It will become evident in what follows that I am using "prophetic encounter" to designate a current religious phenomenon rather than an institution in ancient Israel or an office in the early church. Thus the contemporary Christian prophet demands that we go out from bastions of power and privilege to encounter God where he is to be found: in the center of the revolution. And there to do his bidding, on which the prophet claims to have explicit information.

The prophetic spirit in our times does not make much of other encounters with God. I do not find that this is commonly a theological decision made as such. It is a result of personal stress and of social urgency. From a generic Christian belief that God is encountered everywhere the prophet extracts and specializes the inevitability of encountering the God of utter righteousness. He seems therefore to avoid the embarrassments which cluster around the traditional belief that God is encountered everywhere, could we but recognize him in all things. For so soon as we say God is that being we cannot avoid we are asked, "Why call that being 'God,' to say nothing of 'the God and Father of our Lord Jesus Christ' "? For death is also something we cannot avoid, in any case. So is guilt. And taxes. And conflict. And sex—I hope. Christians are rather notoriously reluctant to call any of these inevitabilities "God." Yet Christians have been rather notoriously prone to claim that God has a hand, and the winning hand at that, in all, repeat all, creaturely inevitabilities. How then, can Christians gracefully decline to answer such a question as, "Why do you not say Death is one of the names of God? You say that God is somehow implicated in death; but you insist that he is Life rather than Death." And so also for sex. D. H. Lawrence strove with rare dedication to convince our parents that sexuality *is* a "name of God." Was it just prudishness that made them shy away from that passionate avowal? Perhaps. But they have also believed that while the right enjoyment of sexuality might well be praise of God, sex as such is not a route of access to him.

The general theological situation of the Christian belief in God seems to be an angular logical oddity. God is honored as the creator of all things—death, guilt, taxes, war, sexuality, whatever. He has not done all things in the same way, but in all things his doings can be made out, somehow. But he *is* not anything he has made or done. The name of nothing in creation can be ascribed to him. Yet there is a way of reflecting upon the eventualities of life, and upon the sheer existence of whatever exists, that is a route of access to God.

I think it could be shown that even the hardiest "revelationist" in recent Protestant theology makes his own awkward admissions of this logical oddity, however ferociously the fans of his theological windmill assail that Don Quixote, Natural Theology. But let us not suppose that any of us gains by perfecting the spread of theological embarrassments. It is more important to learn whether the prophet has a way out of this logical mess; and specifically whether the encounter with God in the center of social revolution is such as to absolve prophetic religiousness from responsibility for showing just what is divine (or God) among the multifarious powers working the dissolution and reconstruction of the social order.

I

I propose to attack this issue, and the larger or more encompassing logical oddity, by reviewing the classical structures of inference.

    I. *Something exists: therefore, God.*

    II. *Something is going on: therefore, God.*

Now let us dress each out a bit.

    I. From the fact that anything exists ("anything" being the blank check for something particular, determinate, finite), it follows that the proposition, "God exists," is a true proposition. Or, in the most abstract terms, *"finite" implies "infinite."*

The second structure (II) can be rendered in at least two different ways.

    (1) The world is made up of processes all of which start and eventually stop. Yet the world does not start and stop. Hence: *change* implies *permanence,* which, spelled with a capital P, is God.

    (2) Something is happening so momentous that it must be God's direct doing. How can God do something *directly* without being *present?* How can he be present without being present somewhere and to somebody?

(1) and (2) seem to have nothing to do with each other. (1)

reflects a cosmological concern like I; and (2) a revolutionary historical one. (1) seems to aim at the validation of a cosmological proposition. (2) seems to aim at the recognition of a Presence—a power perceptibly at work in our history and existence.

The cosmological route (I and II.1) has been in acute disfavor in Protestant theology for well over a quarter of a century. Apparently this state of mind is now well established in Catholic centers, too. Quite apart from the fact that it is a blatant expression of confidence in human reason (cognitive powers) there is a greater embarrassment: there seems to be no valid and instructive way to get from Principle of Permanence to "the God and Father of our Lord Jesus Christ," or from beings to Being. This difficulty can be rephrased. *Whatever avails to render experience intelligible (here the experience of change) does not necessarily expose anything salvific or properly divine.*

It may be that these charges rest upon a serious misunderstanding of the cosmological structures of inference. Were they designed to carry the mind from "intelligibility" to "savior" or "salvation"? Were they supposed to be the launching platform for the ascent of the mind from the general features of experience rightly understood to God Almighty rightly worshiped? Is it not rather the case that "Change implies permanence" only when it has been antecedently determined that change of itself is unintelligible? Many defenders of the cosmological route have indeed operated from that antecedent determination. Or, again, "Things are happening" implies "There is a Source of all action" only when it has been antecedently determined that the preeminent model of "Something is happening" is a conscious volitional subject producing or generating action. Again, many —probably most—followers of the cosmological route have operated from that antecedent determination.

The real inferential structure of the cosmological theists seems then to have been this. Appeal to the data of experience is logically a display of the explanatory capabilities of theistic belief rather than the first step in the rational construction of that belief or the king-pin in its validation. Thus the experience of change, contingency, transitoriness, etc. is an encounter with God himself. This encounter is not a direct unmediated awareness of God as the supreme subject from whom all things come. It is, rather, an awareness of being caught up in something God himself must be doing, that is, *evaluating change, as well as causing it.* This does not mean that God must ask what we must often ask, namely, What is going on here? before we can rationally proceed to appraising it. Let us say, rather, that the "power of God unto salvation" presupposes a judgment on God's part that things are not what they ought to be. Thus the cosmological structure of inference is not as remote and alien to the historical inferential route as many theologians seem to suppose.

Nonetheless II.2 is ostensibly a revolutionary-historical concern rather than anything even remotely cosmological. "Something so momentous is happening that it must be God's direct personal doing. Properly focused and refined perception is able (or ought to be able) to discern God as present in the determination of these great events." It must therefore seem uncommonly high-handed to say, right off the bat, that there *is* an inferential structure embedded in this encounter with him whence comes the "permanent revolution." But I think that is the case. For what is actually *encountered?*

Powers destroying the old world and powers shaping a new and hopefully a better one. The claim of (II.1) is that God is present among them; and that is where he can be known. Indeed (II.1) contends that unless we meet him there we are not going to know him as he really is, at all.

Nothing could be farther from my intention than to minimize the ethical passion evident in this claim. It is a timely and powerful rebuke to religious strategies for private salvation. When there is a world to be won or lost how could a really moral person wish to be plucked as a brand from the burning?

Surely, in this historical moment a retreat to ethical and religious privacy is *eo ipso* a flight from God! If God can be encountered only where "cross the crowded ways of life," it is folly, if not heresy, to suppose that he can be encountered in private self-interested worship. Or, we may add, in sanctuaries sound-proofed against the mounting war of a world in violent upheaval.

Let us agree, then, that the issue is not ethical authenticity. The issue is theological. How is God recognized as *God* in this world of revolutionary upheaval? Is he the true author of revolution, his breath the whirlwind beating against the walls of alienation, the structures of injustice, until they come tumbling down? Or is this rise and fall of empire a rhythm God built into the human commonwealth, there to stay so long as man lives on earth?

These are not the only theological options, but they are the ones which stand in the sharpest contrast to each other. They are also the ones which typify in our time the perennial opposition of Intuition and Inference, in the Christian's knowledge of God. We are therefore justified in devoting careful attention to this contrast.

II

If I say that God is only to be encountered where the revolutionary action is I ought to brace for the natural and inevitable question: How do you recognize *God* in the general turbulence? Since we have agreed to put aside private visions and every other kind of subjective assurance, I should have to say one of two things.

(1) What I *mean* by "God" is a being who is dedicated to destroying injustice in order that the light of love and peace may break out across the human scene in uncorruptible splendor. Consequently wherever I find human beings so dedicated and so energized, I say, "This is God's work," and "Here God is

present." From this it is but a short step to the acknowledgment that "God" is a name for the noblest and most fertile human passions. "God" is the concert of passions focused upon the perfection of the human commonwealth. And surely *this* God is encountered in every such passion and every such concert. About that there should be no theological mystery at all.

The mystery sets in at another point: Why use "god language" at all, if that is the upshot? Is it an accident, a mere coincidence, that the ideological masters and architects of the most massive political revolutions in the modern world have been avowed atheists? No doubt atheism is often a rejection of the church as an institution rather than a systematic metaphysical view, and a criticism of its behavior rather than of its beliefs. But surely part of the meaning of the slogan "the world coming of age" is just the conviction that what man has messed up in his own affairs he can and he must straighten out by himself.

Still, if it were simply or largely a semantic decision involved here our theological worries would indeed be few and minuscule—a matter, that is, of what name to supply to the absolute to which one appeals as the ultimate justification for one's revolutionary posture and practice; for then where I say "God" you might say, "the historical dialectic," and someone else, "the ultimate ethical commonwealth," etc.

But this is not simply a semantic decision. Whether or not the philosophers give their approval to such habits we do habitually suppose that the use of the word "God," when it is serious, puts us into a reality-game, and not just into a language-game. Why would I appeal to the manifest will of God as the ultimate justification for some principle or policy if I were persuaded that *this* God does not exist, is not *there* to have and make known a righteous will? Assuredly, if I believe God endorses some principle or policy to which I am attached, this attachment is likely to be strengthened thereby; but only so far as I hold that the belief is sound. My conviction that I ought to do my duty would hardly be strengthened by my believing that the ghost of

Kant nods approval. For even if I believed that ghosts exist and that Kant might well be hanging in there, I should still be dealing with a morally fallible being (I hope that the ghost of Kant is not offended by that remark); and I cannot and do not appeal to such, living or dead, as an *ultimate* justification for principle or policy.

We have now to return to the question to which so far only one kind of answer, and that an unsatisfactory one, has been returned, namely, how does one recognize *God* in the turbulence of historical crisis?

(2) To this it must seem far more satisfactory to say that God can be counted on to make himself known; and never or nowhere more clearly than when the human stakes are the highest, that is, when the human commonwealth is most powerfully threatened.

We have two good reasons for looking into this viewpoint. The first is the ethical seriousness of the prophets of social revolution. The second is the formidable difficulties which the notion of the self-authenticating character of divine revelation encounters.

III

Let us agree that the most interesting form of the inferential structure sketched above is this: "Something so momentous is happening that it must be God's direct doing. Properly focused and refined perception is able to discern God as *present* in the revolution of our history." Thus to know him as he is we must know where he is. In that encounter alone will come the holy shock of recognition.

Something like this is the gist of the theology of contemporary Christian prophecy. Within this striking religious formation I make out two quite different ways in which recognition of God is claimed, which I shall simply call Type A and Type B.

A. *The prophet recognizes the hand of God in history; and not merely in the history of the "almost chosen people."* As Amos so long ago saw, the hand of the Lord is raised against injustice and cruelty wherever these monstrous enemies appear on earth. The Lord will not stay the rod of punishment whether the culprit is Israel, Judah, Syria, etc. Assyria comes down from the north like a ravening wolf to devour faithless Israel; but Assyria also is destroyed for her own iniquities.

This prophetic message can be formulated in more general and philosophical terms. The result will sound something like this: Every society feels the pressure of Ideality, and specifically the pressure from the ideals of Justice, Freedom, and Peace. And every society responds in its own way to these "pressures." The builders and defenders of an empire know in their bones that Fortune has presided over its birth; and the president deity keeps a jealous eye on the performance of its darling. Thus even empires must hew to a line of rectitude (however primitive this seems to the prophet), or suffer the awful consequence. This much Tacitus sees and proclaims even while Rome was rising to dizzy heights of power and glory. Eternal Rome indeed! He knew that the germs of destruction and death were already at work.

The prophet of the one true God has a broader vision. He recognizes the hand of God in the rise and fall of any and every empire. The prophet discerns a rhythm, a law, in human history. Imagination, fired by evil appetite, conjures an empire in which the many live for the advantage of the few. Given a break here and there, the evil dream comes true; and the happy few may for a while rule the multitudes of the world. But only for a while. The regnum may seem to run forever; but this is an illusion.

It takes a prophet to recognize the arm of the all-righteous Lord in the destruction of empire. What meets the unprophetic eye is the destructive impact of the appetites of people who want more and more of the goodies for themselves, and the diminishing concern for justice and mercy. Or the superior might of another empire bent upon "synthesizing" weaker achievements often accounts for the fall of the one and the aggrandizement of the other. It takes more than the naked eye to recognize a higher justice in that. But the prophet has an answer to these sour generalizations. He claims that God uses the fallible and corrupt powers of man to work the ultimate design of justice, peace, and freedom. The prophet speaks for the righteous God who reigns supreme over the rhythm of empire.

No matter how stirring the performance of the prophet of this persuasion, we are beset by theological problems when we come home from the show. The Christian moralist knows what to think of a *human* agent who deliberately employs or piously ordains the use of evil instruments to achieve a good purpose. Is a presumptively divine Agent *rationally* immune to that condemnation? Moreover, the God who reigns supreme over the rhythms of empire is remote from the dreadful struggles which rend the human commonwealth. So where is the virtue in saying that *in the end* his will prevails; for we have no way of getting at (either to know or to correct) the vision of the end such a God might have, if indeed the "end" of the historical process (the rhythm of empire) is in anything different from the process itself. Through his prophets that God teaches us that injustice does not pay. But history teaches us that making the unjust pay up is an atrociously expensive business, and count the expense in any terms you want. The mills of the gods grind slowly. They also chew up a lot of innocent people. To reply that none is innocent, cheapens the whole game.

We should expect a *Christian* prophet to recoil from these inferences. We should expect—to put it somewhat more affirmatively—the Christian prophet to hold out for a divine intervention in the process of history. For how can he be Christian (if that connotes anything but idealism) if he does not believe and preach that God is really present in the ongoing struggle to deliver the human commonwealth from its besetting evils? So far as we are Christian we expect God to do something more and better than to preside over history. We expect him to be really present in it, in order to make sure that one day his creation will become what he intends all along that it should be.

Thus we are brought to Type B, the prophecy which recognizes God as the supreme Eschatological Presence in the great crises of history, and thus in the revolution which has seized our life.

B. Here the mode of recognition of God appears to be largely intuitive, that is, a direct apprehension of a present reality. The prophetic consciousness, Type B, apprehends God present here and now. God is the sublime eschatological Presence, he who shapes the future for the perfection of the human community and who does this divine work from within the perimeters of the human community.

I think something like this lies behind the burning conviction that one can encounter God only where the action is. This is the commanding prophetic passion of the hour; and it seems to put its subjects in much closer communication with the revolutionary spirits outside the church and the faith than with the defenders of tradition. "God has moved outside the church" is a sentiment heard frequently in the church itself. It is often expressed with such earnestness and single-mindedness that one is reluctant to do anything to modify the passion, such as saying that even the doughtiest defender of the ancient doctrine that outside the church there is no salvation would never have dreamed of denying that *God* is "outside the church." The God of the Tradition is hardly a household deity, even for the household of faith.

Nevertheless the work of theology is not all passion, not even the most admirable passion. It does, I am afraid, require us to ask disconcerting questions, such as, How do you know it is *God* you encounter where the action is? Type B prophecy is very likely to say, in response, something like this. "When you do God's work out there on the action front you just *know* God

is present. It is almost as though we can *sense* him as we are
drawn up into the battle to deliver men from the fetters of
injustice, slavery, war, hatred, etc."

What can we make of this? Several things. (i) It has a certain
mystical air about it. Almost every kind of religious life promises
some kind or degree of community with the Ultimate, provided
that the person who seeks this is prepared to accept the discipline of a community. Granted that the prophet in our day is
likely to minimize the values of the traditional cultic community,
he has his own salvific community, the company of people who
have been "out there" together. In that company one senses the
magnitude of the revolutionary task; and one senses, from time
to time, a sublime Presence permeating that company, healing
the wounds inflicted by the outer world, and overcoming the
alienations which develop in any human society, no matter how
noble its purpose and dedicated its members.

(ii) But another interpretation comes to mind. The prophet
recognizes God in the revolutionary confrontation because he
knows that this is the sort of thing God would be interested in,
to put it somewhat whimsically. Properly instructed by Judaism,
Christianity teaches that God is righteous altogether. If we are
to serve him properly, therefore, we must make every effort to
straighten out whatever is crooked in our life and our world. It
is not enough to be sorry. It is not enough to insist that injustice
is as old as the human story; and that every reform brings in
new evils. God still demands that we "bring forth fruits worthy
of repentance." The first Christian cells laid great stress on the
life of love within their perimeters; but did not intentionally
paper over inequities with amiable sentiments. Yet they did not
grasp the immensity of the eschatological Presence. Nor for
that matter did they dream that one day the church would feel
obliged to accept the reigns of government from the dying
hands of the mightiest of imperial states. The religious and
ethical mentality apparent in the Apocalypse of St. John is
hardly compatible with the assumption of civil governance; and
so the former yielded to the necessities of the latter; and the

church became an empire among the other kingdoms of this world.

God as the eschatological Presence was not defeated by this worldly triumph. He moved out and on, not so much to bring down an imperialistic church as to build up responsiveness to his real presence elsewhere. Eventually the imperialistic church came down—or should we say it is still coming down? The point is, it did not come down through the operation of some "law of history." It came down because the Creative Spirit had gone off and left it.

(iii) Type B prophecy makes much less of *law* in history and much more of the *contingency* of history. The God recognized in the revolutionary upheaval is not the God who presides over the rise and fall of empire. Rather, he is God always present to release the victims of every captivity, ancient and modern. He is on the side of essential freedom. Indeed, he *is* the spirit of essential freedom. As such he cannot have an ultimate regard for Law; it is not at the top of his priorities. Thus type B prophecy is much inclined to treat law and rule as human conventions rather than as divine arrangements, except so far as freedom and love might be spoken of as law-like, e.g., "I give you no law except that you should love one another." It is, I suppose, clear that this is much more like an ethical norm than a law, that is, it is a non-enforceable prescription.

If this account of type B prophecy is reasonably correct then it would be hardly consistent with it to speak of a divine *intervention* in human history in behalf of justice, mercy, peace, brotherhood, etc. "Intervention" still carries too much of the scent of "miracle," the event that suspends momentarily the laws of nature. This conception of miracle gives away far too much weight to the reign of law, either in nature or history or both. So where essential freedom is given the highest priority law ought to be regarded as somehow derivative from freedom.

Thus God as the ultimate supreme Revolutionary does not have to struggle against any legalistic factor in his own makeup. He is the eschatological Presence inspiring and perhaps directing the demolition of institutions and sanctions that alienate man from the brother. God is absolutely free to seek the release of human creativity from whatever obstructs, obscures, or diminishes it.

We have thereafter only to ask two questions put to his prophets. One, is this God also proportionately powerful to enforce his holy will? Two, how does the man of faith distinguish *God* from worldly powers *accidentally* creative-constructive even though they are essentially either destructive or "value-free"?

The two questions are intertwined. If God is identified with the powers undermining the massive institutions of our civilization and their theological-ethical sanctions, God emerges with just so much power and resourcefulness as revolutionary forces in fact display unless we are given some theological grounds for believing that the eschatological Presence is holding vast powers in reserve for the moment he has ordained for their deployment. The type B prophet has not yet come forward with those theological grounds. But from this some fairly curious results flow. For one, a defeat for the Revolution becomes *eo ipso* a defeat of God—not a defeat *for* God but a defeat *of* God. It is not entirely clear that this is the sort of thing St. Paul had in mind in speaking of the "weakness" of God (1 Cor 1:25). And there is another inference: If revolutionary forces succeed only in disrupting the social order, and nothing constructive emerges, or even promises to emerge, God, so far as he is identified with this revolution, seems much closer to Death than to Life, to the shedding of blood rather than to concord, peace, and love.

We can have no doubt that the Christian prophet is made very restless by this sort of discussion, and would move to end it with some such claims as the following.

"But of course as a *Christian* we know that God is entirely on the side of love, justice, and peace. He *cannot* be identified with anything merely destructive, hateful, and anarchical. Nor can he be identified with any "value-free" social process. In the turbulence and tumult of the present hour God is the spirit of love leading the faithful to seek justice for all by the appropriate methods of social criticism and social reconstruction." From this it would seem to follow that the faithful Christian might not applaud the destruction of the social fabric but might yet see in this process something providential, namely, an opportunity to make the case, existentially if not theologically, for self-sacrificial creative love.

Be that as it may, we have still to decide whether the type B Christian prophet is fundamentally and decisively committed to a kind of intuitionism in his claims to have recognized God in the scene of turbulent social change. I think he is, unless he is now prepared to admit that what he calls "recognition of God" *is actually a way of claiming part of the structure of Christian belief to serve as a sanction or warrant for his way of leading the Christian life in the world.* If this is the case we have left intuitionism far behind for any purpose other than a method for grasping a critical situation as genuinely critical. Thereby "encounter" becomes perception of the actual situation, a way of reading off (not sizing up) what we are up against in it. The right identification of the powers moving in the actual situation, and the determination of the right response to and appropriation of those powers cannot and is not in fact left in the hands of Intuition at all. For these transactions, therefore, some other account must be given. I shall try now to give a sketch of that account.

IV

For this purpose let us begin with a primitive distinction between *recognition* and a kind of interpretation I propose to call *claiming*.

Recognition. In recognizing you I put you where you belong. On the basis of past experience I know what to make of you. The signals you have emitted heretofore, the symbolic structures ("language") you have characteristically employed for self-expression, fall into an intelligible and reasonably coherent pattern; so that even if you are at the moment erratic and inconsistent, I know exactly what I mean by *saying* that you are behaving erratically. If I do not know exactly what I mean by that I have not in fact recognized *you*. Indeed, if you behave erratically enough I may cart you off to a doctor, on the interesting grounds that *you* are not *yourself!* That, let us note, is not a metaphysical judgment. It is a moral judgment. It means that your current behavior seriously jeopardizes your own best interests.

Claiming. In the example just given I obviously claim a right (and perhaps even a duty) to act in your behalf; and I claim to know what your best interests are. Both claims are debatable. There are many occasions when they are not in fact debated because any reasonable person can see how the debate would come out, e.g., I am your father and you are a six-year-old boy. But even there the claim is debatable *in principle.* I cannot enforce my claims if I have been convicted of criminal negligence against you. In that case even if I did actually know what would serve your best interests I may be disqualified to serve as an agent for their protection.

There are other instances and kinds of claiming that are nearer the mark for our present theological interests and hopes. Consider this one. I make a claim upon your attention for the purpose of making a claim upon your loyalty and love. I suggest that this sequence is of some importance for the next stage of our argument.

"Listen to me! to *me,* the real being you are inclined to mistake or misread. I have a primordial right to be recognized as I *am* rather than as the (illusory) object of your desires and hopes and fears."

Now this does not obviously mean that the I is *worthy* of attention because of some achievement. The primordial right to be recognized is itself a function of a particular situation. *The claim upon attention, in other words, is the way a given structure operates.* I have in mind the parent-child relationship. The father ought to listen to the son, whether or not the son is "good"; and this takes precedence, oddly enough, over the obligation of the son to listen to the father. The reason for this is simple and compelling. The son depends upon the attention of the father in a way quite different from the way the father depends upon the son; and this is true quite independently of the encompassing social system.

The claim upon attention ("listen to *me!*") is generally made with a view to making a claim upon love and loyalty. This does not automatically mean that the claimant supposes that one thing and one thing only will satisfy the claim. The claimant *may* mean that whatever is done, on the strength of an authentic and veracious recognition, must be done lovingly, even if what ensues is a flat denial of the material claim. We all know, of course, how badly mixed up this business gets in everyday human transaction. "If you really love me you will give me a new car," for example. This is but to say that claims upon love are often exploitive. This, however, has nothing to do with the logic of claiming. Again, that logic is simple: a serious and clear claim upon love and loyalty presupposes a claim upon attention; and the claim upon attention presupposes a capacity for recognition.

Now how much of this logic is available for the illumination and ordering of our business with God? The sketch I am proposing has several components.

(1) Consider first the ancient prophetic formula, "The word of the Lord came to me and said. . . ." What follows (as in the case of Amos) is apparently a direct claim of the self-same Lord upon the loyalty of his people. It is a demand for obedience to the law of the Covenant. It is far from clear, in any of the Old Testament prophets, that the prophetic spokesman for God rests his case upon some extraordinary experience of his own, or that he says God is the object of a direct intuition. The people of the Covenant *are* called to remembrance, to a recognition, if you please: They are the Lord's, and he has always provided;

to them he has "revealed his arm." Thus they are summoned to a recognition of God's claim upon them.

(2) Whatever we make of the theology of the prophet, and specifically whether we believe the prophet has something uniquely informative to tell us about *God* himself, we can make out what sort of human claim is being made by the prophet. The whole history of the people, and beyond that, all of life and the world, are claimed for God. This means that the life of faith consists in part of viewing and construing the whole works as belonging to God. Especially the vital center of personal life, the "heart," is claimed for the tabernacle of the Lord, "the house" or tent of flesh-and-spirit (cf. Jer 31:33).

The affective-volitional depth of the claim thus registered ought in itself be an adequate warning against any philosophical effort to interpret the prophetic claiming as anything like the posting of a hypothesis or a conjecture to be tested by experience and accepted if sufficiently confirmed. The force of the claim, the centers of life upon which it is trained, so far leave nothing to tentativeness or to mental reservation. We are deeply attached to the spirit of tentativeness, of testing in order to see whether the Lord is there at all and not merely whether he is good; but we ought not to begin to explain this in terms of philosophical prepossessions, e.g., an antecedent and binding commitment to open-grid intelligence, revisability of all truths, relativity of all values, etc. I suggest that the beginning of an explanation is much more practical and historical: our century has seen what awful destruction fanaticism can wreak once it occupies the seats of power; and this whether the fanatic is revolutionary or counter-revolutionary. Beyond this is the overwhelming success of science, both in its theoretical probing of nature and its technological reconstruction of our lives. And since science in our understanding is committed to the revisability of all its beliefs and results, we have a model of the open-grid intelligence which honors no absolutes save Intelligence itself.

But what would naturally and clearly lead one to suppose

that religious belief and commitment are but an extension into the depths of feeling and appetition of human curiosity and desire to control so much of human life and the environment as possible? In the religious life we are at once struck by the pre-eminence of the belief that here at last the "sense for the whole" is gratified; or if it is not, one can discover where the deficiency is. I do not mean to suggest that the religious life is one with the conviction that "life is worth living" or with "my life is worth living." The sentiments are too vague; and they are too lightly attached to the decisive centers of human action, at least as they are commonly expressed and received. Rather, the religious life expresses the sense of being able to endure all things and to hope for the best because the power and goodness which sustain the world are here at hand to sustain me. This sense, this conviction, and finally this commitment, do not admit tentativeness into their final composition. Each of us has days of doubt about his beliefs. In each of us the "sense of the whole" unpredictably falters. None of us is spared the experience of proving irresolute, and even treacherous in our decisive commitments. But we are sustained; and not merely endured or put up with. This is the belief that God puts a value on our existence that we cannot cancel, even at our worst, individually and corporately.

I have spoken of this as a belief. It is actually a "construing belief." A construing belief is rather more a *believing* than it is the finished product commonly suggested by *belief*. Thus a construing belief is an interpretation of some aspect of experience. But it may also be a program, a mandate, as it were, for interpreting all of experience and the world. Such I take *believing in God* to be.

(3) The prophet (early and late) is a great one for saying to the Lord God: "If you believe in me you will do thus-and-so." The formula quite naturally leads us to think that the doings constitute a series of inferences drawn off a budget of linguistic units called "beliefs," e.g., "God is love" *implies* "love your neighbor." Now in fact "God is love" does not imply

"love your neighbor" in any easily recognizable sense of implication. Why not? Well, to start with, God is God and I am I;
and unless one has already adopted a theology that cannot or
will not distinguish God from me, I should have to say that
what God is *able* to do entails of itself nothing whatever as to
what I am *supposed* to do. Christians believe that God loves
the whole works, with the possible exception of the Devil and
the damned; but even of them we must say that if God does not
love them they have no *raison d'être,* and therefore in the sight
of God they are nothing. Not, note, *worse* than nothing; because
in the traditional ontological scheme whatever totally fails to be
cannot be the subject of a moral judgment, human or divine.

Furthermore, "God is love" might be taken to mean that God
does not have to put the slightest effort into loving—he *is* love,
by nature or essence. On the other hand "love your neighbor"
stands over me as a prescription, as an imperative. "This is my
commandment, that you love one another as I have loved you"
(John 15, 12). The prescription is notoriously hard to enforce,
whether one thinks of it as commanding a feeling or passion;
or as laying down a policy-norm. I do not mean that failure
to obey the commandment is something the Christian is inclined to take lightly. He may indeed agonize over this failure,
and believe that his repeated failure rightly to love others (particularly his enemies?) is observed with severe displeasure in
heaven; and that sooner or later the divine displeasure will
cut him off from "the land of the living." These dark forebod-
ings and harsh self-accusations are not promising ground for
the seeds of love. So Christians are constantly tempted either
to vaporize the love-commandment or to evacuate it. It is vapor-
ized when "love" becomes a vague amiability and a readiness to
wish well for almost all of God's creatures. The love-commandment is evacuated when one decides that at least one can try to
"do right" by as many of the victims of injustice as one can
manage without disrupting one's own life or upsetting the apple-
cart of established society; and all the while resenting the bloody
mess which other people have made of the world.

For the little it may be worth we might note that we are up against a kind of logical puzzle here, as well. How can a statement about a state of affairs *imply* a prescription for action? Take a humdrum example. Someone has made a mess of my garden. Who ought to do something about it? You say, "The culprit, if you can catch him." You will probably not say, "Whoever or whatever is to blame, the same must make amends, tidy it up, etc." For it might have been the prankish wind, upsetting the trash cans and spreading the contents fortuitously to create the most offensive result. I can hold the wind responsible, in a manner of speaking, but I cannot put the wind under an imperative. It blows where it wills. I might pray that tomorrow it would blow from the opposite direction but the effect of that might be to strew my neighbors' gardens with the same junk. If they knew I had prayed for that it might be a strain on community relations.

So only if the state of affairs is such that human agents are sensibly and enforceably chargeable with its ills, can a statement to that effect be said to imply a prescription binding upon specific human agents. But that means that the very statement about the state of affairs already makes a claim upon ethical conviction and is intended to function as a moral constraint and motive. "God is love; thereafter love your neighbors" does not look at all like that.

Perhaps, then, we are satisfied that the connection between the fundamental beliefs of the Christian and certain actions and patterns of action is not strict implication. Then what is it? It is a kind of inference. It is, actually, a whole bundle of inferences, as I shall now try to show.

(4) Belief in God is a construing belief. It is in fact the supreme construing belief, but only in part because God is believed to be the Supreme Being. It is the supreme construing belief because it commands the widest range of routes of inference from antecedent factors to consequences, some of which function as confirmations of antecedent factors. Take, for example, the belief that God is Creator of all things and Lord

over all. (Even at the analytical level we ought not to construe "Creator of all things" and "Lord over all" as synonymous. For God might have started the show and left it thereafter pretty much if not altogether to its own devices and fate. Secondly, the Lord over all might not have started the show but might have demonstrated his competence and power to run it out to the end, whether or not he has any power or authority to change the end or postpone or hurry it, etc.) This belief is a declaration of intention both to "see" all things as belonging to God and actually so to construe them. Here "construe" is more than a linguistic-intellectual activity. *It means an intention to relate to all things in ways appropriate to their belonging to God.*

(I think it is important to enter a caveat here. This does not mean some kind of generalized application of the I-Thou principle to cover natural entities as well as persons; because the I-Thou, in my view, does not apply monolithically and univocally even to persons. Given forms of society not organized as *communities* (in the prevailing sociological understanding of community) I can and I must relate to those structures in ways appropriate to their nature (their being what they are). Practically this means that it is not morally wrong *sometimes* to treat human beings impersonally, so far as I do not intentionally treat them as less than human. Impersonal treatment is not in itself brutalizing or cruel. Quite to the contrary, it is one of the prescriptions of *justice* that I should be able to abstract a moral concern from personal investment and private interest, in order to assure that persons and groups of persons should get what they deserve. This means that on some occasions I must be ready to act in adverse interest, relative to myself, not because there is someone out there who counts for more than I do, in some absolute scale, but because the pursuit of some interest of mine (and of my dearest group, often enough) has deprived some other being of something more fundamental in the pursuit of a human existence than that particular interest of mine. Thus, it is right that I should surrender some of my property, according to a certain (definite) rule, if my continued possession of it diminishes access of another person to sufficient food, clothing, medicine, work, etc. to maintain or establish him as a viable member of the state. For this purpose it does not matter that I know him personally and am therefore disposed to treat him better—or worse—than the mass of unknowns who have a right to be treated as "sons and daughters of God.")

Thus the vitally important business of determining the appropriate response to God's creatures can be identified as a process of running out inferences, not from some axioms in the mind but from the "dispositions of the heart." Inference as such is a matter of "getting from one thing to another," where the antecedent is something firmly grasped (or, in the case of intellect, clearly known), and the consequent (the being toward which inference runs its appointed course) is something to be made out; and thereafter gathered into the antecedent. The process thus expands and enriches the antecedent. (This fact makes difficulties for the axiom-model.)

The running-out or tracking down of inference, therefore, in the prime instance of belief in God, ideally issues in the recognition of someone or something. I do not know what to make of the other until I know who he is; but I cannot know who or what the other is unless I am pre-disposed to let him be himself, that is, enter the structure of communication carrying his full weight and profile of value. If I am so pre-disposed (this invaluable *pre*-disposition is what we ought to mean by "infused grace producing faith") I can confidently expect the structure of communication itself to be modified by the appearance in it of the other with his full weight and profile of value. His authentic self-expression, in other words, may (quite literally) scare the Hell out of me. The antecedent disposition to affirm his being may be badly rattled by his emergence as he really is. This is a formidable possibility, rather more formidable than the possibility of my discovering personal hostility. *His hostility may be trained upon the structure of communication, because he has learned that this structure characteristically deprives him of some of his value.*

We say therefore that the routes of inference must be kept open to radical criticism and sweeping revision. This necessity goes beyond any effort to cope with philosophical challenges to the structure of belief; for what is being challenged in our time and in ourselves is the good faith of the Christian and only incidentally the structure of belief. It is our readiness to track down or follow out the proper inferences of our professedly good will and overflowing love for all of God's children, that is being most effectively challenged.

The openness thus laid upon Christian faith and conscience is a claim made by God the Holy Spirit. That, of course, is a theological proposition, an appropriation of an element in the structure of Christian belief. It is intended also to provide yet another illustration of the claiming character of Christian faith. To believe in God is to claim the whole world for him; and it is also to claim for him the very ground on which we stand to profess our faith; and it is also to claim for him the sovereign right to command the entire range of our powers of recognition and response.

V

Why then do the Christian prophets of social revolution in our day make so little of the Holy Spirit as a vital link in the structure of Christian life and belief? Perhaps they feel that the traditional structures are obsolete, except for an item or two that can be salvaged as sanction for the revolutionary cause. This conjecture is borne out to a degree by the readiness of the contemporary prophets to claim the "historical Jesus" for the Cause; and Old Testament representations of the God of absolute justice. But how can someone living now have an "existential encounter" with the historical Jesus, unless the prophet is prepared to draw upon fairly abstruse doctrines of the contemporaneity of Christ, à la Kierkegaard? I am sure we can see how a Christian might want to claim Jesus Christ as his ethical model as he wrestles with the harrowing problems of conscience and contemporary society. But this seems very far from the existential encounter with Christ himself. So also for any existential encounter with the Lord God of Old Testament righteousness. Perhaps Moses had such an experience. Judaism has never appealed to the *experience* of Moses as a warrant for the Religion of the Law. Nor has it sought to perfect ways by which the faithful Jew could have some of Moses' experience.

On the other hand, belief in God the Holy Spirit has certain fairly obvious advantages for the work of the prophet. Here is a representation of God, fully and truly God, everlastingly committed to making the Kingdom of God intimate and precious to all men everywhere, through the ministry of the church and through other channels known only to God: and all of this in a way absolutely faithful to the power and form of life manifested in the life, suffering, death and resurrection of Jesus Christ. Here, furthermore, is a recognition of God governing history in his own way, imposing his own "logic" upon the flow of events in the world here below: not thinking as men think, not judging as men judge, ignoring human canons of justice and injustice, having no regard for towering human achievements, refusing to be impressed by worldly pomp and circumstance, granting eternal happiness to some anonymous character who offers a cup of cool water to someone in need, and withholding it, apparently, from a high-minded citizen who has observed every detail of the Law.—Surely here is a religious model of God moving with absolute freedom through the labyrinths created by Man to conceal himself from the piercing invincible demands of divine righteousness. Finally, in God the Holy Spirit faith has a model of God the Interpreter. It is he who brings *recognition,* of himself first and thereupon of ourselves, each bound to the other and to all others in a community of God's creation. Therefore the life of faith, that complex, formidable and withal exhilarating affair of construing all things as belonging wholly to God, opens before us, beneath us, over us, around us.

The Christian prophet, accordingly, would have excellent grounds for insisting upon an encounter with God as his justification and inspiration. This would be God the Holy Spirit, the sanctifying Presence before, so to speak, the eschatological Presence. Here encounter is as existential as you please. For this God is not *out there* as an empirically identifiable entity or power among other empirically identifiable entities and powers. But neither is he *in here* as a feature or quality of the hidden psyche or of the private soul struggling desperately or dreamily to maintain purity against the wickedness of the world out there. Rather God the Holy Spirit, the sustaining and sanctifying Presence, is apprehended as the mediating power rendering Being acceptable to beings, if you want a dash of ontological language. Or, in the language arbitrarily chosen for this occasion, mediating the antecedent disposition of faith to the potential consequences, potential not in the abstract scheme of Being and non-being, but in the context of moral decision. The ethical other, that is, exists in his full profile and weight of value. But what he and I *may become* together in conflict and in harmony, is yet to be made out. Somewhat fantastically I have used the term *inference* for that concrete process by which such potentialities are tracked down. The process or act by which they are realized is, of course, *decision;* and thereafter it is the giving and receiving of promise or pledge.

But perhaps the very openness demanded by encounter with God the Holy Spirit tends to minimize the acceptability or appropriateness of God so represented for the purposes of the contemporary prophet. Perhaps he needs to feel absolutely sure of his grounds. Perhaps he needs an *ultimate* justification for his posture and policies. Perhaps he is pre-disposed to believe that there is only one right course to be taken and endorsed through the thicket of modern life.

Pursuit of such considerations would precipitate us either into *ad hominem* arguments or into psychological exploration. The prophets themselves show some familiarity with both moves. I do not believe that this imparts either dignity or fertility to them —either to the moves or to the persons making them.

VI

Prophetic or otherwise the Christian is still left with a very old and very pressing question. How does he distinguish the presence and work of God from the other powers in and of the world, making for its improvement? Among the prophets there were of old "lying spirits." The faithful community had therefore to discover some way to discern the true prophet, and thereafter to dispose of the false ones. A very similar problem arose very early in the Christian community. I believe it persists into our own life. How ought we to cope with it? I have no novelties to propose and must therefore fall back upon the tradition, as follows.

(1) Whoever claims to have learned something directly from God for the reproof of the faithful community and for the building-up of the human commonwealth must show that he speaks and lives from the "antecedent disposition." If, that is, he does not "speak the truth in love" he does not speak *God's* word at all. This does not rule out any chance of his saying important and productive things. It rules out an effective appeal to the "God and Father of our Lord Jesus Christ," as the decisive justification for his performance.

(2) If the "word of the Lord" has indeed come to him personally, the claims he makes upon powers of recognition and enactment will have an element of novelty. They will be shocking, almost certainly. But the novelty will be a route of inference running from where the faithful now stand (or sit) to where they ought to be. The true prophet, in other words, is not so much concerned with disclosing new objects for acceptance and action as he is in showing that a reorientation of the antecedent disposition is now called for *by God*. No one is

surprised when Jesus says, with the Law and the Prophets, "Love your neighbor as yourself." The surprise comes in the disclosure of the neighbor's identity; he is *anyone* in need of your attention and help. In terms of the particularities of our own situation as Christians in America, we do not need prophets of the Lord to tell us that the black community has an enforceable claim upon our sense of justice. *The double-edged sword of prophetic truth must fall upon the factor of exclusivism in the antecedent disposition of the faithful.* Thus Racism is not the primordial sin of American life. The primordial sin is the division in the antecedent disposition: we all believe that the love of God in Christ Jesus is compatible with attachment to preferential arrangements of many sorts in which Ego and Ego-like are automatically Master. Thus even the Black, and the Red, and the Yellow, is let into the preferential community if he can show that he is *really* like us.

(3) The true prophet of the Lord is therefore the declared enemy of anything and everything that divides the human commonwealth into warring factions. The true prophet is not a breeder of suspicions, hostilities, and alienations. He is an enemy of false harmonizations. It does not follow that he is the friend of disruption.

(4) Both the prophet and the faithful community must therefore work from and with a normative model of the human commonwealth. The working models are inadequate; and they may be corrupt. What then shall we do, to be saved? Shall we encourage the prophet to turn visionary and produce a new model? The visionary is apt to consult Ideality first, as though that wondrous realm of being offered compositional models rather than clues, directives, solicitations, lures, etc.—offered, that is, unitary programs of what-to-do and how-to-do it. That is an ontological mistake. We would not worry about it if it had not had momentous practical consequences.

There is an alternative to the imaginative free-hand construction of a normative model of the human commonwealth. That is the Kingdom of Christ presented, re-presented, and accepted as the ambience of the antecedent disposition of the Christian. So understood, the Kingdom of Christ is not a blueprint for the rebuilding of the human commonwealth. Rather, it *is* the human commonwealth as it is recognized and claimed by Almighty God, the Father of our Lord Jesus Christ.

To this we must add a dash of historical realism. The higher righteousness opened to the antecedent disposition as the guidelines for the inference-tracking of the Christian life does not promise Utopia as the logical and historical reward. It offers instead something inexhaustibly rich: Wherever a person accepts his identity as a member of the Kingdom of Christ, he will surely come to recognize a brother or sister in every human being. Common beneficiaries of the righteousness of God, they can together construe the whole world as the object of God's antecedent disposition. To value the world after the model of God's valuing of it is the ultimate (as it is the fundamental) encounter with God in the conditions of this life.

In the world to come we shall know fully even as now we are fully known. That is one version of the Christian hope. It is for me the most precious, as it is also the most terrifying, because the knowledge of which it speaks is at once so familiar and so wonderful. I mean that knowledge which is the perfection of love.

Gabriel Vahanian

No Other God

As legacy of Christianity, the death of God inaugurates an understanding of the human reality whose advent rises in defiance of the traditional understanding of man as disclosed by faith. In view of this, Feuerbach could write already in the last century: "If I do not believe in God, God does not exist for me." [1] Strike hard at theism as he would, Feuerbach can formulate his thesis by merely adapting to his own use one of the major assertions of the Old Testament. But the propositions with which he concludes his argument oppose him to the Bible so radically that, in spite of his implacable logic, he forces us to wonder what is the originality of the Old Testament when it, too, affirms that without my idea or my awareness of God, God does not exist. Indeed, the latter's originality becomes evident as soon as one compares Feuerbach's position and the New Testament's claim that if I do not believe in Christ, God does not exist for me. It appears then that if Feuerbach's thesis consists in refuting theism on the basis of its own premises, and doing so merely in order to replace it with atheism, by contrast the New Testament challenges the very principle of a conflict between theism and atheism; it takes care to define neither God nor man by opposing them to one another and it even shows that the experience of the human reality as signified by "life in Christ," or, simply, by "Christ," is itself a test of the reality of God. Which amounts to saying,

60

practically, that, for the New Testament, anthropology is no anthropology as soon as it either presupposes or, conversely, excludes God; and that is the reason why if I do not believe in God, it is not God but Christ who does not exist for me. Even granting that on the whole the Church has been able to honor such a claim only by deifying Jesus, what remains evident nevertheless is that for Christianity, as well as for the New Testament, man is man only if he is the "supporting body" of God, his carrier or bearer. Demythologizing God so as the better to question man and his idolatrous imaginations about himself, Christology could not be read as a demythologizing of God unless the experience of the human reality is settled by evacuating God.

I

To be sure, classical Christianity derives its conception of man from two fundamental presuppositions, which are: the innateness of the idea of God in man, and the supernatural nature of the very operation by which man comes to faith. At best, this can lead to thinking either, like Tertullian, that *anima naturaliter christiana est,* or, like Calvin, that sinful man is consequently "without excuse" before God if he is given over to the idols fabricated by his own imagination.[2] At worst, this conception presents the major disadvantage of placing the human reality under the yoke of a double temptation: that of sinking God in the world by making him its supreme datum, and, on the other hand, that of totally banishing him. Placed thus under the sign of an unhappy anamnesis of God, the human adventure can be realized in the glimmer of no other hope save that of an apocalypse through which man's destiny is retrieved. Whether conceiving God as the ground or as the destiny of his being, man comes sooner or later to consider his own existence as a fall or as a debt to be paid by making a sacrifice of it. To be sure, it will also happen that he will settle in history, as though history were itself some vast hyperbole of the reality of God. The hu-

man reality is then transformed into a mere pedagogical exercise whose historicity melts into a design or a purpose—those
of a being as absolute as it is ungraspable. And should such a
purpose and such a design span man's space, they would do so
only in order to raise it into a high place either of memory or of
hope: the world overflows with meaning, and God is its param-
eter; or else history pursues its course, and God is the beginning
and the end of it.

Once deciphered, however, there remains nothing of such a
universe but a text, the chronology of sign-less human reality,
a reality of which God ceases to be the articulation, the one "in
whom we live and move and have our being" (Acts 17:28).

The death of God is the cultural expression of the mutation
undergone by man's self-understanding when God is no longer
the condition, the beginning and the end of it. With the birth
of Christianity the Western world was going to stop confusing God with nature; likewise, the emergence of today's post-
Christian civilization already obliges us to un-learn the necessity
of confusing God with history. This latter confusion, Christianity itself should have, indeed, refrained from indulging, given the
manner of its own affiliation to ancient Israel: it is by the
crumbling of Israel's historical messianism that the fulfillment
of the law results in the gospel and that eschatology is no
longer conceived of in relation to some design invested in the
historical development of a religion and social privilege, viz., the
descendance of Abraham according to the flesh, but in relation to the historicity of man (Jn 8:31-59; Rom 4:1-25).
There is no history other than of that which is inauthentic.

Not only, then, can this historicity no longer be conceived of
either as the realization of some "meditation of the life to come"
(Calvin), or as the precomprehension of the reality of God, but
it denies both at once by the very fact of its contingency.[3]
Evicted is the reality of God, overpowered as it is by the world's
as well as by man's own reality. God no longer twists the world
out of nothing into significance. Nor is his eviction done in the
name of an autonomy for which the world or man could hence-

forth serve as proof; it is done to the advantage of a "polynomy" of meaning wherein the meaninglessness of the world is immersed. From the standpoint of the autonomy-heteronomy duality, meaning and meaninglessness oppose or exclude one another; by contrast, polynomy implies that the world's capacity for meaning does not depend on the absence of meaninglessness. Meaning no more consists in what meaninglessness cannot abolish, than does faith in the elimination of doubt: faith consists in the polynomy of meaning which the world can attest if it is created *ex nihilo* but not if it emanates from a *primum movens.* Just as the gospel does not result from the abolition of the law but is what the law ends in, so also polynomy of meaning does not abolish the world but is what the world anticipates when the world becomes creation. Of course, we must be careful here not to understand by "creation" a sort of cosmological point of departure for the world: even in Genesis, if there is no world except through the word which brings it off as creation, it is because God does not become a cosmological hypothesis; creation is what happens to the world when God speaks, when the world itself speaks of God. As for the anteriority of God, this seems merely a temporal way of speaking of his otherness in relation to a world which, *ipso facto,* may no longer be considered divine. In any case, one thing is certain when trying to penetrate the meaning of Genesis: it is not the world in itself which presupposes the reality of God.

Seen from this angle, the traditional understanding of man appears in a considerably different light. Granting that it was determined by the presupposition of the existence of God, one must also concede that the reality of this God had no meaning outside of given situations: without the faith which, despite his tribulations, Job finds the means to confess, his story is simply the story of a life, the holiness of which is precisely not sufficient to explain this faith, and it is because his comforters tried to explain one by the other, that Job was led to exclaim: "I know that my redeemer lives" (Job 19:25). Job realized that he would only have been able to affirm exactly the opposite if he had listened to his comforters. At most, he would have disposed of an explanation of his faith *ad absurdum*. Somewhat like the Christian, so to speak, who today would appeal to the outdated problematic of the Church and its historicistic Christian ideology. Or who, rather, would admit the death of God as the ultimate secret of the alienating religiosity which Christianity has despite itself nurtured down the centuries. Which is why, incidentally, in rejecting Christianity, the man of the twentieth century is equally tempted to question the perennity of the sense for religion.

The Christian conception of God and of man have both been, indeed, so firmly predicated on the presumption of the innateness of religion that a quasi-indissolubility has in effect been operating between them. I do not know if, as Bonhoeffer pretends, we are moving toward an age totally divorced from religion.[4] Nor am I convinced that this would follow from the logic of that methodological atheism which is today required from any form of thought, theological thinking included. Indeed, one must not confuse the cultural crisis of conscience we are undergoing with the conflicts, whether social or religious, which distort as much as they manifest the nature of this crisis. There is crisis only when the impact of the future on the present cannot be explained through the mere logic of ideas handed down from the past; there is only conflict when there is aroused a desperate attempt to hold the future accountable, at any cost, to this logic of received ideas. Thus, because we find it difficult to accept the notion that the process of humanization if not of hominization has always been somewhat artificial inasmuch as it has been dependent on art or on culture no less than on nature, we are shocked by the resolutely artificial character of today's human technology. And yet, whatever the mode of humanization, is not the motive always the same? Is it not a certain consciousness man has of being irreducible? As for the sense for religion, it could be that its manifestations will at the most be modified by the appearance of a new type of *homo religiosus*. Had not, indeed, Feuerbach himself already sensed this when, in the last century, although in a slightly different perspective, he wrote with discernment: "Today's atheism is tomorrow's religion"? [5] As Cassirer said no less correctly: *"Religio una est in varietate rituum."* [6] Not that I in my turn would wish to advocate the quest of some meta-religion. But, whether it is a question of the mystagogy of whatever religion or that of magic, pure and simple, or whether it is a question of folkloric rites, the human reality brought to life by religious experience transcends the varieties of the latter. After all, if man has occasionally known progress despite religion, because of it, also, history is irreversible, even if the key to it is constituted neither by the progress of the sense for religion nor by its decline. For it is the experience itself of the human reality which is irreducible. It matters little, therefore, that the religiosity which has so far mediated the truth is, today, found to have become irrelevant. Provided, of course, that man has himself not become estranged from us: "Lord, when did we see thee hungry and feed thee, or thirsty and give thee drink? And when did we see thee a stranger and welcome thee, or naked and clothe thee? And when did we see thee sick or in prison and visit thee? And the King will answer them: Truly, I say to you, as you did it to one of the least of these, my brethren, you did it to me" (Mt 25:37-40).

II

No, the death of God does not refer *merely* to a cultural phenomenon about which we would be reassured if only we would denounce the alienating character of theism or of God as existential hypothesis, as some would-be critics have presumed rather naïvely. In the death of God, what must be dealt with is a mutation of the understanding of the human reality and, accordingly, of faith itself, a mutation whose real meaning none of these critics seems to have grasped any more than they have measured its consequences. For, in the last analysis, the death of God concerns nothing less than the impossibility of anchoring the archeology of our being, still less the genesis of the Christian faith, in the historical Jesus. Without God, Jesus is nothing more than a story, hardly a biography; at most, he serves as a pretext to the historical account of the emergence of a religion. And even if it were possible to liberate the powerfully contagious image of a "man for others," without God we would be missing what the tradition has confessed in proclaiming him "Christ," namely: insofar as man can be claimed as God's supporting body, through Jesus himself no other God is revealed than he who is "God for man."

The dilemma of a Christology without God is not so much that it eliminates God, even supposing that such a notion belongs to residual mythological thinking. It consists in neglecting an essential element of the Christologies of the New Testament, with respect to the incarnation, namely: the history of Jesus is as alienating to me as Israel's was to the man for whom the law and the prophets are fulfilled in the gospel. What gives value to the diverse Christologies of the New Testament is that they end in an anthropology and not in any ultimate effort to retrieve Jesus; they correspond each to a different problematic connected with one another by the question of how the God of Abraham, Isaac and Jacob can be the God of Jesus Christ, and mine. I mean that in speaking of Christ or of the word made flesh, the New Testament is not worried about ratifying the theism in whose mythological categories it seems inextricably enmeshed, so much as to designate the human reality as "divine condition." In so doing, the New Testament certainly demythologizes history just as the Old Testament had demythologized nature, but in neither case does this demythologizing exact any *sacrificium intellectus,* simply because the reality of God is not dissolved into man's. Because the New Testament Christologies avoid, indeed, historicizing God, "Christ" can be God's permanent significant in the very terms of the historicity of every human being. Otherwise, faith would be dealing only with Jesus, an historical character whose private life did not seem to interest either the gospels or the epistles, still less the Apocalypse, and from whom the death of God alienates us even more.

Without God, Jesus is no more than an historical character, sad and glorious, fierce but impotent, an epitaph of the human consciousness. Let Christology be determined by such an image of Jesus, and it could not justify itself without endorsing the decrepitude of the Christian faith. Surely, it is not in and of himself that Jesus is Christ. Nor can one say: he is Christ because he is my Redeemer, except if the reality of God is not disintegrated in that of man.

Though stemming from an obvious theism as to its vision of the world, the New Testament does not depend on it for the conception of God which governs the Christologies. The same holds for anthropology; the conception of God which determines it in the New Testament is such that Christ signifies not the deification of Jesus but the accomplishment of God's deed in man and for man. It is there then, in Christology, that the crux of the problem is located. And from that point, the whole question is to know whether the Christology of the New Testament can be understood to imply that the problem of God is either resolved or dismissed, or whether, on the contrary, it is by virtue of the anthropological orientation of its Christology that the New Testament introduces the problem of God in the sphere constituted by the experience of the human reality. To answer this question, it is necessary first to clarify what "God" signifies for the New Testament in particular, and for the Bible in general.

In the first place, we will point out that if the Bible consolidates its speech about God, thanks to the categorical scaffolding built on the theistic problematic to which it subscribes, theism itself is not what ultimately interests biblical thought. At the risk of disturbing some preconceived notions, we have no choice but to acknowledge that theism is not in itself necessary to biblical thought; what other meaning indeed could the affirmation have that constitutes the very foundation of the New Testament according to which God cannot be conceived except in terms of Jesus? To say that the word is made flesh or that God becomes man means nothing, it would seem, unless truly the flesh or man constitutes the "divine condition," and unless God

cannot be thought, and lived, except through the contingency of
the flesh, through whatever experience any man may have of
his own reality. All biblical thought, in spite of the diversity
often attributed to it and as often glossed over, insists on that
point. At any rate, we can see the proof of it in the fact that,
contrary to thought patterns we refuse to call into question, the
Old Testament concepts of God presented to us from beginning
to end vary among themselves as much as the Christocentric
monotheism of the New Testament differs from the monotheism
of the Old Testament. By contrast, what remains constant is the
anthropology.

It is true that for the Bible anthropology means something
quite different from what it usually does today. Whereas today's
anthropology focuses on the structures by which man grasps
his being-in-the-world, biblical anthropology sees in this
event itself the hinge of the presentness of a God who is only
by "being-here." In other terms, anthropology governs the logic
of the biblical discourse about God as much as it is shaped by this
logic of faith: God is not therefore a manner of speaking of man
in capital letters—any more than anthropology is a simple ap-
pendage of theology. Indeed, can one speak of creation and, in
particular, do so in the sense meant in Genesis, if it is necessary
that what determines man and the world must also negate them?
It is therefore no wonder that, far from seeing in man God's
antithesis, the Old Testament goes so far as to call him a God,
though without impugning the otherness of God. So also, the
notion of creation implies that the world is no vestige of the
presence of God, nor even the epiphany of an ungraspable God,
but the dwelling place of his Name, the paradigm of his presence. There, it seems, is the reason why classical Christian
theology was able to consider the Church as the body of Christ:
the man who is grafted thereto is the one for whom creatureli-
ness is at stake in any given historical situation, outside of which
it is not possible to conceive of God without falling into speculation or theodicy. Israel itself was not the chosen people except
insofar as it was not able to justify itself by or through its own

history. Sacred history is not a history parallel to that of other nations, nor even the supernatural envelope of that of Israel as a nation. But it signifies the possibility of renewing a destiny in spite of both the meaningfulness and the meaninglessness intrinsic to all previous historical unfolding of that destiny. When Israel identifies itself with its history, it ceases to be the chosen people. Live as it would, then, in the expectation of the Messiah, the latter needs only arrive for Israel not to recognize him. Indeed, the Christ event constitutes the denial rather than the end of that sacred history with which Israel is fettered. At any rate, the Christ event cannot be considered as the end of that history except, perhaps, insofar as Jesus represents the most radical denial of the ethnocentric messianism around which the history of Israel, it seems, sought to center itself. Nothing is less sufficient than having Abraham for father. Faith still is necessary, and the one sent from God still must be recognized when he comes. In other words, it is not fidelity to the faith of the fathers which was found wanting in the contemporaries of Jesus. On the contrary. But confusing this fidelity with the "meaning" which in their eyes the history itself of Israel had acquired, they were blinded by it instead of being liberated to become, with Jesus, the contemporaries of God. And yet, that is what the God of the fathers had always claimed, through his very promise to be with them everywhere they would be, *to be there* with them, no matter what the given historical situation.

Tied to the history of Israel, the reality of God is not exhausted with a history which is destined to pass away. The God who is, who was, and who will be, is he who *being-here* gives me also the possibility of *being-here;* he is that through which I assume the historicity of my contingency.

III

"God by himself is not God," says Barth in *The Word of God and the Word of Man.* "He might be something else. Only the

God who reveals himself is God." [7] Similarly, by himself Jesus is not Christ: we are insistently reminded of this by the very structure of the Apostles' Creed, where Christology occupies only the second article, and not the first, even if for the New Testament faith in God is predicated on faith in Christ. Otherwise, God would only be a myth, and the Christ event would not be the "denial" of man's imaginations about God, nor would it be the "true light which enlightens every man that comes into the world," or the word through which the world is made but which the world does not know (Jn 1:9-11).

It is true, in the Christ event, God hides or even suspends his divinity. That is to say, he does not act as a God should, at least according to man's imagination. He does not die. Not even in order to rise again, as is the case in certain myths of antiquity where such a strategy is justified by the desire to explain and to complete the gap between God and man, between man and himself: where, basically, God is a God who retrieves himself at the expense of man. On the contrary, if in the Christ event it seems that God is impoverished, it is because he no more disdains the poverty of his creature than he begrudges him his grandeur; it is because he is-here only in terms of a faith the very experience of which constitutes the human reality in its empirical dimension, and because the very facticity of the human condition is what is assumed by faith, and "victory by which the world is overcome" (1 Jn 5:4). Just that is what the New Testament means by the impossibility of believing God without believing in Christ. Since Caesarea Philippi it is not possible to confess God without confessing Christ; nor is it possible to confess Christ without confessing God. But to confess him through God does not mean describing him under the aspect of this or that concept of God, as do those who identify him as John the Baptist, or as Jeremiah or some other prophet. It means that we must take him for what he is, the man in whose life God becomes God for man, a man for whom the human reality is an account rendered by the reality of God: "When they had arrived in the region of Caesarea Philippi, Jesus asked his disciples this question: 'Who do men say that the Son of Man is?' And they said, 'Some say John the Baptist, others say Elijah, and others Jeremiah, or one of the prophets.' 'But who do you say that I am?' Simon Peter replied, 'You are the Christ, the Son of the Living God.' And Jesus answered him, 'Blessed are you, Simon Barjonah, for flesh and blood has not revealed this to you, but my Father who is in heaven' " (Mt 16:13-17).

As flesh and blood alone, Jesus is only an ideal man, whose charisma is undoubtedly exemplary, but not sufficiently so—far from that—for the faith to draw from it the symbol of its authority (Mt 21:23-27). As flesh and blood, even Jesus' authority over his disciples is repaid at the hour of the passion by the denials of Peter and the cowardice of the others. But it is not God who dies on the cross; it is the idol of those, not unlike the rest of men, for whom God dies as soon as he is worshipped. All our gods are idols and in particular the God who dies: [8] "Why do you call me good? None is good but God alone" (Lk 18:19).

Without God, Jesus becomes at best an idol, and ceases to be a man as the title Christ itself implies, or the early Christological definitions painfully attempted to bring to light: it is not by the historical exemplarity of his life that Jesus is Christ, but through the historicity of a given human reality, mine, which is "condition" of that Christ which Jesus is. Even in the divinity of Christ, it is the humanity of Jesus which, being at stake, is the condition of that divinity. Moreover, it is not in an attempt to retrieve Jesus that the Church attributes divinity to him, but rather in order to underscore the historicity of the believer. Here, no doubt, it will be objected: Does this not imply the ruin of the *ephapax Christi*—of the uniqueness of Christ, the notion that Jesus Christ is the only son of God? In order to reply to such an objection, it is sufficient, I believe, to indicate that the *ephapax Christi,* not being a mythological but an historical event, could not be distinguished in and of itself from what gives uniqueness to every other historical event; for God alone is unique, and he is the ground of man's possibility to be himself, by being for others what God is for man: man as the supporting body of God.

Admittedly, Jesus does not hesitate to identity himself in terms of his relationship to God or even to identify himself with him: "The Father and I are one" (Jn 10:30). But he also states in what this identity consists. He and the Father are one only to the extent that he has not come to give testimony of himself but of him who sent him (Jn 5:30ff; 8:13ff; 18:36-37). They are one to the extent that in the work accomplished by the one sent by God, and to the extent that in the Christ event itself, it is a question of the tangibility of God. As Vinet wrote: even while theology seemed to be concerned with diminishing God, it did not reduce God to man so much as it sought to guarantee the objectivity of grace, the grace which is constitutive of the human reality.[9] In other words, theology is in truth simply a matter of anthropology, but an anthropology in which the human condition is described in such a way that God is its regulating structure, and that, on the other hand, without that "condition," God could not be believed in. When Isaiah writes: "I am the Lord, and besides me there is no savior. I declared and saved and proclaimed, when there was no strange god among you; and you are my witnesses" (Is 43:11-12), Simon Bar-Yochai gives the following interpretation: "If you are my witnesses I am God, and if you are not my witnesses I am not, so to speak, any longer your God." [10]

If there are no witnesses, then there is no God. The same thought is expressed by Paul after listing all the witnesses of the risen Christ: "For if the dead are not raised, then Christ has not been raised. If Christ has not been raised, your faith is futile . . ." (1 Cor 15:16-17). If the experience which man has of his reality is not also its ultimate contestation, then man is no more than the gratuitous act of an absolute negation. But the resurrection signifies precisely the contestation of any experience of the human reality such that it would negate itself by sinking into the abyss of a God who annihilates it. Therefore, St. Paul maintains that, rather than culminating in the death of God, the Christ event implies exactly the opposite: the reality of the living God which becomes one flesh with man's. And in the cross, it is not God who is edged out of the world, as Bonhoeffer contends,[11] but our idols. For God is no transplant to be ultimately rejected by the human body; he is the ineffable, and the new man in Christ has no other name than his own by which to name him: "For there is no other name given to man, by which we can be saved" (Acts 4:12).

It is appropriate here to remember the affirmation by which we began our theme: the death of God blocks all return to Jesus. We then tried to show that (a) if traditional Christology itself goes bankrupt with the death of God, every attempt to raise from the ashes a Christology without God is doomed to failure, for the simple reason that the anthropology which thus underlies it now is merely predicated on the non-existence of God, instead of his existence; (b) if with the death of God, biblical anthropology, of which theology was as it were the "far side," can be appealed to again because it, too, understands the human reality as the condition of God, Christology becomes what permits me to acknowledge what separates me from Jesus and estranges him from me; at the same time Christology enables me to assert how—the human reality being itself condition of God—the God of Abraham, Isaac and Jacob, the God of Jesus can be mine. For without God, Jesus immediately ceases to be accessible to us. If man does not as such attest the reality of God, Christ himself is not risen and "empty also is our faith" (1 Cor 15:14). Without God, Jesus is a miscarriage of history; and rather than liberating him from the *chromo* to which myth and the supernatural have reduced him, a Christology without God can only confirm Jesus in a role of anonymous saver, from whom the death of God alienates us, irretrievably.

What then is faith, or what, indeed, is the Christology of the New Testament if not a certain understanding of man centered on his liberation from all psychologies, all anthropologies, and all theologies necessitated by the persistence of a sense for religion which ends up by alienating him? Not that in the final analysis the New Testament and the Old Testament are based on an understanding of man which would be either timeless or the condition *sine qua non* of biblical thought. On the contrary: when, for example, one considers the prophets of the Old Testament, their importance does not consist in claiming that they represent the ideal of all that is noble in the human being, or that they would be the *homines religiosi* par excellence; their importance consists rather in "the fact that in addressing their contemporaries they exhort them to concrete action, an action which could demonstrate their fidelity to the history that God puts at their disposal." [12] There is no faithfulness to God which does not involve the obligation to assume these cultural tasks which are concomitant with it. There is no faith which does not demand, as a sign of faithfulness to God, the obligation to assume the secularity through which, precisely, this faithfulness can express itself. This is, moreover, where secularity and secularism are differentiated.

But let Christianity retreat from the frontline of secularity, and it will but change into a religion of mysteries, the very antithesis of what it has claimed to be for twenty centuries. More or less fossilized and deprived of public character, Christianity would become the parasite of a segregationist spiritualism which would be worth little more than the ghetto to which its tradition has condemned it. As Vinet said, "To believe in God, and not to be able to draw from it any practical consequence, is, if you wish, to believe in God, but it is also to be without God." [13] If Luther had good reason to protest against works supposed to facilitate entry into heaven, it does not follow, either, that in neglecting these one should cut oneself off from the world. Just as "faith without works is dead" (Jas 2:26), and just as without man's witness, that is, that by which man conquers his humanity, there is no God, so also a Christianity which did not know how to renew its cultural vocation, soon would itself be endorsing the death of God, and denying Christology—that approach to man as act of faith which gave it birth.

IV

I have tried to show that in shifting the emphasis from the concept of God as *ens necessarium* to the biblical concept of God *pro nobis,* one need not be driven into pure subjectivism but perhaps one might be led to view the historicity of man as "divine condition," as that kind of presence in the world, through which the world, by becoming what "becomes" the creation, becomes the field of the tangibility of God. The mystery of the incarnation has less to do with the virgin birth of Jesus than with the possibility the new man has *hic et nunc* of living out that which he can only outlive, experiencing his new birth, that is, of becoming that which he is not. It is solely to this that all the Christologies of the New Testament are directed: Christologies whose different formulations were made necessary by the different historical situations of those who conceived them and for whom the Messiah, Christ, was an act of God more than an historical personage. In the New Testament as in the Old, it is always the human reality which is conceived as the "divine condition," or, to borrow a phrase from Teilhard de Chardin, as the "divine milieu." God is bound up with man to such an extent that without the latter's adoration he no longer is, so to speak. That is why he is not bound either by the world *qua* nature or by the messianism of any history, no matter how sacred. But in binding up the reality of God with the historicity of man, biblical thought signifies that no historical situation, even the one brought about by the disavowal of a particular religious tradition, is in itself alien to the reality of God, a reality of which Christ is the objectification: the darkness of Good Friday could not occlude the glory of Easter. The reality of God is given with that of man, yet without being contained entirely in it, since man himself is more than man, inasmuch as, confined as man is in a concrete historical situation, he has a past and a future only in terms of what the present can and must make possible. Nor can the very experience of the human reality corroborate the empirical data, of which it is composed, except if faith is constitutive of it.

On this condition, one may affirm that the Christian faith centers on Christ only in the measure in which the new birth (re-generation) is a co-generation, one in which the realization of man is revealed as a demonstration of God's otherness. Accordingly, human existence is considered from the biblical point of view at once as nature and as history, or rather as flesh and spirit, as an empirical datum on the physiological or biological level and as a spiritual or eschatic reality on the level of faith. Support of the spirit, the flesh is not for that less distinct from it. The spirit is identified as flesh, but it is not identical with it. And if, in a similar manner, it is through man that God is identified, in Christ this identity of God through which alone we are to be saved (Phil 2:9-10) reveals God's otherness. Not that we find here the *deus absconditus* so dear to mystics. God's otherness has nothing to do with the notion of a God who would negate himself in order to be and who is only by negating himself. It is concerned rather with the possibility that man has, as *dasein,* to contest all the false gods in whose name he sighs after the living God. Man can have no other god but the one in whose image he is created, and that God has no other image but the one which reflects his otherness. Moreover, this image is not composed of the natural and historical qualities of man, for man himself is other than the totality of his contradictions. It is a gift. And what man so receives is not a gift unless he really has also a right to it. But he has no right to it unless such a gift remains free, unless God remains *totaliter aliter:* and God cannot remain wholly other, unless hominization is not a negation of God, or unless anthropology is not an emptying out of theology,[14] and unless eschatology is not fixed into a history, even salvation history. That is why Barth was right in saying that the image of God is an eschatological reality; yet, that is true only if Jesus himself is not divinized and only if

Christ is the objectification of the reality of God from the standpoint of faith alone. The unity between the Father and the Son,
underlined so often by John (10:30-38), can signify nothing if
not that man has access to God, and has it precisely as man,
one whose life in Christ is revelatory of God: if the dead do not
rise says St. Paul, our faith is vain.

V

Far from substituting Jesus for God (either by making him
per se the manifestation of God on earth, or by an atheistic
retrieval of his person and his work), the New Testament affirms,
rather, that man, as such, and with the whole of creation, proclaims God's presence. For God is not an absolute, but the one
whose otherness is revealed in my way of being in the world.
Otherwise, faith would amount to believing that God is here or
there, this or that—in a word, a God who dies.

If it has always been said that the Trinity was the Christian
doctrine par excellence, the reason was not because it fulfilled
the need to maintain the identity of God across history so much
as because it allowed insistence on the historicity of man as
condition of faith as well as insisting on the human reality as the
divine condition. It being therefore a question of Man himself,
on this view, man can assume such a contingency only at the cost
of faith.

Confirmation of such a point of view is given, I am convinced,
by all the Christological developments which have taken
place since the writing of the first New Testament text. Even,
and perhaps especially, in acknowledging the role of Christology as that of a hinge between the doctrine of God and the
doctrine of man, one should not lose sight of the fact that, even
in a gnosticizing or adoptionist perspective, the essential element of the second article of the Creed was to show that through
the human reality the reality of God is what is at stake. In this
sense, the Johannine conception of the Word made flesh does

not prove relevant because of an insistence of sorts on the supernatural character of the divine intervention in the destiny of man. Rather, this conception attempts to stress the Old Testament's twofold affirmation, namely: it is, on the one hand, through the *flesh*—in other words, through man's historical situation more than through some history of which he would only be the machinery—that man is not estranged from God; and, on the other hand, God being thus neither what precedes man, nor *he-who-is* as an absolute, he is God for man only if he *is here* with man. Such a concept of God will no doubt be objected to on the grounds that God's reality is made to depend on the contingency of man, or of the world. I believe it works differently. Indeed, the criticism of the proofs of the existence of God has always underlined the fact that the concept of an *ens necessarium* in its turn necessitates the eternity of the world. And if one considered that the "world-ification" of the world as well as the humanization of man did not reveal God's *being-here* except in terms of his otherness, his contingency upon the world dispenses us from the necessity of appealing to the eternity of the world for an authorization to affirm this otherness of God of which eternity was the symbol. As far as I know, the pre-existence of the Son of God has never derogated from the contingency of Jesus as historical existence. Quite the contrary. Indeed in order that, as St. Paul says, authentic man may conduct himself according to "the dispositions that one has in Jesus Christ," he must certainly also be that "condition of God" which Christ attests when he does not consider it a prey but assumes it in its most perfect expression: the human reality.[15] The Christian tradition has throughout insisted on God as he who reveals man to himself. In Christ, what man reveals to himself is the humanity of God, a humanity which goes so far as not to reject even that by which God is negated (2 Cor 4:11; 5:11).

But neither the world nor man is that which in itself can negate God. That is how we must understand St. Paul's contention that the consuming of meat sacrificed to idols could not affect the integrity of the believer, for the simple reason "that there are no idols in the world and there is no God but One" (1 Cor 8:4-6), the one whose world is not an emanation but a creation, that is to say, a freedom which can neither be explained nor resolved by the antithesis of autonomy and heteronomy. That is why the reality of the new man in Christ, as Paul understands it, can smash only idols; it is not resorbing into God (as in the emanationist theories); indeed, man becomes that which he is not only if God remains wholly other than the idol man makes of him and would worship were it not contradicted by the very experience of man's own reality and, like an idol, smashed.

NOTES

1. Ludwig Feuerbach, *The Essence of Christianity,* New York, 1957, p. 200: "The existence of God must therefore be in space—in general, a qualitative, sensational existence. But God is not seen, not heard, not perceived by the senses. He does not exist for me, if I do not exist for him; if I do not believe in a God, there is no God for me. If I am not devoutly disposed, if I do not rise myself above the life of the senses, he has no place in my consciousness. Thus he exists only insofar as he is felt, thought, believed in—the addition 'for me' is unnecessary. His existence therefore is a real one, yet at the same time not a real one; a spiritual existence, says the theologian."
2. Cf. Calvin, *Institutes* 1/13/2.
3. Just as gadgets become needs, so also to the extent that God is necessary to the world, he is superfluous to it.
4. Bonhoeffer, *Letters and Papers from Prison,* New York, 1962, p. 162.
5. Feuerbach, *The Essence of Christianity,* p. 32.
6. Ernst Cassirer, *An Essay on Man,* New York, 1956, pp. 98-99.
7. Karl Barth, *The Word of God and the Word of Man,* New York, 1957, pp. 202-203.
8. Cf. Jacques Maritain: "L'idole est dieu et n'est jamais tout à fait dieu," "Signe et symbole," *Revue Thomiste* (April, 1938), pp. 315.
9. Alexandre Vinet, *Etudes sur Blaise Pascal,* Paris, 1904, p. 210: "A en juger par les apparences, la théologie a eu plus souvent affaire à la tendance qui cherche à diminuer la Divinité qu'à celle qui cherche à diminuer l'humanité."
10. *Pesikta derabbi Kahana,* p. 102 (I owe this information to Poksar Manfred Vogel); cf. Franz Rosenzweig, "Atheistic Theology: From the Old to the New Way of Thinking," *Canadian Journal of Theology,*

XIV (1968) 2, pp. 79-88; Henry Slonimsky, "The Philosophy Implicit in the Midrash," *Hebrew Union College Annual* (1956), pp. 263-264; Zohar III, 93b, Guy Casaril, *Rabbi* Siméon Bar Yochai et la Cabbale, Paris, 1961, pp. 104, 109.

11. Dietrich Bonhoeffer, *Letters and Papers from Prison*, p. 219.
12. Rudolph Bultmann, "Die Bedeutung des Alten Testaments für den christlichen Glauben," *Glauben und Verstehen I*, Tübingen, 1958, p. 323.
13. Vinet, *op. cit.,* p. 243.
14. Cf. Clyde A. Holbrook, "The 'Death of God,' American Style," *Journal of the American Academy of Religion* XXXVI (1968), no. 2, pp. 123-125.
15. Phil 2:5-11. Cf. in particular Pierre Bonnard, "L'Epître de Saint Paul aux Philippiens," *Commentaire du Nouveau Testament,* Vol. V, Neuchatel-Paris, 1950.

Raymond Panikkar

Nirvana and the Awareness of the Absolute

There have been many attempts to express the awareness of the Absolute. Two of the main attitudes could be summed up in the expression *transcendent transcendence* symbolizing the Semitic trend proper to the Jewish-Christian-Islamic and modern post-Christian tradition, and *immanent transcendence* proper to the bundle of religions which we call Hinduism.

The Buddhist approach is startling. It does not fit into the above-mentioned typology. It would rather say that the true awareness of the Absolute is to have none.

Let us quote a passage of probably pre-Buddhistic times:

"8.—Now a dispute once took place between the Spirit (*manas*) and the Logos (*vāc*) as to which was the better of the two. Both Spirit and Logos said, 'I am excellent!'

"9.—Spirit said, 'Surely I am better than thou, for thou dost not speak anything that is not understood by me; and since thou art only an imitator of what is done by me and a follower in my wake, I am surely better than thou!'

"10.—Logos said, 'Surely I am better than thou for what thou knowest I make known, I communicate.'

"11.—They went to appeal to Prajapati for his decision. He, Prajapati, decided in favor of Spirit, saying (to Logos), 'Spirit is indeed better than thou, for thou art an imitator of its deeds

81

and a follower in its wake; and inferior, surely, is he who imitates his better's deeds and follows in his wake.'

"12.—Then Logos (*vāc*, fem) being thus gainsaid, was dismayed and miscarried. She, Logos, then said to Prajapati, 'May I never be thy oblation-bearer, I whom thou hast gainsaid!' Hence whatever at the sacrifice is performed for Prajapati, that is performed in a low voice; for Logos would not act as oblation-bearer for Prajapati." [1]

This was a fundamental option. By and large, I would dare say that India decided in favor of the primacy of the Spirit and the West for the Logos. The consequences are far-reaching. I would like to exemplify a single instance and would like to beg that what follows be understood in the light of the just-quoted text.

Most religions have to do with God to such an extent that to speak of an atheistic religion seems to be a contradiction in terms. Yet around the sixth century before Christ, at that time when humanity seemed to be awakening to self-consciousness in a reflexive fashion, when men began to develop a critical attitude, there appeared some religious reforms, Jainism and Buddhism, which claimed to establish a whole norm of life with no reference to God. These reforms, although they excluded the existence, the essence, the name and the reality of God, soon became authentic religions. It could even be said that the elimination of the name of God is, for the Buddha, the supreme religious undertaking.

Much has been written about the so-called Buddhist atheism and many hypotheses seeking to explain his silence have been proposed.[2] I would simply like to indicate here what seems to me to be the fundamental attitude of the Buddha on the problem of the name of God, an attitude which was at the origin of the whole Buddhist tradition and which could well have exceptional importance for our present time.

To be brief, I shall introduce the problem with no reference whatever to the surrounding Brahmanism, to the religious ferment, and to the multiplicity of gods at the time of the Buddha.

I would only cite one verse of the Bible that will situate us *in medias res:* "You shall not utter the name of Yahweh your God to misuse it." [3]

Why?

Because one cannot speak of God but may only invoke him, because talk about God does not belong to current language, because his name is justified only in the vocative, because he is not an object like others whose name cannot be linked to other names, and because respect and adoration are due to him. That is the traditional answer of nearly all the religions.

Now the Buddha goes further. He tells us that any speaking of the name of God, that any talk about God, and even all thought, are just so many blasphemies. According to the Buddha it would be pure hypocrisy to forbid the making of images of God or the speaking of his name if it were permitted to think of him at the same time. Of what use is it to cast God from the imagination, from the pen, the lips, or from the walls, if one retains the thought of him? He will thus tell us: because God can only be named in vain, because every name of God is a vain name (a false name, if one wishes to follow the modern translation), because no name attains to God, since God is beyond all possible naming. Now all that is, is in one way or another nameable, and being is the last object—or the ultimate subject, if one prefers—of all that is named. God cannot be named, nor even can he be called "being"; that would be to kill him, to destroy him as God, by situating him among the things of this world. God does not *have* a name because he *is* not. That is what Buddhism will defend to its very last consequences.

"Why do you ask my name?" [4] says the man, the angel or the god who wrestles with Jacob. There is no need to emphasize the importance of this text and others like it [5] in the Christian tradition in general.

One cannot ask the name of God either because one does not have the right to do so, for God has a hidden name, a secret name, which he reveals only to the initiate, etc. (this alternative seems to have been the line followed by the Christians and

Islamic tradition) or else because he has no name. It is this second alternative that the Buddha chose and which he pursued to its extreme. We shall now attempt to examine it.

I

The Buddha's attitude is well known. He does not answer questions on the ultimate nature of things. He refuses to allow himself to be brought into purely speculative discussions, for they do not lead to deliverance from suffering and they distract us from the existential and concrete meaning of life. The famous parable is well known: when a man is pierced by an arrow, to concern oneself with conjectures on the direction whence the arrow came, the nature of the arrow, the possible motives for which it was shot, the identity of the guilty man, whether he was in the right, etc., will be the cause of the wounded man's death well before there is time to answer the questions that were raised.

To understand the Buddha's attitude it is possible to distinguish a double level in his silence.

1. The Silence of the First Degree: The Silence of the Answer

No answer to the question on the nature of the absolute can possibly give the desired information since the question itself cannot be absolute—for we are relative, limited, contingent. If it is said that nirvāna does not exist, one falls into the existential contradiction of trying to show and to follow a path toward something that does not exist. If one says that nirvāna exists one falls into a series of inevitable contradictions. Basically that would be dealing a fatal blow to transcendence, for it would be rendering it accessible to our thought or to our speech. At the same time one falls into a speculative contradiction, for the existence of an absolute should explain the burning questions that man raises, resolve his difficulties and save him from the contradiction.[6] Yet life and philosophy, experience as well as thought bear witness that such is not the case. It is thus necessary to maintain silence if one does not want to fall into a contradiction. Silence is the sole response.

Nevertheless, it is not out of fear of committing himself or out of fear of falling into logical contradiction that the Buddha remains silent. Quite to the contrary, his silence is irksome to people, and, according to the spirit of his time, it can well be said that failure to elaborate a new theory amounted to casting oneself from the company of cultivated and spiritual men. His silence is a greater commitment and also more eloquent than any theory whatever.

The Buddha wishes to teach us to know silence, to love it and to grasp its message. He speaks of the noble silence and says that the monk is a lover of silence. He thereby indicates to us that the reality of speech, that the world of signs and of expressions can be surpassed. Concerning God total silence must be kept. Neither his affirmation nor his negation can lead us to attain the threshold where divinity is found, or can also not be found. His message invites us to surpass the world of signs and the world of words, of speech, the realm of the *logos*. You will come to divinize the logos, he would have said, if you persist in seeking to penetrate everywhere by the power of your discourse. That is what has happened in the West, where by reaction man has fallen prey to the other extremity, of antitheism. Without myth, the logos becomes an absolute, it divinizes itself, and a divinized logos destroys its very self.

As for the excuse that the logos speaks to us only of the existence and not of the essence of God, of the "back" of God and not of his "face," of an indication and not of a localization, of an analogy and not of a univocal concept, of an image and not of a notion, of a name and not of a reality, and that we can grasp the name of God as the ersatz of the non-comprehension of his being, etc., this the Buddha would refute as the worst example of spiritual and intellectual hypocrisy, as the religious farce that speaks of something which is affirmed to be unknown. The

game must be played clean, the Buddha would say, and he was
to attract crowds who were tired of complicated religiosities.

To say that for God all is clear, to affirm that the contradictions, the tearings of human life, its injustices, its sufferings and
its scandals are but appearances that have been deformed by
our ignorance or by our sin (since for God in his happiness all
goes well, all is just and good), to seek to convince us that we
must accept, with blind belief, that in God all the contradictions
are resolved, and that we must content ourselves to know only
his existence, all this is for the Buddha a striking example of the
weakness of the established religions that perpetuate a state of
things (organization, cult, castes, etc.) for very mixed motives.
Buddhism would add that to defend the possibility of knowing
the existence of God and to close off the content of his essence
is equivalent to postulating his existence from motives that have
nothing to do with God, but that stem from the desire that man
has to find a crutch outside of reality. Buddhism says that it
can well do without the God hypotheses, without in that way
falling into the contradiction that affirms the most important
thing about God, his existence, and denies the knowledge of his
essence. What is the meaning of an existence whose essence
cannot be known?

But the Buddha does not stop there. He does not pretend that
his silence is the adequate answer. He does not fall into the
trap, so often found in the history of human thought, of believing that all the others up to his time have been wrong and
that it is he that will bring forth the true solution. In a word,
silence is not the Buddha's answer. He does not answer by silence. To think this way would be to misunderstand him and to
follow him only on the outside, as a pure philosopher and
simply out of intellectual curiosity.

To ask the name of God means to ask his identity, to en-
close him in our categories, even if one says that his name is
secret and unknowable. According to the Buddha he has no
name; because there *is* nothing that *has* this name. There is not
even any meaning in saying that God is identical to himself;

because he has no identity, he cannot be identified by a name. The principle of identity would destroy him. There can be no God identical to God—to himself. But the Buddha is not an agnostic; he is an Enlightened One. It is here that the modern age and contemporary Buddhist studies generally fail to grasp his spirit, reducing him to a thinker, a philosopher, or a great humanist, forgetting that he was above all a prophet, a mystic, a saint. I would propose to call his silence a silence of the second degree.

2. The Silence of the Second Degree: The Silence of the Question

The Buddha's silence is neither a methodology, nor an answer; it is not a new theological or philosophical system. The Buddha does not answer by silence; he does not answer. He remains silent and gives no hermeneutic of his silence but only of his refusal to answer. He explains why he does not rally to the views of this party or that one, he gives reasons why he does not share the belief of those who say that the soul exists after death, and also why he is not of the contrary opinion. He gives the reason for his refusal, but he does not expand upon his silence. He says categorically that he is not of the opinion of those who say A, nor of those who say non-A, nor of those who at once affirm and deny both A and non-A.[7] He does not give a positive opinion, he goes over every possible opinion and he denies being of whatever opinion there may be. Nevertheless, he does not give his own opinion. He is silent, but his silence is not an answer to the question.

What the Buddha does is to make silent the question, to silence the question, to pacify the questioner by showing him that his question has no meaning, or rather that he does not have the power, and hence the right, to phrase such a question. He puts the question in crisis, in a way, and thereby even the questioner. He puts the question in question, and thereby also the questioner who had identified himself unduly with his question. The question appears anguishing when man identifies himself with his reason and loses the global perspective of his human situation. The entire message of Gautama reduces itself to making men understand that to torture oneself over the so-called major questions of life is the great human fallacy, the source of misery and the price paid for the utopia of believing oneself in the right, and worse yet in the duty, of piercing the mystery of existence. Such an ideal is the fruit of human pride. What the Buddha requires is a realistic sense of acceptance of reality just as it presents itself, a total confidence in life, in what is given to us, without seeking to replace reality with our own ideas. His faith is a cosmological faith, his hope is the elimination of every future, and his love is the compassion for men of flesh and bones, our contemporaries, and not an ideal entelechy that exists nowhere.

When man will have discovered by himself that he has nothing to ask, that the question on ultimate reality has no meaning and that in spite of that he is neither a rebel nor discouraged, yea despaired, then man will begin to understand the message of liberation of primitive Buddhism: the total acceptance of our human condition, of the real contingency in which we find ourselves. It is not a matter of resigning oneself to never surpassing the human condition; it is rather understanding that what we must do is to better it, and that if it must be surpassed, that does not depend absolutely on us, and that if it must not be surpassed, every effort to do so will lead us to alienation and will only increase our misery. The entire message of the Buddha tends to render silent, to silence our desires. It is often said, but it is easily forgotten that the most intense desire or thirst, as the Buddha himself says, is the desire to transgress reality, to evade the human situation: to attach oneself to life is just as unreal and deadly as to wish death, no matter what the motive. The thirst for non-existence is to be eliminated as well as the desire for existence.

"Blessed are the poor in spirit" is what the Buddha wanted to say; not the poor who seek and beg, but the poor in spirit, those who in their spirit do not want to jump beyond themselves and believe that they can become as gods. The Buddha does not discourage human and secular initiatives, but he will not recognize as a true religious undertaking the evasion of the human condition by whatever means at man's disposal.

If there is a transcendence, it will take care of itself; that is the Buddha's message in summary. And if it does not exist, it is useless to mistake oneself. But there is more to that. Transcendence, if it exists, is so very transcendent that it surpasses both our thought and our being, and thus also any attempt whatever to name it. To name the absolute would be, for the Buddha, the great blasphemy. The Buddhist apophasis is an apophasis at once ontic and ontological. Silence is taken seriously, and not as another form of expression or speech. In the last part of this study I will try to explain this with a dialectic borrowed from the Buddhist tradition.

II

"Is the principle of sufficient reason insufficient for naming God?" Castelli asks us at the end of his introduction to the colloquy on *The Name of God*.[8] Here then, according to the Buddhist tradition, is the Buddha's genial answer.[9]

Buddhism will tell us without hesitation that it is by virtue of this same principle that we must renounce naming God, and thus also to asking anything whatever about him. He cannot even be named without sinning against this principle, which is the basis of all rationality. How can one postulate a sufficient reason that is other than and superior or exterior (God) to that of the very principle of sufficient reason without presupposing *ad infinitum* such a series of principles? Before seeking to grasp the Buddhist dialectic, I would like to make a brief excursus in order to situate the problem in the history of religions.

1. The Dialectic of the Name of God

I shall summarize my point.[10] We could discover a sort of dialectical play in what concerns human relations with this superior principle, which we agree to call God.

I would like to highlight the following moments. I would request that they not be considered chronological milestones, but, if I may use the expression, *kairological* moments.

(a) Before the cultural and religious complexity of the so-called great (higher) religions, each god is a local god with a local name, which is a proper name. To know the god is to know his name, and vice versa. The act of faith is the act of invoking the name. This name has usually been revealed in the myth.

(b) There is an early realization, either by an encounter of different traditions, or by a deepening of the mystery of God, that God has several names. The first reaction is to consider a plurality of gods corresponding to the plurality of names. Thus the harmony between the name and the thing is not broken. To each name there corresponds one god.

(c) True polytheism, however, cannot be upheld for very long. The plurality of gods, guaranteed by the plurality of names, leads to the discovery that there is a basic unity among the gods, that they are, in one way or another, but the different manifestations of a single and unique supreme power. Thus it is that the innocence of the name is in process of being weakened. Each name of God does not exhaust the divinity, since there are other names that also refer to the divinity. Men begin to suspect that the name of God is not God, or rather that his name is not *the* name of God, but *a* name of God or the name of *a* god. The name of God does not express God, so to speak. A break, a hiatus appears between the name and the thing. It is truth that bridges the gap.

(d) It is at the same moment when the divine name suffers its first crisis due to the fact that the plurality of names suggests a plurality of gods that the tradition of the hidden name of God begins its course in the history of religions. The names of God are not his true name. His true name is hidden, it is secret and reveals itself only to him to whom God wants to reveal it. It is to his devotees that the divinity uncovers his true name. The revelation is the revelation of this name. One hears it said even today, in Christian theology, that Christ is nothing else but the revelation of God inasmuch as he is the true name of God outside whom there is no salvation.

(e) The essence of the secret name is that it is unknown. In the beginning man could rest content to say that it is unknown to the uninitiates, but soon man becomes aware that the secret name represents something more than the divine whim to remain hidden, or the selection of a small group (as the part of the divinity) to whom the name would be revealed; there is an awareness that God has a name which in itself is hidden, so to speak. One thus arrives at the highly suggestive formulation of the name of God as simply an interrogation. God is the question that is always open, his name is the simple question about him, to find him means to seek him; to know him means not to know him (to name him means to invoke him as an unknown god with an unknown name), for his name is the pure and simple question. God is not a substance and he has no name, but he is a question, he is a simple pronoun and even an interrogative pronoun: *Who?*

(f) The next moment of the kairological dialectic is of more than historico-religious interest. A good deal of the contemporary reflection of mankind rests perhaps on this point. If God is the transcendent, the non-anthropomorphic, the ever Other, the interrogative pronoun, the question, the search, the road ever open and beyond, a suspicion enters the mind of man: at bottom is he not really questioning himself rather than interrogating God? Is not the question about God in its depth the question about man? Is not anthropology the true theology? Is not the question on God the anguished quest or the hope-filled question of man concerning himself, about the meaning of his life, of his destiny? Is it not really the Self that is sought?

(g) The dialectical process does not end there. At this point Buddhism brings us its contribution. Since there is no appeasing answer to the question about God or about Man, on the meaning of life or on the explanation of the mystery of existence, will not silence then be the true response? Does he alone who knows how to be silent understand the mystery of the real? We have arrived up to this point in our presentation and even up to the following point.

(h) Silence as an answer remains nonetheless suspect, since every question requires a decision and a choice. Silence can appear to be cowardly, a lack of courage to take a position and to rid oneself of atavic remains. If silence is a sign, it is a sign that is very weak and very vague. It can be acceptable as a moment of transition inasmuch as one does not dare to destroy all the idols at once, but it does not satisfy the human mind. It is here that our last point appears: silence as a question and not as an answer. Man has come to silence the question; it appears robbed of meaning. Man no longer asks, he lives, he has regained innocence on a higher plane.

(i) This would be the last moment of this sort of dialectical circle. One returns to daily living, as the tenth of the Zen tableaux, the seventh mansion of Saint Theresa, or any affirmation of nearly all the mysticisms shows. God is immanent and transcendent, existent and non-existent, and at the same time he is not. There is nothing more to be said. God is that about which there can be no talk. Discourse on God is basically inauthentic; it is only in the interior cell where the logos is silent that the Father can be adored in spirit and in truth.

This is not irrationalism, fideism, or religious romanticism. The Buddha leads us by the hand, and I would want to develop his dialectic further very briefly.

2. The Reduction of the Silence

In many instances the Buddha does not impose silence, but he wins his adversaries by converting them to his way, not by a reduction to the absurd of the reasoning of others but by what I would like to call a reduction to the sublime. It is for that reason that those who come to question him are not only won over, but they are converted, and very often they enter the order of *bhikkhu,* in Sanskrit *bhikṣu*). Nevertheless, on rare occasions he reveals the dialectic of his thought by directing the attention of his interrogator to the meaning of the question itself.

"When a bhiksu, Sirs, knows thus and sees thus, would that make him ready to take up this question as intelligent (and intelligible)?" he often asks after a long discourse on the absurdity of holding any opinion whatever on the ultimate problems of the human condition.[11]

I would like to analyze just one text. To the question repeated a thousand times in the dialogues of the Buddha concerning some information on the meaning of life, the Buddha answers the monk Rādha in this way:

"Rādha, you can grasp no limit to this question." [12] "That question is beyond the compass of an answer." [13]

But it is worth translating the text in full.

"Thus have I heard:—The Exalted One was once staying near Savatthi, in the Deer Park.

"Then the venerable Rādha came to the Exalted One. Having done so, he saluted the Exalted One and sat down at one side.

"So seated the venerable Rādha thus addressed the Exalted One:—

'They say, "Māra! Māra! lord. Pray, lord, how far is there Māra?" ' [14]

'Where a body is, Rādha, there would be Māra or things of the nature of Māra, or at any rate what is perishing. Therefore, Rādha, regard the body as Māra; regard it as of the nature of Māra; regard it as perishing, as an imposthume, as a dart, as pain, as a source of pain. They who regard it thus rightly regard it.

'And the same is to be said of feeling, perception, the activities and consciousness.'

'But rightly regarding, lord,—for what purpose?'

'Rightly regarding, Rādha, for the sake of disgust.'

'But disgust, lord,—for what purpose is it?'

'Disgust, Rādha, is to bring about dispassion.'

'But dispassion, lord,—for what purpose is it?'

'Dispassion, Rādha, is to get release.'

'But release, lord,—what is it for?'

'Release, Rādha, means Nibbāna.'

'But Nibbāna, lord,—what is the aim of that?'

'This, Rādha, is a question that goes too far. You can grasp no limit to this question.[15] Rooted in Nibbāna, Rādha, the holy life is lived.[16] Nibbāna is its goal, Nibbāna is its end.' " [17]

This is reduction to the sublime. He does not say that the question has no meaning. How could he say that when it is the anguishing question for a good part of mankind and the very torture from which, according to the Buddha, he has come to liberate us, the torment of useless anguish and of suffering without reason? It is not an absurd question.

It is not a false question either. There are no false questions, properly speaking. It could be a contradictory question and in that sense false: a question which negates itself in its very asking because it is founded on a contradiction. But that is not the case.

Those who ask this question are not considered weak in mind by the Buddha nor are they sinners against logic. The most profound parallel which I can find—and I hope that I will not be found amiss—is that between the Buddha's attitude and the cry of Jesus: "Father, forgive them for they know not what they do!" When he finds himself before the Absolute, man truly does not know what he is saying nor what he is doing.

Let us imagine the question: "What is God?", for that is basically the question at hand though nirvāna be the problem of the dialogue quoted above. The Buddha answers that the question itself cannot grasp its proper limits, that the question does not know what it is asking. We must be careful in our exegesis. The Buddha does not say that the man who raises the question does not have something very positive in mind when he asks. He believes he knows it. He is asking about the Absolute, about God, about the last things, about eternity, about nirvāna, etc. And he who asks will never be mistaken in his asking. He knows very well what he wishes to know. What is truth? That is the question that Pilate asked of him whom he called "Man" and he also obtained nothing but silence.

What the Buddha is saying is that the question itself is not capable of defining its limits, that the question asks nothing, for it does not know where the request leads or what it asks for. Let us suppose that I answer the question "What is God?" by saying "Mu!" How would I know that this answer is not a satisfactory answer if the question itself does not know, and cannot know, what it takes in and what it leaves out? If I ask the color of the stone hidden in Sakyamuni's pocket, I have an idea of the limits of the question. I do not know the color of the stone, nor even all the colors, but I do know what a color is, and I am able to distinguish a color from a sound, or anything else. The question, in a word, already contains the answer ontically; the question determines the very level at which the answer is an answer, and through which the answer must pass, so to speak. The question fixes the limits of the answer and also gives it its conditions of intelligibility. Only what it is possible to ask is asked because the limits of the answer are already known.

It is for this reason that in many religious traditions it is admitted that to seek God implies having found him already, and that to ask about him means, in a way, to know him already. The unquestionable cannot be questioned; and if the Absolute is questionable it is no longer absolute. In other words, the real question about the nature of the Absolute cannot grasp its limits, can offer no ground by which the answer might be verified, as modern terminology would put it. The question does not know what it is asking; it is not a question.

That comes down to saying that I am asking nothing, and not just nothingness. That comes down to destroying the question, for in asking nothing there is no more question. All the meaning that I find in the question is a meaning that I inject into it, the meaning that the questioner gives it, but certainly not the meaning of the question itself.

And now we are near the end of the Buddha's catharsis. The meaning of the question is not that of the question, but the meaning that the questioner gives it, his anguish, his insecurity, his doubts. He projects in a question a problem that the question does not contain and cannot contain or support. What is to be done in that case?

What the Buddha does is very clear. He makes us understand

that the real question destroys itself, and in so doing it ceases to be a question and frees us to go directly into the path of deliverance. To be sure, by destroying the question he has also destroyed the questioner, the little ego who had identified himself with his question. What is to be done then? To make man aware of his limits, to center him on what he can do, not to distract him from his human task, not to allow him to become dissipated in his speculation, to make him lose his ego which makes him believe he is a little god. The Tathāgata repeats his theme constantly: to show man the path to deliverance. He removes man from the obsession with orthodoxy in order to return him to *orthopraxis,* to the eightfold path, which leads us to liberation because it eliminates the obstacles—in a word, contingency—and is not preoccupied with the rest.

Must one then renounce all intelligibility? Neither Buddha nor Buddhism would say that. I have just sought the dialectic of the matter: the very question destroys itself as a question. But this is an existential operation in which reason by itself can do very little. How does one get the logos to silence itself? Of course, the logos must not be made silent, but it must simply recognize that there is a gate which it must not cross, that it can eat of all the fruits of paradise, save one: that God cannot be named. Much more: man must recognize that there is no need whatever to name God, that the question is not even raised, and that if it is raised, that shows me that I am falling into the *hybris* of believing myself to be a little god who can question God and ask him to explain himself or to justify himself.

These are all metaphors. The question is also raised at an altogether deeper level: at the very level of being and of Being. God certainly is not in any of the senses that we could give to this concept. But Buddha has not said it in this way, for he never loses sight of the existential and personal levels on which he is speaking. He sets forth no theory. The problem of God does not lie in the realm of theory. It does not belong to the realm of the word, but to the kingdom of silence.

I would answer our philosophical query in this way on the part of the Buddha: the principle of sufficient reason forbids us to name God in any way whatever.

The new question would be this one: Is the man who no longer questions still a man, or has he become an angel? or a beast?

The Buddha does not reduce the word to silence, nor does he speak of a word of silence, but rather he helps us to discover the silence of the word: the Buddha smiles!

III

I leave aside here three problems, which I state thematically:

(1) Is it still meaningful to speak of God, when one has understood what the Buddha says? Can the name of God be considered a stage in the awakening of consciousness of mankind? Can there be faith without an object?

(2) Can lost innocence be regained? Is salvation possible without thought of God? Can man cease to raise the ultimate and definite question?

(3) Would the Buddha be in agreement with someone who would not speak to him of God, but who would add that the word (*logos*), the image (*icon*) is the other pole required for the dialogue, and which is called "man"? Can there be a cross-fertilization between silence and the word? Would it be the smile?

NOTES

1. *Satapatha Brahmana* I, 4, 5, 8-12. Julius Eggeling (tr. & ed.), *The Satapatha Brahmana*, Delhi, Motilal Barnasidass, 1963.
2. Cf. R. Panikkar, *El Silencio del Dios,* Madrid, 1970. The reader will find the appropriate scholarly notes and historico-religious apparatus in this work.
3. Exodus 20:7. The Jerusalem Bible translation is very significant: "You shall not utter the name of Yahweh your God to *misuse it,*

for Yahweh will not leave unpunished the man who utters his name to *misuse it.*" The Vulgate gives: "Non adsumes nomen Domini Dei tui *in vanum;* nec enim habebit insontem Dominus eum qui adsumpserit nomen Domini Dei sui frustra." The Septuagint uses the same expression in both cases. Cf. as points of reference: Leviticus 19:12; 24:16; Deuteronomy 5:11; Ecclesiasticus 23:9; Matthew 5:33-35; James 5:12.

4. Genesis 32:30 (29 in the Vulgate and Septuagint): "Cur quaeris nomen meum?"

5. Cf. Judges 13:18: "Cur quaeris nomen meum, quod est mirabile" and the relation that Christian thought has found between these two texts and those of Psalm 8:2 and 10 and Isaiah 9:6, etc. The Jerusalem Bible translates the "mirabile" ($\theta\alpha\upsilon\mu\alpha\sigma\tau\acute{o}\nu$) as "mysterious."

6. I do not resist the temptation of quoting the "Buddhist" answer of Jesus when he refused to say by what authority he was acting, if even the "high priests and the elders of the people" did not know if the baptism of John was by heaven or by man. Cf. Matthew 21:23-27.

7. The fourteen propositions which the tradition attributes to the Buddha and which he affirms not to uphold are the following:
   1-2-3-4: the world is, is not, is and is not, neither is nor is not finite in time;
   5-6-7-8: the world is, is not, is and is not, neither is nor is not finite in space;
   9-10-11-12: the Tathāgata exists, does not exist, exists and does not exist, neither exists nor does not exist after death;
   13-14: the soul is, is not identical with the body.

8. Cf. *L'Analyse du langage théologique: le nom de Dieu,* edited by E. Castelli, Paris, 1969, p. 22.

9. Even if the texts upon which I am basing myself were not spoken by Gautama himself, they are ancient texts of the purest Buddhist tradition.

10. Cf. the contributions of Bettina Bäumer, "Le nom secret dans l'hindouisme," and Marina Vesci, "Ka, le nom de Dieu comme pronom interrogatif dans les Veda. La demythisation du nom de Dieu," in the above-mentioned volume edited by E. Castelli, which furnish the details of what is here condensed in the dialectic of nine points.

11. Cf. for example *Mahali Sutta* 16 and 19, i.e., *Digha Nikāya,* VI (16 and 19).

12. *Samyutta Nikāya,* III, 189. F. L. Woodward (tr.), *The Book of the Kindred Sayings,* The Pali Text Society, ed. Mrs. Rhys Davids, London, 1954, Vol. II, p. 156.

13. *Samyutta Nikāya,* V, 218: Mahā-vagga, IV, 5. Jaravaggo 42, 2—Unnabho Brāhmano. Cf. the translation by F. L. Woodward, *The Book of the Kindred Sayings,* Pali Text Society, London, 1965, Vol. V, p. 193:

" 'Nibbāna, brahmin, is the resort of release.'
'But, Master Gotama, what is the resort of Nibbāna?'
'The question goes too far, brahmin. That question is beyond the compass of an answer. The aim of living the holy life, brahmin, is to

plunge into Nibbāna. It has Nibbāna for its goal, Nibbāna for its ending.' "

The Pali text says here: ajjha-parām, brāhmana, panham, na-sakkhi parayantam gahetum. Other texts say accasarám (i.e., transcendental), instead of ajjhaparam. The Nalanda edition in devanagari says accayāsi. Cf. the analysis of the text in the following notes.

14. Māra is a mythical personage in the life of the Buddha, the evil one, the tempter, and also death.
15. Cf. the Pali: accayāsi, rādha, panham, nāsakkhi panhassa parivantam gahetum. Nalanda Edition. The Pali Text Society gives assa instead of accayāsi.
16. Nibbāna gadham hi, rādha, brahmacariyam vussati. It is interesting to note that what the translations render as the "holy life" (pure life, in the text), is brahmacariyā.
17. Samyutta Nikāya, III, 187/189. (Khandha-vagga, II, 1). I have relied on the translation of F. L. Woodward in the volumes of the Pali Text Society, *op. cit.*, III, 155-156.

E. L. Mascall

Awareness of God and the Christian Doctrine of Man

Is man alone in the universe or not? Miguel de Unamuno is quoted as having said that this is the overshadowing question for man.[1] In this he is, I believe, entirely right, but it must be added that it is a question in which the vast majority of modern men and women show very little interest. I shall therefore begin by discussing the phenomenon of the atheism of contemporary man.

It will, however, be well to remind ourselves at the start that not all modern men and women are atheists. This is important because it is frequently assumed by writers who consider themselves to be objective and enlightened that belief in God is an extremely rare syndrome and that, like other syndromes, it is the sign of a clearly morbid condition. People who profess belief are, the assumption runs, either knaves (such as ministers of religion) who are making a good thing out of it for themselves or are fools who have been imposed upon by the knaves. It therefore needs to be said that there are, even in this latter part of the twentieth century, a very large number of people, not notably either villainous, thick-headed, credulous or immature, who believe that there is a God and conduct their lives in accordance with this belief. It must nevertheless be admitted that such people form a very small minority in the world of

100

today and that to the great majority of our contemporaries theism —belief in God—is taken as being either obviously mistaken or of no consequence one way or the other.

Contemporary atheism is, I suggest, of three main types, though they merge into one another and are not mutually exclusive. In accordance with their dominant characteristics I shall denote them respectively by the adjectives "reasoned," "willed" and "assumed." By "reasoned atheism" I mean a conviction that there is no God which has been arrived at as the result of a serious and diligent consideration of the arguments for and against his existence, with the conclusion that the latter definitively prevail over the former. It may, of course, happen that the enquirer will conclude that the available evidence is insufficient to settle the question one way or the other. This is the position commonly denoted by the term "agnosticism," and in its authentic form it is a very painful condition in which to find oneself; for to be unable to make up one's mind on so fundamental an issue as the existence of God can hardly fail to be a source of deep distress. In actual fact, those who describe themselves as agnostics do not usually appear to be in a state of either indecision or tribulation. Such people, I suggest, are not for the most part genuine agnostics at all, but a kind of atheist; they have in fact assumed that the atheistic position is *prima facie* in possession, and the absence of conclusive arguments either for or against that position is taken as leaving it in command of the field. It is worth noting at this point that disbelief, quite as much as belief, is open to the charge of wishful thinking, for God, as he is traditionally conceived, is not only man's beatitude but also his judge.

> "There is no God," the wicked saith,
> "And truly it's a blessing,
> For what he might have done with us
> It's better only guessing." [2]

Thus wrote Arthur Hugh Clough, and, to quote a more recent writer, Clive Staples Lewis:

Some people talk as if meeting the gaze of absolute goodness would be fun. They're still at the Munich stage of religion. Goodness is either the great safety or the great danger—according to the way you react to it.[3]

There are disadvantages, as well as advantages, in having a God, and it is interesting to notice that atheists, while they are ready to accuse believers of making God a consolation for the miseries of this life—"pie in the sky when you die"—are equally ready to accuse them of postulating a deity of a vindictive and bloodthirsty character such as no decent man could tolerate. A Christian will, of course, assert that God's kindness and severity are two complementary aspects of his nature or, rather, with Dante, St. Catherine of Genoa and C. S. Lewis again,[4] that they are manifestations of his nature as absolute goodness according as he is either accepted or rejected by his creatures. At least it may be suggested that the accusation of wishful thinking cuts both ways. Here, however, we are infringing on the other types of atheism which are the subject of this lecture. At this point we need only repeat that it is possible for a man to come to disbelief in the existence of God as the result of a process of argument, even if we judge that such reasoned atheism is uncommon and that the arguments which are involved in it are fallacious.

The second type of atheism, that which I have denoted by the adjective "willed," is one which, whether or not God is believed to exist, is primarily motivated by a deliberate rejection or repudiation of God as a being whose very existence would be abhorrent. Its mildest form is exemplified by the German philosopher, intellectually an agnostic, who held that we cannot be sure whether God exists or not but that if he does exist it is a misfortune. Its most extreme form is found in the radically perverted and contorted wills of the devil and his fallen angels, who, in the scriptural phrase, both believe and tremble,[5] those whose wills and intellects are set in precisely contrary directions, who know one thing and will the opposite, who know with certainty that God exists while willing, vehemently though altogether inefficaciously, that he should not. This inherently self-destructive psychological condition has received brilliant and horrifying expression in C. S. Lewis' famous little volume *The Screwtape Letters.*[6] In the human realm it is manifested in satanism and blasphemy, in the strict sense of those words, in which they signify not merely profane language and behavior directed against a deity who is believed or assumed to be non-existent but the deliberate defiance and renunciation of a God who is only too terrifyingly known to exist.

Willed atheism of this pure or extreme type, in which the will is exerted in direct opposition to the intellect, is fortunately rare, and the natural end of its deliberate and persistent practice can hardly be anything but mental disintegration and insanity. Much more common is the type which combines a willed rejection of the idea of God with an intellectual conviction, or at least an assumption, that God does not exist. This may not always be entirely easy to identify or diagnose, for somebody who disbelieves in the existence of God and also holds that belief in God's existence is socially or psychologically pernicious, may very well dramatize his position by using language which suggests that he is engaged in active warfare against a really existent being called God. Thus such phrases as "the war against God" are often ambiguous; what is being warred against may very well be simply a distorted or inadequate notion of God which the professed atheist rightly or wrongly believes some or all theists to entertain. Furthermore, there may conceivably be no necessary logical connection betweeen atheism and the various metaphysical, economic and political doctrines which have in practice been associated with it. Thus Fr. John Courtney Murray has raised the question whether dialectical materialism and atheism are inevitably connected. He writes as follows:

It is quite obvious, and it was openly admitted by Marx, that atheism is the postulate of dialectical materialism in the Marxist sense. It is not at all obvious, even though Marx did not admit it, that atheism is the conclusion of Marxist dialectical materialism. If this theory of reality is held to be only a philosophical-scientific theory; if it is therefore held to be open to further critical development, as all such theories are; if, that is, Marxist dialectical materialism is not transmuted, by the alchemy of a political will to an atheist society, into an immutable dogma as has happened in the Soviet Union; if all this is the case, it may well be that dialectical materialism is open to the theist conclusion.[7]

Clearly a vast number of questions suggest themselves here. If it is an open question whether dialectical materialism necessarily leads to atheism unless it is associated with a particular type of political mentality, a fruitful dialogue between Christians and Marxists may well be possible. Indeed the first steps toward such a dialogue have already been taken in such a discussion as that between Karl Rahner and Johannes Metz on the one hand and Paul Garaudy on the other which is contained in the book entitled *From Anathema to Dialogue.*[8] One may mention also the conferences held in Germany by the Society of St. Paul since 1965. Garaudy the Marxist admits the service that Christianity has performed in awakening and keeping alive man's yearning for a transcendent reality. It was wrong, he holds, only in teaching that that yearning can be satisfied; in his view man has to learn to live in this world with an inherent yearning for a supramundane reality that does not exist; and this, he maintains (somewhat paradoxically, one might think), can in fact provide the dynamic for social progress along Marxist lines. How far such an interpretation of dialectical materialism would be accepted by other Marxists it is difficult to say. Nor is it easy to judge how far such an atheism is "reasoned" and how far it is "willed," but that there is a considerable willed element in it can hardly be disputed. I must resist the temptation to follow up this particular line of dialogue, fascinating as it is. Fr. Murray does not refer to the Garaudy thesis, and indeed his book was published before the thesis was formulated; it is, however, relevant to our present concern to observe that he took the case of Marxism in order to illustrate his contention that atheism is a willed rather than a reasoned position. I quote from him again:

My own proposition, derivative from the Bible, is that atheism is never the conclusion of any theory, philosophical or scientific. It is a decision, a free act of choice that antedates all theories. There are indeed philosophies that are atheist in the sense that they are incompatible with faith in God. But they are reached only by a will to atheism. This will, and the affirmation into which it is translated ("There is no God"), are the inspiration of these philosophies, not a conclusion from them.[9]

I hesitate to go all the way with Fr. Murray in his assertion that atheism is always willed. I believe that it is sometimes reasoned, even if the reasoning is defective, and I also believe that it is sometimes of the much more perplexing type which I shall shortly discuss, which I have denoted by the adjective "assumed." Nevertheless I have found his discussion quite remarkably illuminating and I recommend wholeheartedly his small book—*The Problem of God*—from which I have quoted. It was in fact by reading it that I was myself brought to recognize how large a part is played in modern unbelief by the will in contrast with the intellect.

Perhaps the most notorious example of a willed atheism is that of Friedrich Nietzsche but it will perhaps be more instructive to consider the case of our contemporary, M. Jean-Paul Sartre, for this is extremely self-revealing. His starting point is the assertion that the world in which we exist, and our own existence in it, simply do not make sense; this assertion is dramatized in the celebrated episode in the novel *La Nausée* in which Antoine Roquentin characterizes the root of the chestnut tree as superfluous, gratuitous, contingent and absurd. It is relevant to notice that the first three of these four adjectives designate precisely that feature of finite beings on which traditional theism constructs its "cosmological" argument for the existence of God and it claims that by so doing it removes the appearance of absurdity. That is to say, it asserts that the existence of the world makes sense if, and only if, it is seen as conserved by the creative will of self-existent Being. Sartre, however, will not take this way out, for to him the existence of God would imply an intolerable restriction of human freedom. Man can only be free if there is nobody—not even God—who can claim his obedience. Faced, as he believes, with the choice between God and freedom, Sartre chooses freedom even at the price of absurdity; and indeed he emphasizes and exaggerates the absurdity in order to be quite sure of retaining the freedom. The freedom for which Sartre campaigns is, nevertheless, a freedom of a depressing and distressing kind. There is nothing joyful or self-fulfilling about it. It leaves each man tortured and defiant in a heartless and hostile world; it is poles apart from the Christian freedom which is not contrary to, but identical with, obedience to God: *cui servire regnare est,* as the collect pregnantly expresses it.

It is not altogether easy to decide whether Sartrian atheism, willed as it undoubtedly is, includes an ostensibly reasoned element. It is charitable to hope that Sartre is not blaspheming a God whom he believes to exist but is attacking the pernicious consequences which, in his view, belief in God carries with it. It is nonetheless relevant to suggest that if Sartre *did* believe that God existed, his protestations and denunciations would become even more vehement; for, bad as it may be for people to believe erroneously that there is a being who demands the surrender of their freedom, it must be ten times worse if such a being actually exists. The question, however, remains: Does Sartre plump for atheism and absurdity because he sees no other way of justifying the absolute freedom which for him is the supreme human value, or does he plump for absolute freedom as the only human value that remains in a world which he is, on other grounds, convinced is altogether absurd and godless?

More striking than even the atheism of Sartre is the so-called "Christian atheism" of which much has been heard in recent years, especially in the United States. God, we are told, is dead, and the Church must accept this fact and indeed must rejoice in it and embrace it. It must be admitted that those who proclaim the death of God do not always appear to distinguish between the idea of God and God himself; this confirms one's suspicions that for may religious people God has never been anything more than an idea. Nor is it always easy to know whether those who speak of God as being dead believe that he was ever alive, though we do not normally use the adjective "dead" to describe a being which has never existed. Dr. J. C. Cooper, in his book *The Roots of the Radical Theology,* has in fact listed no less than ten distinct senses in which the death of God has been understood by the different writers who announce it.[10] These range from moderates such as Gabriel Vahanian, for whom the death of God simply means the alleged inability of modern people to find the idea of God either interesting or relevant, to extremists such as Thomas Altizer, according to whom God used to exist but has annihilated himself in order to emancipate his creatures, and who agrees with Nietzsche in identifying God with Satan. There are signs that, even in the land of its origin, the death-of-God theology is itself showing signs of approaching demise, but it is to our purpose to observe that Altizer does not think it sufficient that a Christian should merely disbelieve in God; he must positively and passionately will God's non-existence, and there is even a suggestion that unless a large enough number of people do this there is a dreadful danger that God will come to life again. Here we have as clear a case of willed atheism as could be imagined, and it is interesting to remark that it claims to be the only authentic form of Christianity, in spite of the fact that Christ himself believed in God. *Mais nous avons changé tout cela.* It should perhaps be added, as making Altizer's position slightly more comprehensible, that he appears to hold a type of metaphysical idealism of Hegelian origin, according to which beings and ideas are ultimately identical. It is in any case difficult to believe that so-called Christian atheism could command very much of a following except in countries where membership in some religious organization is still an accepted element in the pattern of social life.

I must now pass to the third type of atheism, which I have denoted by the adjective "assumed." This is the position of those who have never seriously considered the question of the existence of God and have assumed without reflection that the non-existence of God is so obvious that any investigation of the arguments for and against would be a sheer waste of time that could be better occupied in other ways. This appears to be the position of most English people. (I have used the word "appears" because the majority of English people, while professing no form of definite belief and indulging in no visible form of worship, are revealed by opinion polls as still wishing that their children should be instructed in the Christian religion. Whether this is due to the notorious English lack of logic, or to a feeling that religion, even if false, is a safeguard against juvenile delinquency, or to a vestige of belief still lingering in the English mind, is not easy to decide.) This assumed atheism usually, though not quite invariably, goes with a belief, equally assumed and not argued, that the life of a human being ends with the death of his body, that there is no life other than "this life" and no world other than "this world." Here we have, I think, a clue to what may well appear to a theist as a quite incomprehensible indifference on the part of most of his contemporaries to the most important and fundamental question with which a man or woman can be confronted. This indifference is, I would suggest, without any rational basis at all; it is the result of a conditioning process to which modern civilized man has been subjected in a world that is almost entirely dominated by scientific technology. In saying this, I am not implying that there is anything especially irreligious about either science or scientists; as far as my own observation goes, scientists are, as a body, rather more religious than the mass of the population. It is not a question of scientists or science or even technology as such, but of the psychological impact, upon people who are not scientists, of the amazing proliferation of technology during the last hundred and fifty years. Our attention has been more and more directed away from ultimate questions about the ground and purpose of the world and of human life toward proximate questions as to what we can do with the world and its contents. Not "why is there a world and what are we for?" but "what can we do with the things that surround us?" is the question that is dinned into our ears, and we have become so accustomed to turning to scientists and technologists for the solution of our problems that we treat as non-existent any questions that scientists and technologists cannot solve. Furthermore, the whole pattern of life changes so rapidly that the concerns of one generation are likely to be dismissed without further consideration as irrelevant and obsolete by the next. The young have, of course, always been ready to dismiss the views of their predecessors and their older contemporaries as stuffy and out of date, but the range of assumed obsolescence has contracted very markedly. It is no longer a matter of a generation, but of a lustrum or little more. Many of the young, and of those of their elders whose chief preoccupation is to keep level with them, reject as virtually antediluvian anything in the realm of art, literature, music or philosophy that is more than five years old. This tendency is, of course, encouraged by the vast commercial interests which thrive on planned obsolescence and which largely control the media of communication. I do not wish to indulge in the elderly occupation of bewailing the behavior of the young, but only to point out the effect on all of us of the necessity of keeping up with an ever accelerating process of change in the technologically dominated setting in which our life is lived. In this frenzy of change in the temporal sphere not only is there little time left for considering ultimate questions, but also we are psychologically conditioned not to think about them. And not to be able to think about ultimate questions is surely a pathological state for rational beings to be in. Some will perhaps urge that in any case the question about God, involving as it does the recognition of a transcendent reality beyond the things that our senses immediately perceive, requires a certain sophistication which it is too much to expect from the generality of mankind; but to this it might be answered that ordinary people in much less sophisticated societies than our own seem to have found little difficulty in it. However this may be, it is certainly surprising to find a complete lack of interest in the question of a future life, since the one certain event which everyone has sooner or later to face is death. Religious people have often been accused of using their religion simply as an insurance against the flames of hell; it is not obviously more reasonable to assume, without any consideration whatever, that there is nothing beyond death or that, if there is something, it will not depend in any way on the seriousness with which we have taken it in this life. This is surely a morbid condition, and it indicates, as nothing else could, the extent to which our minds have been conditioned by the ever accelerated pressure in the realm of the secular. It is with this *assumed* atheism, rather than with an atheism that is reasoned or willed, that the Church has to reckon today.

Given this situation, the prevalence of assumed atheism should, on reflection, be less mystifying to the orthodox Christian than it appears at first sight. For, if the Christian doctrine of creation is true, the presence of God as the never-absent ground of his creatures can hardly be evident to a casual glance. If God's creatures were unsubstantial wraiths, clothing God's being and entirely transparent to him, it would be impossible to look at a finite being without seeing God; God himself would be the primary object of our perception. If, however, the Christian doctrine is true, creatures are anything but wraiths; they are real and substantial entities to which God has given all the reality and all the relative autonomy that it is possible for a creature to have without ceasing to be a creature. God has, we might say, given them everything that he has except his incommunicable self-existence. Nothing is therefore easier than to look at them and see nothing beyond them; indeed, as the prevalence of pantheism and of idolatry in human history shows, it is only too easy to mistake them for God. It is necessary to consider them in an attitude of quiet contemplation and penetration if one is to get beneath their sensible surface and apprehend them in their true status as the creatures of a transcendent God. It is therefore understandable that, to minds which have been conditioned in such a way that this attitude of contemplation is extremely difficult and even its possibility is virtually unrecognized, God, in spite of his universal presence, will simply not be seen to be there.

Now there is, of course, a noisy party in all Christian communions, not even excepting the Roman Catholic, which, while not going all the way with the so-called Christian atheists, alleges that, in a world whose mind has become thoroughly secularized, the Church itself must thoroughly secularize its thought and action. These persons frequently echo the assertion of the Marxists, that, by directing attention toward a future life, religion diverts human efforts from the urgent task of transforming the material world. Some of them, like Dr. Harvey Cox in his book *The Secular City,* while not themselves rejecting belief in God, assert that Christianity, in repudiating the pagan notion that the world is divine, is logically committed to the view that the world is godless and entirely autonomous, both *de facto* and *de jure*. Others, while stressing their belief in God, assert or assume that his concern is entirely with this world, with the corollary that there is nothing beyond it for any of us. Thus a recent book of essays entitled *Conflicting Images of Man,*[11] which was published in the United States as a defense of belief in God against the more extreme "radical" theologians, contained only one reference to the fact that men die; as far as the rest of the book was concerned we might all be immortal or, if not immortal, have no future beyond the grave with which we need now to concern ourselves. This quiet assumption can infiltrate unobserved into unexpected quarters; it is instructive to read the Report of the 1968 Lambeth Conference with an eye open for it.

We must, I think, ask ourselves very seriously what lies behind this assumption, the assumption that in a secularized world the Church and its message must become completely secularized. At its worst, it is, I believe, sheer ecclesiastical opportunism.

People who despair of maintaining the Christian institutions in a world which seems to be increasingly indifferent to Christianity may try, as a last desperate expedient, to ensure their survival by turning them into organs which the world may, by its own standards, accept as being relevant. Apart from questions about the morality of this policy, it would seem to turn the Church into an organization for doing in an amateur way tasks of immense complexity which the secular institutions are able to do more efficiently and professionally. It is paradoxical that those who wish to ensure the Church's survival on these terms are usually highly contemptuous of the way in which, in the past, ecclesiastics have often been ready to compromise with the secular outlooks and purposes of their own day. Side by side with this element of opportunism there is frequently a large dose of intellectual laziness. To think out in detail the ways in which the Church can try to make its beliefs about God and man effective in a highly complex secularized social order is an exacting and complicated task; it requires not only a thorough grasp of the Christian verities but also readiness to enter into sympathetic, humble and penetrating dialogue with experts and specialists in science, sociology, law, medicine and many other branches of professional life. It is much easier simply to put the Church's organizations at the disposal of the dominant popular trends.

It would, however, be both unfair and unkind to suggest that the movement for a complete secularization of Christianity is entirely governed by such discreditable motives as these. Partly, at least, it arises from a theological error, which is very evident in the book of Dr. Cox to which I have referred; this is the assumption that in rejecting the pagan notion that the world is divine one is committed to holding that the world is godless. With this there goes the allied assumption that to bring God actively into the world is to depress and diminish the spontaneity and originality of man; this second assumption is often fortified by clichés about man having now come of age and having achieved maturity. There are, it must be admitted, certain aberrant views of the relation between God and the world that would justify this attitude. The eighteenth-century view known as deism is one, the extreme voluntarism of some late medieval theologians is another, and a third would be provided by a similar voluntarism which characterized some Protestant thinkers. These views look upon the creative act of God as being exercised by a sheer act of omnipotent command, as a result of which the world has come into existence, endowed with certain properties and certain inbuilt energies and principles of action, but having no continuous real relationship with its creator. Clearly for such a doctrine any genuine intervention of God into the created world would dislocate its working and would be a thorough nuisance. Again, on these views, if God exercised any real influence upon the minds of men, this could only result in a suppression of their freedom; this was, of course, what Jean-Paul Sartre perceived. The matter is, however, entirely different if we hold, first that the world and its contents exist from moment to moment only because God is incessantly conserving them with their genuine but dependent activities, and secondly that, just because God and man are personal beings and not blind mechanical forces, God's influence on the minds of men results not in the suppression but in the liberation and enhancement of their freedom and their spontaneity. If this is true, as I believe it is, Christians should react to a secularized civilization, not by capitulating to its basic assumption that the very notion of God must be excluded in order to leave man free to achieve his own beatitude but, on the contrary, by assuring the world and demonstrating in their own lives that man becomes more and not less free when God is the dominant principle of both his thought and his action.

I may seem to have digressed very widely from my central theme, namely that of contemporary atheism, but I do not think that the digression has been irrelevant. For if contemporary atheism is for the most part of the type that I have denoted by the adjective "assumed," it is of primary importance to diagnose

the nature and cause of the assumption in question, as a pre-
liminary to forming a strategy and a tactic for dealing with it.
We should not allow ourselves to be daunted by the fact that
the task with which we are faced may be one of extreme difficulty. Still less should we make this an excuse for capitulating
to the assumption ourselves. If this assumed atheism is basically
not the result of a process of reasoning but rather of a process,
albeit unplanned and unforeseen, of psychological conditioning,
it may be necessary for this conditioning to be undone before
anything like a mass movement back to the Christian faith can
begin. Conceivably the confusions and frustrations of the world
today may be the first signs that such a reversal is on the way,
but it can hardly be a speedy or a comfortable business. There
may be a long period during which Christians will have to live
their religion not only for their own sake but for that of the
rest of the human community. The "co-inherence" which was
such a profound feature of the religion of the novelist and poet
Charles Williams may become the dominant concept of the
Christianity of the near future.

It will, I think, be useful at this point to inquire about the
way in which, on the basis of Christian theism, we should expect the existence of God to be discernible. This is important
in view of the fact that Christian apologetics, especially that
of the cruder sort, has widely appealed to the evidence of events
alleged to be miraculous. These may range from alleged answers to prayer to alleged divine punishments meted out upon
impiety. There was a widely used book in the last century which
attempted to prove the existence of God from the alleged fact
that generals who attacked their enemies on the Sabbath (interpreted, of course, as Sunday) invariably lost their battles. Apart
from the great difficulty of proving that an allegedly miraculous
event is in fact due to an interference with the laws of nature
there is the further fact that, during the last two centuries, more
and more previously unexplained phenomena have been
brought within the scope of scientific explanation, so that those
who located God's activity primarily in the gaps that science

had hitherto not succeeded in closing have found themselves left, as time has gone on, with fewer and fewer gaps in which to locate it. The progress of science has certainly deterred from religion those for whom God would at most be merely an agent who, in answer to prayer, confers benefits or prevents calamities which cannot be acquired or avoided by more mundane means. It must, however, be noted that even in the ages when people applied directly to God to cure disease or change the weather, they did not disbelieve in the normal operation of natural causes. Medical and surgical remedies, however crude in comparison with those of the present day, have been known and used throughout the history of Christendom, and the folklore of all the Christian nations has been rich in maxims concerning the weather. Christian teachers and preachers, too, have spoken in terms of condemnation of those who only turn to God for things which they need and which they cannot obtain in any other way. Ecclesiastical authority has rightly been skeptical of alleged miracles, not least because of the difficulty of knowing whether or not an unusual effect falls outside the operation of the normal laws of nature. There is a well-known story of Pope Pius IX's rebuke to a lady who alleged that she had been miraculously cured of rheumatism in her leg by wearing a stocking that had once belonged to the aged pontiff. "My daughter," he said, "I have been wearing two of my stockings for years and my rheumatism has got steadily worse. Thank God for your cure, but it is not a miracle." If one believes that the ordinary course of nature runs on independently of God, no doubt one will attribute exclusive importance to miracles as evidences of God's activity and hence of his existence. If on the other hand, in accordance with traditional Christian teaching, one believes that the natural order itself operates only because it is conserved by God, miracles, if and when they can be reliably identified, will be of very much less importance from the point of view of evidence. We may remember that Jesus himself, while he performed many miracles as acts of compassion and even pointed to them as signs that the Kingdom of God had appeared, was severe toward those whose primary concern was with their unusual character. "Nothing can be called a miracle," wrote St. Thomas Aquinas, "in relation to the power of God." [12] It is significant that the classical arguments for the existence of God, of which the "Five Ways" of St. Thomas are typical, are all derived from the normal orderly behavior of the natural world; none of them makes any appeal to the miraculous. This does not imply that miraculous events, that is to say events which God produces otherwise than by the normal operation of natural law, never occur, but it is fortunate for us that they do not occur very often. M. Rémy Chauvin has observed that if God worked miracles every five minutes, all science would be impossible, but that at the rate at which he works them science and religion can painlessly co-exist. [13] As I have written elsewhere:

Miracles may be expected to occur more frequently in a religious context, especially that of the Church, which is the continuing body on earth of the Incarnate Son of God, than in a purely secular one. The setting of the laboratory is one in which, so far as is humanly possible, the scientist isolates his experiment from all influences other than that which he is interested in investigating. Divine intervention would be such an extraneous influence, and, although it is perhaps the only disturbing influence against which the scientist cannot in principle erect an absolute barrier, we may expect that God will respect the nature of the task on which he is engaged and will not make it unnecessarily difficult by *ad hoc* manifestations of his power. Scientific research is difficult enough in any case, without the scientist having to take account of miracles. The matter is quite different when the setting is not that of the laboratory but that of the Church, for here the context is not that of the secular but that of the supernatural. . . . There are furthermore situations of a mixed nature in which the two settings overlap and intermingle; the increasing co-operation between the clergy and medical and psychological practitioners in dealing with the sick provides just an instance. In such a case the task of discrimination will be increasingly difficult, but the principle is nevertheless clear. [14]

Theoretically, then, Christianity has nothing to fear from the advance of science and technology, but in practice it is faced with a very difficult task. The committed Christian today must thoroughly involve himself in the concerns of a secularized civilization without slipping into its secularist outlook. For the sake of civilization no less than of his own spiritual integrity it is essential that he should not shrink from this vocation but should accept it with courage and humility. He will be encouraged if he recognizes that the secularist interpretations of life, whether Marxist or scientific-humanist, rest upon a glaring logical fallacy. While holding that individual men and women cease to exist when they die, these systems are accustomed to speak in glowing terms of the glorious future awaiting an entity designated by the word "Man." Man in the past was miserable and frustrated, either because of his lack of understanding of the forces of nature or because he was exploited by priests, kings and capitalists. Man today, at least in the more enlightened regions of the earth, is very much happier than he was, and at some future date Man will be enjoying a condition of virtually unbounded happiness, with all his needs, both material and cultural, supplied by the good things of this life. What must be recognized is that on secularist principles the word "Man" in these different contexts does not designate the same being. The man who was miserable in the past is not the man who is happier today and neither of these is the man who will be so gloriously happy in the future, for each of these men ceases to exist when he dies and each of them is dead long before the next one is born. The secularist story of Man is a sheer imposition; it has nothing to offer the individual man or woman at all. "There are times," writes Daniel Callahan, "when life is just awful: boring, stupid, brutal or trivial. The promise of the future does not always, nor can it, drive out the pain of the present. Some people are going to die tomorrow. That is their context, and they want to know why." [15]

It is this situation of the individual man, face to face with death, to which secularism of all kinds has nothing to say; but it is to him that Christianity, with its doctrine of creation by

God and redemption in Christ, can speak in tones of assurance and hope. And because it can speak to the individual man, it can also speak to human society as a whole. The story of Man, which is a fairy story and a myth in the mouth of the secularist, becomes sober truth in the mouth of the Christian. For the Christian does not believe that each man ceases to exist when he dies; the story of Man is the story of the progressive incorporation of redeemed humanity into the Body of Christ. This is the vision that Pierre Teilhard de Chardin saw when he identified "Point Omega," the climax of human evolution, with the Total Christ, the "Christified" human race. It is strange that Teilhard's admirer, Sir Julian Huxley, should think it possible to retain Teilhard's vision without Teilhard's faith in Christ.

The Christianity that can speak to a secularized civilization, a civilization permeated by what I have called assumed atheism, will not be a secularized Christianity, a Christianity that has succumbed to the assumptions and valuations of secularism. It will, however, contain within itself a theology of the secular, that is to say a theology which, on the basis of the Christian doctrines of creation and redemption, interprets not only the religious but also the mundane concerns of man. It will involve that positive, and at the same time discriminating, attitude to the technological age for which Fr. Chenu has so eloquently pleaded in his book *Faith and Theology* (*La Parole de Dieu*). Far from condemning technology as such, it will see technology as providing man with new and wonderful means for realizing his vocation as God's vice-gerent in virtue of his creation in God's image. And, by showing to our contemporaries a more coherent, hopeful and exhilarating vision of human existence than they now possess, we may hope to free them from the bondage of their secularist and atheist assumptions.

C. S. Lewis has written: "In modern, that is, in evolutionary, thought Man stands at the top of a stair whose foot is lost in obscurity; in this [i.e., medieval Christian thought], he stands at the bottom of a stair whose top is invisible with light." [16]

These two conceptions seem to me to be complementary rather than contradictory. It may be one of the most important tasks for theology in the immediate future to make the synthesis. Man may well be standing on the landing where the two stairways meet.

NOTES

1. Cf. Harvey Cox, *The Secular City*, New York, 1966, p. 242.
2. A. H. Clough, *Dipsychus*, pt. I. v., in *Poems*, New York, 1895.
3. *Broadcast Talks*, London, 1942, p. 32. Published in New York, 1943, as *The Case for Christianity*.
4. Dante, *Hell*, iii, 1; St. Catherine of Genoa, *Treatise of Purgatory;* C. S. Lewis, *loc. cit.*
5. James 2:19.
6. New York, 1943.
7. *The Problem of God*, New Haven, 1964, p. 94.
8. New York, 1966.
9. *Op. cit.*, p. 95.
10. Philadelphia, 1968.
11. New York, 1966 (William Nicholls, ed.).
12. *Summa Theol.*, I, cv, 8.
13. *God of the Scientists, God of the Experiment*, Baltimore, 1960, p. 86.
14. *The Secularisation of Christianity*, New York, 1966, p. 210.
15. In *The Secular City Debate*, Daniel Callahan, ed., New York, 1966, p. 99.
16. *The Discarded Image*, Cambridge (England), 1964, p. 74.

Gregory Baum

Divine Transcendence*

In the main theological tradition, divine transcendence referred to God existing in and by himself, apart from and superior to cosmos and human history. To acknowledge divine transcendence in this perspective meant to affirm the existence of a supreme being above time, living in eternity and ruling the course of history from this beyond. Because of this view of divine transcendence, it was possible for theologians to think of God as a supernatural and suprahistorical person, to speculate on his knowledge and his will, and to suppose that in his providence history was completed till the last day.

I

While Christian theologians have always taught that God is both transcendent and immanent, the Church's central teaching and preaching tended to deal with his transcendence first of all and then only, by way of supplement, to refer to his immanence in the world. Once the theologian thought of God as a fully

---

* Since the lecture, originally given at Fordham University, introduced a theme developed at greater length in a book, since published, entitled *Man Becoming,* the author has revised the manuscript to make it a more adequate reflection of his present views.

constituted subject apart from and superior to history, it became impossible for him to get him back into history again.
God necessarily became the outsider to human life. Both in
theology and preaching the prevailing image of God was that
of the eternal father in heaven, who at certain chosen moments
graciously intervened in the lives of men to set them on the
path of salvation.

This view of divine transcendence inevitably led to the radical
distinction between the sacred and the profane. The sweep of
human life and history was regarded as profane or secular. It
was the work of man. It was simply human. Yet the moments
and places at which the gracious God intervened in the lives of
men were radically different from the ordinary course of human life. They were sacred. In these sacred times and places
God offered his divine salvation, there he made himself available to men, there they were able to leave the world behind
and surrender themselves to him in worship. Christian theology
and, more especially, Christian practice considered human life
divided into two distinct sections, namely the secular (man's
day-to-day existence comprising his relationship to other people and the building of the human world) and the sacred
(man's religious side including his relationship to God in faith
and prayer, and the supernatural life communicated in the
sacraments).

I hasten to add that the great theologians always taught
that in Jesus Christ the radical distinction between the sacred
and the secular had been overcome. What is revealed in Jesus
Christ is that human life is the locus of the divine. God is
present to man not simply in his religious moments and at
religious places but in the faith, hope and love that constitute
the substance of his human existence. While this was taught
by the great theologians, it did not influence the mainstream
of teaching and acting in the Church. The Thomistic humanism,
for example, never became part of Catholic spirituality on a
wide scale. Liturgy, canon law and the various institutions in
the Church reflected the sharp division between the secular and

the sacred, and it was through these social elements that the Church was a more effective teacher than through the more sophisticated expressions of her doctrine.

Catholic life, we remember, was filled with symbols of the radical separation between the secular and the sacred. A layman, for instance, was not allowed to carry a priest's chalice unless he used a cloth. The altar boys in the sacristy, knowing that it was wicked to touch the sacred vessel, would play games of temptation and bravery and, while the priest was not looking stealthily touch the chalice with their index finger. Implicit in these actions and even in these games was a definite view of what divine transcendence means.

Because of new forms of religious experience many theologians from the last century on, often supported by a new religious sensibility among the faithful, have rejected the above mentioned view of divine transcendence and the radical distinction between the sacred and the secular associated with it. Already at the end of the eighteenth century, before he had worked out his system of philosophy, Hegel called the idea that the infinite existed apart from and above the finite "the bad infinity." [1] Hegel thought that this was the view of God presented in the Old Testament. There, according to Hegel, God was pictured as the Lord of history, living in an eternal heaven and ruling the world from above. (Biblical scholars today, I wish to add, deny that this is the God-concept of the Old Testament.) Hegel thought that while this view of God was in principle overcome by Jesus Christ, it was especially in the modern age that such a view of the infinite had become wholly unacceptable to man. If God was thought to exist in some other realm apart from the reality in which men live, then this would invalidate history as the locus of men's crucial decisions and lead them to escape from the concrete to the abstract. What better view of the infinite did Hegel, at this early period of his life, propose? "The good infinity" was the idea that the infinite was present in and through the finite, without absorbing the finite, without being identical with it, without becoming limited by it or enclosed by it. Hegel's polemics against "the bad infinity," we note, anticipated the death-of-God literature of the last decade.

From the turn of the twentieth century on, there was an increase in the number of theologians who refused to look upon God as a fully constituted subject apart from and superior to human history. While these theologians did not accept the Hegelian system, they were profoundly influenced by the new *Weltgefühl*, the new developmental consciousness of the human world, to which Hegel had given expression. As these voices became stronger they found a responsive echo in the Christian community. The great German scholar Ernst Tröltsch regarded God as the *Lebensgrund*, the divine ground of human life, who could not be conceptualized as a being over against man and his history. Divine transcendence, according to Tröltsch, did not refer to the being of God in and by himself, but rather to the inexhaustible character of the divine ground, out of whom the new ceaselessly came to be, yet who could never be fully expressed in history. Paul Tillich, a brilliant and original student of Tröltsch, brought this theological trend to the United States. During World War II, Dietrich Bonhoeffer found powerful words to express this new perspective on divine transcendence. He wholly rejected the two-spheres approach to human life, i.e., he refused to regard human life as divided into two sections—the secular of man's day-to-day life, and the religious of man's spiritual contact with God. There is only one sphere of life, Bonhoeffer held, of which the gracious God is the deepest dimension. He is the beyond in the midst of life.

In the Catholic Church it was above all Maurice Blondel, at the turn of the twentieth century, who inveighed against what he called "extrinsicism," that is, against the idea that the supernatural could be conceived of as a reality extrinsic to man and his history. Since it was man's vocation to assume responsibility for his history and involve himself in the action that made him more truly human and simultaneously constituted his human world, it would be irresponsible for him to turn away from history and be concerned about a being existing in and by himself in a superior world. If God was truly a sovereign outsider to human life, no modern man could become a believer. What Blondel tried to show, by contrast, was that God was in fact present in human life. Man comes to be through a process, in which God is redemptively involved. Every man, through the dynamics of his action, is carried forward to a crucial option in regard to life, in which he *either* opens himself to the infinite and thus enters into his true humanity *or* locks himself into his finite house and in this way undoes the foundation of his humanity. God or, in Blondelian language, the supernatural is present to human life as the possibility of man's true humanity.

A similar trend is found in the Catholic theologians and philosophers of the twentieth century who made the so-called transcendental turn. These thinkers shifted their interest from the object of knowledge to the presuppositions of knowledge in the knowing subject. Thus, in line with this shift, they theologized about God not as the divine object of man's mind and hence as an objective reality, but rather as the divine presupposition in man's mind and heart enabling him to be in touch with truth. Here God is no longer necessarily conceived as a supreme being over against man, existing in and by himself, but rather as a supreme principle operative in man in every act of knowing the truth and every act of true love. Here again, then, human life cannot be defined in purely human terms: God enters into the definition of man. Divine transcendence refers, therefore, to a dimension of history—to the deepest, hidden, gracious, ever surprising and incomprehensible dimension of men's lives.

This trend is followed by several contemporary Catholic theologians in North America. The best known among them is Leslie Dewart. For Dewart God is not a fully constituted subject existing apart from and above the cosmos. God is present to the cosmos as the matrix and orientation of its evolution.[2] Other thinkers, such as Eugene Fontinell and Eulalio Baltazar, following their own, independent philosophical methods, also reject any attempt to objectify the divine.[3] In this context I might also mention my own study.[4]

II

Is it possible for theologians who wish to remain faithful to Scripture and the Church's tradition to reject wholly and systematically the object-subject model in the understanding of man's relationship to God? The object-subject model is so useful in our understanding of the world that we tend to take it for granted as the only mode of reflecting on reality. As soon as we speak of the God who has revealed himself in Jesus Christ, we tend, by a habit of the mind, to objectify him, i.e., to think of ourselves as finished subjects faced by a divinity who, through this revelation, has become an object of our mind. But is this really the meaning of God's self-revelation in Christ? Are we not told, rather, that God is present to us in our faith in him? According to the Christian message, God moves us from within and addresses us from without. This means that men are not fully constituted subjects faced by the divinity, but that God is present in the listening and responding by which men constitute themselves as subjects. The object-subject model, therefore, seems to be misleading when applied to man's relationship to God.

We recall here the beautiful teaching of St. Thomas that faith is produced in the Christian through the twofold action of God's Word: the internal Word sounds in his conscience and the external Word, revealed in Christ and preached by the Church, addresses him from without. Faith is created in man's heart only as the inner and the outer Word resound simultaneously. Man's relationship to the divine Word, therefore, cannot be described by the object-subject model. God is present within and without man as he enters into salvation. There is no human standpoint from which the divine Word is simply a reality facing man; God is this reality facing man only if he is simultaneously a reality within man creating a certain consciousness.

If we cannot apply the object-subject model, so useful for getting around in the world, to the knowledge of God, what can we know of God? St. Thomas' solution is well known. While Thomas negated *simpliciter* the application of this model to the knowledge of God, he approved its use *secundum quid* and analogously. Thomas, as is well known, first of all negated all and every similarity between God and the perfections of creatures. God is wholly different from his creation. God is not a substantive, not a being, not a person, not a subject, not an object of the human mind. In other words, the object-subject model cannot be used in theology. But what positive statement can then be made about God? Thomas held that a certain similarity, despite the greater dissimilarity, did exist between God and created perfections and that, because of this similarity, positive statements about God were possible. While it was more true to say that God is not a substantive, not a being, not a person, not a subject, not an object of the mind, it was also true, according to a certain analogy, to affirm that God is a substantive, a being, a person, a subject, and hence an object of the mind. Keeping the limits of this analogy in mind, it was possible, therefore, to use the object-subject model in theology. As long as we recall that the dissimilarity is always greater, and hence the negation always more true, the statement that God is an objective reality, apart from history and over against man, communicates some truth about God. Thus it was possible in Thomistic thought to objectify God analogously.

The Thomistic analogy is derived from a metaphysical hylomorphism that has been widely abandoned by theologians. Theologians have questioned, moreover, whether this doctrine of analogy really sheds much light on the doctrine of God. It has certainly not prevented the easy objectification of the divine. By applying the object-subject model, albeit in analogy, in theological reflection, it has encouraged theologians to think of people and their history over here and of God as the supreme being facing them over there. While this was by no means the necessary consequence of Thomistic theology, it remained present as a tendency and influenced the treatment of topics such as divine providence or the relation of time and eternity.

Many modern theologians influenced by Existentialism have tried to reject the object-subject model in their theology more consistently. God, these thinkers said, may in no way be conceived as an object of the human mind. He is not a reality that can be described in terms drawn from our experience of the world of things. We must resist the unhappy tendency, built into our practical rationality, to reify interpersonal relations in general and the divine-human encounter in particular. The only category to be used in speaking of the divine is one drawn from the intimate relationship of man to man. God is not a reality to be referred to in the third person: he is not an "it" nor a "he." God is a "thou" who speaks to us and to whom in turn we address ourselves. The I-thou category alone is adequate for theology.

While this theological approach had many advantages, it did not solve the problem. For if we say that the I-thou relationship is the model to be used in theology, then we seem to set up God as the divine subject facing man, the human subject, and again conceptualize God as a fully constituted subject independent from and superior to human subjects. We thus continue to divide human life into two separate sections, namely the secular sphere where men create community and build their world, and the religious sphere where they encounter the invisible other, the divine thou. The subject-subject model of Existentialism does not really save us from the substantivization of the divine. For this reason, the Existentialist thinkers have often said that the divine thou does not face man as an independent subject but is present to them in and through the human subjects they encounter in their lives. But if this is so, then the divine thou enters into the constitution of these subjects and, correspondingly, also of myself as subject, so that it becomes quite impossible to apply any more the subject-subject model to God's presence in human life. If God is present in the process by which I become myself and the process by which others become intelligent

and feeling subjects, then it is simply impossible to say anything about God in terms of the subject-subject model. For this
model presupposes that two subjects, each existing in himself,
meet one another and enter into communication. But this is precisely what we cannot affirm in regard to man's relationship to
God: God and man are not two fully constituted subjects, each
existing in himself, who meet and enter into communion. God is
the matrix of the human community and thus of man's becoming man. God is the ground of the I-thou relation and hence
cannot be conceptualized in terms drawn from it.

Is it possible to speak of God while rejecting resolutely the
object-subject as well as the subject-subject model? This is
demanded today. For if God is in and through man and his
world, then man may not turn from these to another sphere to
find God there. There is no other sphere. There is no alternative
to present reality. The God who has revealed himself in Christ is
in and through human history, without ever being identified
with any aspect of it. God is operative in the becoming of man
and his world, yet without ever being bounded by this process,
without being caught up in it, or in any way necessitated by it.

The divine presence, we hasten to add, is not a created gift
which God extends across the infinite distance separating time
from eternity. This would indeed be "a bad infinity." The Christian message is that God's gift to man is God himself. The word
he addresses to man is he himself. God's entire presence in the
lives of men is his own self-gift. God is his own gift to man. He
offers not part of himself, but offers himself as he is in himself.
Is this not what the creeds signify when they say that the Son
and the Spirit are "consubstantial" with the Father? Word and
Spirit, operative in the human community and the building of the
Church, are not only from God: they are consubstantial with
the Father: they are God himself. We must conclude that according to the Christian message, the presence of God in human
life is God himself. There is no God somewhere behind this
presence, making himself known across a distance; no, God is

his own presence to man. This is what he is in himself: his gracious presence in human life.

This position, we note, is obviously not pantheistic. Pantheism usually refers to the view that God is so all-embracing that the world is either wholly identified with him (cosmic pantheism) or is basically illusory and unreal (acosmic pantheism). Pantheism has no doctrine of divine transcendence. According to the Christian message, however, God is present to human life, yet never identical with any moment of it. The divine presence is in and through all of history, without ever swallowing up this history or being swallowed up by it. God's presence remains free. Seen in this perspective, he is no longer the sovereign outsider but the sovereign insider to history.

While, in the central theological tradition, divine transcendence referred to God's existence in and by himself apart from history, in the new perspective *divine transcendence clarifies the mode of God's immanence.* In this perspective divine transcendence does not point beyond history to eternity but refers to a dimension of history, qualifying the whole of it, a dimension which is never exhausted or absorbed or determined by history but remains the power for overcoming the present and bringing forth the radically new. Here divine transcendence does have a relationship to time: it establishes time and overcomes it. We conclude that in this new perspective, divine immanence and divine transcendence refer to the same divine presence in human history. They signify the more-than-human in human life. God's immanence refers to his presence in and through human life, and his transcendence qualifies that this presence is never one of identity.

III

What terms shall we adopt to clarify the meaning of divine transcendence? What concepts remain for us if we resolutely reject the object-subject and the subject-subject model in theology? There is no reason why it should not be possible to work out an ontology that enables the theologian to speak of a reality that is in and through all things and enters their constitution without absorbing them or being absorbed by them. This has been tried many times. What I wish to do, however, is different. Since ontology has become a difficult subject for people today, since we have lost the metaphysical confidence that inspired men of previous ages, it is necessary to develop a language about the divine that abstracts from the ontological question. If I may use the distinction between the ontological and the ontic, drawn from Phenomenology and brilliantly used in Langdon Gilkey's *Naming the Whirlwind,* I can state my position quite simply: the need of contemporary theology is to speak of God and his transcendence, not in ontological terms raising the issue of being, but in ontic terms dealing with the possibilities of human life. Is it possible to speak of the divine simply by rendering an account of various modes of human existence, modes where the divine is absent and modes where the divine is present? Is it possible, to use the ordinary language of the pulpit, to speak about God simply in terms of sin and grace?

The answer to this question is Yes. Since, as we mentioned above, the grace of God in human life is God himself, since, in other words, the gift through which men overcome the powers that undo their humanity is not a created reality but ultimately the self-communication of God as he is in himself, it is possible to speak about this God in statements having to do with human brokenness, with conversion to new life, and with man's glorious destiny.

Talk about God in the Christian perspective is, in the first place, good news about man's salvation. Without denying the possibility of developing a theology based on ontology, I insist that there is a primary necessity for learning to speak of God and his transcendence in salvational terms. Statements about God are, in the first place, not information about an invisible reality making man more learned about things divine, but initiation into salvation. The message about God is meant, in the first instance, to transform man's consciousness.

Let me add at this point that the application of the object-subject model to the understanding of man's relationship to God has a highly problematic effect on man's consciousness. For if a man holds that God is a being apart from and superior to history, living in a supernatural realm, then he will turn away from the world of men and his own life to seek this God in separation from his daily experiences. This man will interrupt the conversation with life itself, in which alone God addresses him, and turn his ear to God apart from history, where his Word is not sounded at all.

I have elsewhere shown in detail that statements about God are messages of salvation relevant to human life.[5] What I wish to do here is to apply this theological approach to the doctrine of divine transcendence. Since the Christian Church speaks of God's presence to human life in the trinitarian formula as Father, Word, and Spirit, I shall expound the threefold meaning of divine transcendence in human life.

First, God transcends human life as judgment or critique. Through the divine Word immanent in life man is ever summoned to discover his idolatrous inclination. Man, the sinner, is always tempted to elevate a finite element of his experience into an ultimate norm, in the light of which to evaluate the whole of reality. Even if the modern age no longer encourages the primitive forms of idol worship, man remains tempted, by an absolutizing tendency operative in his life, to single out a finite element of the world, attach himself wholeheartedly to this element, draw it into the center of his life, defend it compulsively as the most precious thing, and measure the whole of his experience in its light. While preachers have always denounced the possibility of money, power, sex or success becoming an absolute value for people, we have come to realize that even religious men are not safe from idolatry. Even the Church can become an idol. Even the dogma through which we come to know God's presence to us can be elevated to be the supreme value: we may be tempted to worship the human witness to God, i.e., dogma, rather than the divine presence to which this dogma testifies.

We are never totally free of idolatry. Many of our cultural and religious values have entered our consciousness in a pervasive and yet subtle way that we actually identify them with God and defend them as if they were divine. While God is present in the important experiences of our life—in the love and the truth whereby we grow in our humanity—he can never be identified with any of them. God is always different. Despite his presence in them, they remain in need of further redemption. God's presence remains critique. The divine Word immanent in human history (and present in a privileged way in Israel and in a definitive and unconditional manner in Jesus Christ) ever reveals the hidden dimension of man's self-deception and destructiveness. People are always confronted by the divine summons calling them to self-knowledge. In particular, the divine Word reveals to men their unconditional attachment to things that are conditional. There is nothing in history apart from Christ that may be identified with the unconditional. History is not its own measure. God's self-revelation in his Word is, therefore, a judgment on history.

We note that divine transcendence is not information about God. It is not a concept which we integrate into our intellectual life. It is rather an initiation into a new awareness. To acknowledge divine transcendence is a salvational process, a conversion, by which we discern the absolutizing or idolatrous trend in us and in our culture, repent of it, and move away from it into a more gracious future. Yet we recognize that even this future will remain in need of further redemption.

From this it follows that divine transcendence is not necessarily acknowledged by the person who makes a public declaration regarding it. It is a strange irony that the people who loudly affirm the transcendence of God are not necessarily the ones who most readily submit their idols to a critique. Because God is gracious and ever surprising, it is even possible that people who deny divine transcendence in their words and refuse to recognize a norm beyond history are in fact open to the ongoing critique summoning them and willing to discern the self-aggrandizement present in their greatest loves and the self-deception contained in their highest truths. (We even read of ecclesiastical leaders who loudly defend divine transcendence and suspect modern theologians of having abandoned it, while they surround themselves with symbols of divinity, regard incidental developments in the Church as absolutes, and reveal an unconditional attachment to the historical forms of their own authority. Accepting divine transcendence means to acknowledge that all of history, including ecclesiastical life, is in need of an ongoing critique.)

Who, then, acknowledges divine transcendence? Perfectly, only Jesus. Because he discerned the idolatrous in his society, because he saw through what was going on even in the institution founded and operated in the name of God, he was hated by society and eventually crucified.

Let us now move to the *second* aspect of divine transcendence. God transcends history as the irreducibly new. History is not simply a series of effects produced by causes wholly in the power of man or determined by natural forces. History is not determined by factors of the past and the present. It is not simply the unfolding of an inner law or dynamism placed into man, nor the work of a purely human freedom and spontaneity. Divine transcendence is the good news that, due to God's presence to history, the new actually takes place. In personal and social life, there are the significant moments when the future is not simply drawn from elements that preceded it, but comes about through a creativity that transcends man's own resources. These significant moments are called *kairoi* in the scriptures. What takes place at these moments are conversions, either personal or social, at which "the new," graciously entering the history of man, enables him to leave the destructive past behind and move creatively into the future.

The new happening in human life assumes remarkable visibility in the conversation and cooperation between people. Truthful and open communication in a community tends to produce insights and strength, which far exceed the input of any of the members. We may express this by saying, "One plus one is three." Wherever two people are in true conversation, what takes place is not reducible to the sum of their efforts. The new actually takes place in their midst. The bond that unites man to man in charity is not simply a human gift, not due simply to the expansion of the human spirit, but according to the Church's teaching, it is God himself, the Holy Spirit.

The good news, then, that God is transcendent means that despite the awful games we play, despite the traps we set for ourselves and for one another, we are never wholly caught in a dead-end street: the new will take place. Tomorrow is not completely determined by our own resources, by our mistakes, our blindness, our sin; the good news is that tomorrow will be different from today.

While the irreducibly new can easily be discerned by the man of faith in private life and in small groups, the new is also offered on a wider scale in the pivotal points of history. Here, too, divine transcendence means that tomorrow will be different from today. Society is never wholly caught in the inherited patterns. Even here a crisis occurs, even here a new consciousness may be created and the course of future history be changed. Even here are death and resurrection.

Third, God transcends man and his world as orientation. Thanks to the Word and Spirit present in human history, man is appointed to a glorious destiny. The orientation of his life is not produced by forces that are natural to him; man is carried forward by an orientation that transcends him and his powers. Man is as yet unfinished. Thanks to the presence of the Word and the Spirit in the process of his self-making, man is being moved toward a gracious destiny. In other words, man's creation is still going on. When we speak of man's creator, we do not think of what happened in the past as much as we think of what happens in the present and will happen in the future. God the Father is creator. Thanks to his presence, man is being carried forward toward his destiny; creation is still taking place in him.

Thanks to God's presence to him, man is a being with a destiny. He is not exposed to the coincidences of uncontrolled forces or wholly dependent on the wisdom and power proper to him. Borne by the Father's presence in him, he is established as son. He belongs. His orientation is divine.

God's presence as Father is, of course, closely. related to his presence as Word and Spirit. Man's orientation is never a set goal, either as a straight line or as a predetermined curve; the goal is, rather, ever renewed and transformed. Whether we think of man as person or as society, we must affirm that through critical points of crisis and resurrection his orientation is ever new and transcends the goals visible to him in the present.

God's transcendence, looked upon in this perspective, is a principle that transforms history. The divine in human life is that which actually makes us critical of the past, detaches us from the destructive patterns and limiting concepts inherited by us and now crushing our vitality, generates new possibilities of human life, and reorientates the course of our development. This process, we hasten to add, has no ceiling. Man's orientation is truly divine. It is the Father's presence to him.

In the preceding pages, we have tried to describe in simple words what divine transcendence means to the Christian. We have translated divine transcendence into the good news for men in a developmental world troubled by sin, fear, and the other enemies of life, God is transcendent, we repeat, not in the sense that he exists in and by himself apart from the superior to history, but in the sense that his presence in human life is ever different from human life as ongoing critique, as irreducible newness, and as orientation beyond man's powers. This is the otherness of God. If the divine transcendence is thus understood, it does not lead man to interrupt his conversation with life and search for his salvation in another world; it rather leads him to listen to life itself, to his own deep experience, in order to discern in it the divine principle by which he enters into personal transformation and even that by which his society and culture are forever brought to transformation. God is transcendent because he is present to human life and history as liberator.

NOTES

1. This expression is first used in Hegel's *Systemfragment*. Cf. F. Copleston, *A History of Philosophy*, vol. 7, part I, Image Books, 1965, pp. 200-202.
2. L. Dewart, *The Future of Belief*, Herder & Herder, 1968, and *The Foundations of Belief*, Herder & Herder, 1970.
3. E. Fontinell, *Toward a Reconstruction of Religion*, Doubleday, 1970, and E. Baltazar, *God Within Process*, Newman, 1970.
4. *Man Becoming*, Herder & Herder, 1970.
5. See note 4.

Part Two

Faith and Hope
in the Future

Piet Fransen, S.J.

Hope and Anthropology: Is There Still Prophecy in the Church?

The general theme chosen for the Bea Lectures this year is "Faith and Hope in the Future." It would have been difficult, I think, to choose a more proper theme, for there is no doubt that our faith today is being shaken and our hope put in distress because of the crisis which is threatening the very substance of our occidental culture, and of the Church as well.

During Vatican II the bishops went on discovering very slowly the Church was not an end in itself, but was first of all sent to the world in participation of the unique service of the salvation of Christ. In this light I dare to say that it is really comforting and consoling—even, I think, reassuring—that the Church herself now, far from keeping aloof from the pains and tragedies of our contemporaries, is on the contrary fully immersed in their doubts, their anxieties and their divisions. I can understand that some Church authorities and some groups inside the Church might feel rather shocked, and even horrified, to find themselves suddenly so involved with the troubles of our time. They are probably ashamed of it, and feel dirtied and betrayed. We

138

agree with them when they think that this very critical situation might become dangerous. Nevertheless we are still convinced that before anything else, this situation provides a unique advantage of bringing us nearer to our brothers and sisters all over the world.

Groping for a better future amid human concerns and problems in the twilight of our common human situation of ambiguity might indeed, as Jean-Paul Sartre says in one of his plays, give us "dirty hands." But was it not an illusion of our former Catholic ways of life and thought to think that we at least, in our little ghettos, were able to keep our hands clean? Clean hands indeed! Were they not betraying the fact that we were doing nothing at all, or at least that we were not concerned with the real problems of our days?

The general theme suggested for this lecture is rather large: Hope and Anthropology. One could tackle it in a speculative and technical way, in a dialogue with such people as Ernst Bloch, the German Marxist philosopher and Jürgen Moltmann, the German theologian of Tübingen University. One could try to show further how the theological problem of hope does possess a true "anthropological" dimension.

"Anthropology" is quite in fashion today on the continent. As a matter of fact, I suppose that all of you are aware of the semantic evolution in the use of the word "anthropology" today under the influence of continental thought. Anthropology referred, up to a very recent past, to any form of research and work on the origins of the human species and the first cultural vestiges and traces emerging from this very distant past. Anthropology is now getting a broader philosophical and theological meaning. In short, our semantics are returning to the etymological origin of the word: anthropo-logy means any kind of reflection on man's existence as such. An anthropological approach to any subject means that kind of methodological conviction and practice by which we think that there is no valid human knowledge about anything when it is not approached and observed in its effect upon human existence, our existence being as it were the only existing mirror we have in and through which we look at reality. Therefore theological anthropology means the study of this human existence insofar as it is affected and liberated by God's revelation and his creative salvific love in grace. "Hope and anthropology" would mean any kind of reflection by which we discover that the revealed virtue of Christian hope has indeed a real human dimension, a human perspective which does not prescind from the so-called "supernatural" reality, but is the very dimension in which this supernatural reality comes to life in our existence.

There is no doubt that this new theological concern and methodology, that even this new theological language which it entails, is one of the most important features of the theological renewal of our days. We could therefore have enlarged upon those speculative and hermeneutical problems in a more technical way. We have chosen, however, a more direct and practical approach, enabling us to apply this view of modern theology, not in a too abstract and uncommitted way, but in direct relation to the very immediate problems of our days.

So I am asking the question here: Is there still prophecy in the Church? This general question entails a rather personal scrutiny of our own conscience: Is there still prophecy in my *own* life? And, is this prophetical inspiration authentic and true? Is it real prophecy or simply dissent for dissent's sake?

Prophecy is a form of human existence, as we shall see, and has therefore a true anthropological pattern. Prophecy is related to hope, though not in the way we might normally expect whenever we still understand prophecy as a kind of miraculous foreboding or prediction of future events. Prophecy, as we shall see, is related to the future, because it is liberating this future at the very moment when it is bringing us nearer to God in the present.

I

Prophecy is an ambiguous term, especially nowadays when

so many are using it for all kind of things. It is one of the words which are "in," at least among people who still value using Christian language.

In a fully secularized society one should use, I suppose, any other word which might seem proper and relevant: inspiration, gift of vision, deeper insight. We are probably not always aware of the fact that the protest movement and the revolts in our universities and in many parts of the world possess a prophetical streak or vein, the more remarkable in that our individualistic past has accustomed us to look at prophecy as a deeply individual concern. We have lost the awareness very common in Old Testament times—that prophecy can express itself through a community of men, that it has indeed a corporate dimension.

It may therefore be of some use to determine, or at least to describe, what we mean in this paper by the word "prophecy."

We can start with a rather modern use of the word among sociologists. Sociologists of religion frequently call Christianity a prophetic religion. This means that empirically, from the outward observation of the doctrines and the practice of Christian people as a sociological group, Christianity as a whole tends to show certain common characteristics which may be labeled "prophetic." It shows, I think, a religious form of life and thought whose basic dynamic and cohesive power is thought to come down from a divine initiative, from a divine reality and truth which claim more authority and value than the magical, the ritualistic, the moral, the institutional or whatever other values which seem to shape, hold together and sustain different forms of religious life we know from history. In other words: Christianity as it appears in history, as it sees itself, as it tries to live and to embody itself in doctrine and practice, does possess and show a decisive dimension: a very personal relation from God to men, taken as the very source of its activity and life, and the source of its continuous renewal and reform. For other corporate forms of religious life show a strong tendency toward immobility and stagnation. True Christianity shows a kind of congenital unrest and dissatisfaction with accepted doctrines and practices, an inborn urge to go *beyond* some accepted pattern of thought and action because of a deep experience of the presence of a God who necessarily transcends whatever kind of man-made religion.

The decisive point in this description is the notion of a basic inspiration which comes down from a divine initiative, reality and truth—a rather vague description, as a matter of fact, of what theologians call Revelation. Yet can we say that God has spoken to us? And more fundamentally: *Can* God speak to us? And if he can, how does he speak to us? This is the crucial point where the modern anthropological approach in theology has its unique value.

Sociologists and historians of religion know that there was and always is an idea of some *mediation* between God and men, a go-between, what the Germans nowadays call "eine Vermittlung." The very notion of a transcendent God already entails the necessity of some form of mediation. But this is also true when we look at the relations between human beings on the horizontal level of our earthly existence. We are not evident to one another. We are not even evident to ourselves. One of the most fundamental characteristics of human life, a true anthropological quality of our existence, is the need for different forms of mediation to discover our selves, to reach out to the others and to approach God himself.

We may call it the true *symbolic* nature of human existence as such. We use the word "symbolic" in its full sense, not with that meaning we inherited from a very rationalistic age, which betrays itself so easily in the common objection: "It is only a symbol!" Human existence is necessarily symbolic existence; more so, it is a symbolic action, in and through which we express and realize at the same time ourselves, our relations with others and our encounter with God.

Human beings can never be reached except in and through human symbols. And this basic experience of our existence has an important role to play in any true anthropological approach to the faith mystery of Revelation, the Word of God to men. The Word of God cannot come to life and reach us except from within personal dialogue, as Edward Schillebeeckx stated in his paper about "Faith Functioning in Human Self-Understanding" (*The Word in History,* ed. by T. Patrick Burke, New York, 1966, 41-59). We will explain this further in the course of this paper.

At this point we still want to keep to that more general phenomenon of prophecy which we can meet in many forms of religion. Wherever the divine being is thought to reach a human community in order to speak to it, we always meet some human beings who receive a mission by which they feel empowered *to mediate between God and men,* that is, to communicate by means of their own words and actions whatever God might be thought to be "revealing" to humanity. This activity of mediation implies, of course, first of all, a divine initiative of election, of choice and mission, and finally of "inspiration." But no mediation is possible, that is, the divine cannot actually reach other human beings without an active cooperation of that man who has been chosen and sent, and whom we therefore call a mediator.

In the Old Testament, or more precisely in the Greek translation of the Old Testament, that kind of religious mediator was called a prophet. Indeed the Greek word "prophèmi" means to proclaim, to announce publicly and solemnly, to speak out with authority. The public, solemn and authoritative character of their pronouncements is strongly tied to a deep inner experience of being sent by God himself to speak out to his people.

Prophecy, therefore, did not mean primarily to announce the future as is commonly thought. This modern semantic evolution in meaning comes from a false interpretation of the activities of the prophets in the past. Actually the prophets of old were indeed sometimes referring to a certain "future," but this reference had only a secondary meaning and role. And even the future they were alluding to was of a very special nature, much more the projection of a present faith and confidence than a clear statement about particular future events. Von Rad in his studies on the prophets emphasizes the fact that strict eschatological language can be found only in the very latest books of the Bible. And even then we know how this so-called eschatological language, which we also meet occasionally in the New Testament, was a special literary form characterized by a florid and exuberant symbolism which is rather arduous to interpret correctly now after so many centuries. Sometimes indeed a prophet alluded to a particular event in the very near future, but this kind of prediction was only proferred and accepted as a guarantee, a proof of the authenticity of the prophetic message about God himself. Therefore a truly prophetic message is primarily a message about God and his ways with his people, and this in a given situation in history. It has never to do with a kind of abstract or systematic teaching, but it is an interpretation of the basic belief in God in his Covenant and its meaning for the particular situation confronting the people the prophet serves. One could say that the real prophet manifests the faithful presence of God behind the facts of history. In his words the deeper meaning of whatever happens to the community of Israel is brought to life, attaining unique transparence, which is different from the common opacity of human life.

Decisive now for our topic is the teaching of the New Testament, especially in the Acts of the Apostles, St. Paul and St. John. For the New Testament writers, the word "prophecy" still possessed the various meanings it had acquired in the Jewish theology after the Exile. Interesting for us is the fact that the rabbinic tradition, in the centuries before Christ, commonly complained that there were no more prophets in Israel. Sharply outlined against this historical teaching of the rabbis we discover in the New Testament a renewed awareness of prophetism, even if the word was not so much used as in former times. The most striking message of the Apostles after Pentecost is the announcement and the common conviction that from now on the Spirit of God, which the rabbis already considered the source of prophetism, would be given to and would dwell in *all* members of the new community assembled around faith in the risen Lord. St. Peter quotes the prophet Joel on the day of Pentecost: "And it shall come to pass in the last days, says the Lord, that I will pour forth of my Spirit upon all flesh. And your sons and your daughters shall prophesy" (Acts 2:17). This is doubtless a new doctrine, a new awareness of the living presence of the risen Lord among his people by virtue of his Spirit, though one has to acknowledge the fact that this common conviction of the primitive Church was not unrelated to the doctrine of the great prophets of the past. The great prophets of the fifth or fourth century before Christ had already announced this universal presence of the Spirit of God as the peculiar mark of the messianic age. The primitive Church, convinced that it was the messianic community "of the last days," was indeed able to find a confirmation of its common experience in the doctrines of the great prophets of Hebrew history.

It is not our task to elaborate upon this biblical theme. The last Vatican Council, restoring the fundamental dimension of the Church as the People of God, has broken with the fairly commonly accepted illusion that the Holy Spirit should be the *exclusive* privilege of the sacred hierarchy of the Pope or bishops, or even of the roman curia as the living embodiment of papal primacy. Serious theologians had always rejected that false conception, refuted for that matter by so many facts of history. It is probably not unnecessary to say that if our faith possesses some truth, this truth may be expected to manifest itself somewhere and somehow in the history of the Church. It might be very difficult to prove from the facts of history that any particular group in the Church has indeed manifested a deeper insight in the divine mysteries than others. But we know from our daily experience, even after the Council, that there is still in many places quite a gap between the conciliar doctrine of the Church and real life, where patterns of behavior and thought, attitudes of life and forms of authority from bygone ages, continue to shape the life of the Church.

Up to now we have already gathered a few aspects about the nature of prophecy. It is based upon the initiative of God. It implies, secondly, a personal cooperation of the prophet himself. Finally, one of the basic convictions of Christianity is that prophecy is not the privilege of any elite group or institutional authority, but is shared by the whole community. The first two points provide us with the theme for the central section of this paper: God's initiative and the cooperation of man. The third point supplies us with the real motive for caring about any answer to our initial question: Is there still prophecy in the Church? This question regards us all! Nobody is allowed to waive it as irrelevant for his own life as member of the Church.

We would like to add a final remark. Under the influence of individualism and especially of romanticism in former centuries, we are prone to consider any form of deeper inspiration as a form of very personal and unique experience. We have the same idea about artistic and literary inspiration. The uniqueness of this inner, deeply personal notion has further promoted a certain image of the "artist" in which any form of eccentricity or Byronic solitude might become more important than the inspiration itself. The experience of other cultures and even of our occidental history shows that artistic inspiration is not necessarily connected with pathology. One might think that this image of "secular inspiration," if we may use the term, has indeed infected our image of the prophet. There is no doubt that a prophet, even in a very tragic situation, may still remain a normal and balanced human person. There is a further fact to be recognized: that prophetism can be the expression of a group, of a living community, and not exclusively the explosion of one's neurotic idiosyncrasies. Like every other human being, a prophet, and any artist for that matter, can suffer from particular neuroses which may color his appearance and speech. But let us once for all cast off this romantic image of a hypersensitive, tortured personality as being the inevitable price one has to pay for the higher gift of deeper personal inspiration.

II

The most obvious feature of prophecy as taken from the writings of the great biblical prophets and the saints is the sudden and surprising unexpectedness, the fully unmerited and gracious irruption, as it were, of God's call to prophecy. One may call it prophecy's ex-static character. The prophet is taken from the daily humdrum of his comfortable life, out of himself as it were, and out of the security of his social surroundings and the accepted habits and opinions of his milieu to go out and to witness for God and about God and his relations with men. I am not so much thinking of one actually leaving his family and circle of friends and acquaintances—which as a matter of fact may have had a real symbolic value—as of a loosening, deep in one's heart, of the many ties which chain a man to conformity, respectability and other products of social pressure. The prophet is no more his own master. He belongs to somebody else, which as a matter of fact is quite different from belonging to some abstract idea on which fanaticism thrives.

That is the deep reason why prophecy can never be institutionalized. Prophecy is essentially charismatic, a sudden unpredictable grace, and is therefore, from its very origin, alien to any form of established and socially organized structure. In other words there are no human rules or tricks for fostering the emergence of prophecy. For God is not limited or bound by our rules and cleverness. Or again, the real meaning of its "unpredictability" is that we on our level of activity are unable to "manipulate," to bring it about by means of our techniques, our sagacity or organization.

Therefore the image of God which the prophets share is not so much the God of the established religion, the God of rituals and morals, but the Holy One, fully free in his choice and love, above all petty schemes and rules of man-made religion. We shall have to return to this later in the course of this paper.

In the meantime we might be getting a little uneasy and doubtful about one point in our description of prophecy. This aspect of a fully free and gracious initiative on the part of God's calling can easily be understood whenever prophecy remains a rather rare and extraordinary event in the history of a religious community. But it looks rather improbable as soon as one wants, as we do, to emphasize the fact that prophecy can be shared by a whole community, as Christianity believes it is. It is remarkable that St. Augustine already suffered from the same delusion. At the end of his life he defended the idea of a limited predestination to grace, because, so he thought, whatever is given to all members of a group becomes automatically a right, and ceases to be a gratuitous gift.

This objection betrays a rather primitive and anthropomorphic approach to the mystery of God. It is true that a grace given by a king or by the state to all citizens is very soon going to change into a right. But our relation to God is quite different. Before God we never acquire any right in the strict sense of the word. Even our so-called merits, as St. Augustine said and as was repeated by the Council of Trent, are fundamentally his gifts. But even more important for our topic is the fact that God's grace and election are always reaching us as a community, in our togetherness, that is. There is no doubt that God distributes his gifts of prophecy according to his divine will, but no prophet, even the highest, is elected and sent for himself. He is always sent to the others and for the others, because prophecy is essentially a gift and a grace for the whole People of God and, through this community, for all men.

The "newness" of prophecy cannot be threatened by the fact that this gift of the Spirit is promised to the whole Church and all her members. The Church as any other human community is always attracted and tempted, one should say, by the need for security, stability and continuity, and these characteristics seem to be guaranteed by accepted habits, established patterns of behavior and thought. Psychologists and biologists know how any disruption of an established custom or habit creates a sense of insecurity and even a deep-rooted anxiety. For the Church those forms are either ritualistic or institutional and authoritarian. Therefore the Church is always threatened, as any other religion for that matter, by ritualism, by legalism, by institutionalism. The People of God, moved and attracted by the motions of the Holy Spirit, must have the courage and the religious faith to risk leaving the comfortable frame of established religion, and to approach God's Majesty and Holiness each time anew in the nakedness of faith and commitment.

This view introduces us farther into the mystery of the Church, where all members are called to prophecy, each according to God's free love and his own cooperation.

We have described prophecy in its "irruptive" character, we should say, which means that prophecy is not bound by the rules of men, not even by those endowed with religious authority. We shall now proceed to analyze the very origin and nature of the prophetic motion.

We already established the fact—as such quite evident if only we dare to leave our doctrinaire fog—that God cannot be conceived as talking to the prophets as men talk to one another. And the outward or inward visions and apparitions we meet in the writings of the prophets don't bring us nearer to a solution. On the contrary, no religious tradition was so deeply convinced of the invisibility of God as the Hebrew tradition, especially that of the great prophets. Even the New Testament echoes this centuries-old tradition, as when St. John writes: "No one has ever seen God; the only Son, who is in the bosom of the Father, he has made him known" (Jn 1:18). We are perfectly right to paraphrase this statement of St. John's and say: "No one has ever heard God; the only Son . . . he has spoken to us." In the same spirit the writer of the first Epistle to Titus says "that God dwells in an unapproachable light" (1 Tit 6:16). That God is not to be seen or heard by human eyes or ears is also stated by St. Paul (Col 1:15), when he describes the glorious titles of Christ. The first is that "he (Christ) is the image of the invisible God." And indeed the only way to see and to hear God on earth is to look at and to listen to Christ, who is God-for-us-all, the Immanuel.

But if this is true, we have seemingly no right at all to present prophecy as rooted in the Word of God to the prophet. Prophets are not excluded from the common human condition. By the way, it is true that we use too easily and rashly such sentences as "God is speaking to us."

God has his own way of reaching the human conscience; he has his own language, which shares God's very nature. If God is present in our life in his very absence, if his presence is deeply real and effective while being hidden and elusive of any endeavor to manipulate it or to bring it into our own possession, his language is at the same time silence, his Word is at the same time wordless. Every human translation or expression of it is at the same time a betrayal. But to know this is already the very core of prophecy.

Positively, God speaks to us through the delicate and forceful motions of his Spirit, who guides our inner feeling and "taste" toward an ever deeper sense of God's presence and loving attraction. This inner motion can be compared with a kind of instinct, a deep inner prompting, a true inspiration by which the prophet is given a taste, a feeling, a deeper insight into the divine meaning of what is happening about him. One could say that through this inner attraction of grace the prophet sees whatever is happening around him in a new light and with new eyes. He gets a new insight that reaches down to the very depth of reality and history where it rests in the creative hands of God.

There is no pure prophetic inspiration, simply out-of-the-blue, one might say. It is always an inspiration about something, that is, about whatever is happening inside or outside the prophet himself—in short, about the real meaning of human history. The prophet is the man who by God's grace is indeed discovering the "kairos," as we say nowadays, the real meaning of any event. Where man is groping amid the darkness and the meaninglessness of human history, amid stupidity, craziness and madness, the prophet is perceiving the deeper meaning behind the darkness, the senselessness, and even the insanity of human relations. For history rests above all upon human relations and human encounter.

But since this language of the Spirit in our hearts is wordless and silent, the prophet is not necessarily freed from the burden of human tragedy. On the contrary in this colorless light, in this wordless word, in this absent presence he often suffers more from the impact and weight of human tragedy. The evidence of human tragedy gets radicalized by the very fact that he perceives in the depth of his heart the divine meaning. The prophetic transparence of human history makes the contrast between light and darkness often harder to bear, more painful to accept.

Since this almost instinctive perception cannot be compared with a clear sight, a kind of lucid vision where everything suddenly falls into its proper place and manifests its true cohesion in clear-cut concepts and words, any prophetic inspiration is in need of interpretation. This happens as soon as the prophet himself tries to express his own experience with human symbols, in human language and symbolic activities. But this very language of the prophet can only be understood in truth where the people, listening to him, are in some way or another *sharing* his experience. In a certain sense a prophet can only be understood by another prophet, or, at least, by those who participate more or less in his own experience of grace, that is, of God's living and loving presence. This latter point needs little stress for our contemporaries, who are aware from the many forms of philosophy of language that no language can be understood outside a *common* experience belonging to both parties.

At this point we are now capable of understanding the real role and the decisive reason for any corporate prophetism in the Church. It is simply that God takes us as we are, as he created us, that is, respecting the deepest laws of our existence in togetherness. Man is fundamentally a relational being, that is, he realizes himself, he matures and grows into an ever richer humanity in and through the encounter with others. That we exist together, in a community of thought, action and freedom, is not something which should be *added* to any consideration of our individual personal perfection, as a possible *further* enrichment and expansion. Our togetherness is simply the other facet of our unique existence. There is no opposition between individual perfection and togetherness; they are only two aspects of the same reality, that is, our human existence. And we Christians are allowed to see this deepest law of our existence as a very far and imperfect image and reflection of the divine perfection itself, where the three divine Persons co-exist in the same intensity of their own identity and togetherness. The Father is the Father only in the fact that he is the Father of the Son, and the Holy Spirit exists only by the intensity of his being the Spirit of both.

This fundamental unity of communion and individual perfection gives us the reason why man exists, we may say, in and through his language which is one of the fundamental means of encounter and relation, in and through the various symbolic activities by which he reaches out to the others and receives their replies. Truth, freedom and the other forms of human achievement are, all of them—and necessarily so—the result of human collaboration and encounter. That is also the reason why history, resulting from human encounter, is the normal form of human existence. We are in search of truth and we discover it slowly and arduously together; we grow toward a deeper freedom together. This truth is evident for our technical age. The hundreds of technicians, engineers and scientists working together at the center in Houston in saving the three men of Apollo XIII are one of the most striking symbols of this human truth. It is a pity, and even a tragedy, that scholars in the so-called human sciences, especially philosophers and theologians—it is a pity and a tragedy that Christians themselves, the members of the hierarchy, the members of the roman curia, are still unaware of this profound reality. Simply to think that one man with a relatively small staff of technicians and bureaucrats at the Vatican is capable of solving the many problems of a worldwide Church is, in this light, a thoroughly amazing illusion. Collegiality in its daily exercise, the communion of faith in its many forms of "consulting the faithful," as J. H. Newman was already stressing more than a century ago, is for the Church not a luxury, a play one might indulge in whenever one has nothing else to do, a concession to transitory democratic illusions, but as necessary as water for fish and air for any living being.

The same applies to prophecy. The only guarantee we have of a true interpretation of the deeper divine attractions and incitements is precisely the confrontation in dialogue and mutual understanding with the interpretation of others with a similar experience. We are even allowed to contend that there is no true interpretation of prophecy outside our togetherness. And therefore the current interpretation by the curial theologians of the definition of papal infallibility by Vatican I as being irreformable "ex sese, non autem ex consensu Ecclesiae"—that is: "by itself, and not because of the agreement of the Church"— is, in this light, philosophical nonsense and theological heresy. The only possible meaning of this tenet is precisely what was intended historically by the Fathers of the Council in 1870: that the Pope did not need, in the exercise of his charism of infallibility, the juridical consensus of the assembled body of the bishops (which was the Gallican doctrine the Council wanted to condemn). But as an absolute truth, a kind of metaphysical statement about the prophetic charism of the Pope, the tenet is indeed an untruth.

There is no true interpretation outside our togetherness. The New Testament and the ancient Church used another word, but meant the same thing. They used the word "koinonia" or, in Latin, "communio," which we still use in its English form: "communion." The Eastern Churches still keep the notion of "koinonia" as a basic ecclesial concept, which in the Russian Churches acquired a new value and meaning in the word "sobornost," "sobor," signifying synod, assembly. And the famous, nowadays so disputed word "collegiality" as applied to the bishops in communion with the Pope has no other meaning than that the hierarchy too, instituted by Christ, cannot be sure of hearing and interpreting the Word of God outside the deep togetherness of all the bishops with the Pope of Rome, or outside communion with the whole Church. Collegiality is nothing else than that "communion of faith" which is the law of the whole Church, as seen and applied on the level of authority and of teaching ministry.

Collegiality has nothing to do, as a matter of fact, with an unwilling or hesitant concession to the democratic spirit of modern society. We believe in those democratic rules, because we believe, in the long run and through many temporary weaknesses so typical of democracy, that a compromise attained through the participation of all members of a nation functions better for the common good and is better adapted to secure a more mature development of our culture than other more autocratic forms of government and management. We may accept, of course, that the need for a democratic government and the need for the collegiality of the Church have a common philosophical background in human nature. But in their very nature both forms of life are quite different, and do not follow identically the same rules of polity. When emphasizing the decisive role of communion and collegiality in the life of the Church we reach a more deeply rooted necessity and law. We affirm that we cannot meet God alone, that we cannot listen to his Word, that we cannot discover his divine will in solitude, because God is addressing himself to us as a family, as a community, in our togetherness and fellowship, even when the voice of his Spirit is necessarily moving and stirring the very core of the individual's heart and conscience. In other words, for God as well as for man, personal inspiration and corporate interpretation are two facets of the same reality of grace and charism.

After three or even five centuries of an ever growing and spreading occidental individualism, our Western cultures have to rediscover the deep bonds of unity which hold the human race together, but now unity which does not degrade or absorb individuals into itself, as happened in former times. The human race, to "come of age," indeed needed this crisis and even this distortion of Western individualism. We had to discover the real dignity of each human person, whether rich or poor, weak or strong, powerful or dependent, titled or common. For outside human dignity there is no way to build a real community. Therefore we have to hold together these two truths: the unique dignity of the human person, and the fact that this dignity is in some important ways a gift and a fruit of real community. What we are we owe in large part to our parents, our family, the small community we live in, the many people we live with. This implies an infinite variety of human relations, from faithful solidarity in living and working together to the highest forms of human encounter in love. To reduce our human relations to the famous I-Thou relation would imply, as Harvey Cox contended in *The Secular City,* an impoverishment of our human reality.

It is no different with the Church, so that nowadays such theologians as P. Schoonenberg are suggesting the profound idea that God normally gives his divine grace, the most personal of his gifts, in and through human interpersonal relations. In his own words: "We are given to one another in the movement of grace." Interpersonal relations are the normal, one would almost say the usual, "sacramental" way God's grace reaches us in the very depths of our personal existence. Again, in the movement of grace the individual person and the community are but two facets of the same reality. This does not mean that we are for one another the source of grace—which would be a sacrilegious thought, grace being in its very essence the loving and creative presence of God in our life. But our mutual and manifold human relations are the normal channels, created when man was created as he is, through which the flow of the divine Presence reaches us. Therefore prophetism has indeed a personal and almost intimate dimension, but a corporate one as well.

Returning to our topic we conclude that, owing to man's nature, which God respects in his so-called "supernatural" motions of grace and redemption, prophecy takes its origin from

156   PIET FRANSEN, S.J.

that very inner movement of grace and is at the same time a
corporate reality. It can only start with persons who were prepared by their human environment to listen to God's inner
motion, and it can only find its true expression in that dialogue
where any true interpretation of the divine attraction becomes
humanized, that is, achieves a humanly understandable form in
language and life. This conclusion does not contradict the other
aspect of prophecy where, being the result of the free gift of
God, prophecy varies infinitely in its expression, in its intensity
and power. God gives each one his own vocation and grace,
according to his free choice and our personal collaboration.

A final remark. If we stressed the unity of personal inspiration and prophetical interpretation and its expression in the community, this does not mean that there are not tensions between the
prophet and the community he lives with. As in many other aspects of life there is always a tension between our personal inspiration and the fellowship inside a society. Those tensions are
rooted either in our sinfulness or in the fact that the movement
of life is slowed down by our limitations as finite and material
beings. So it happens that the prophet has to live during a certain
time, or even during his whole life, in the tragic solitude of a
misunderstood busybody, a stupid fanatic or a crazy madman.

We have seen how and why prophecy, incited in us by the
divine initiative, has to be at the same time a corporate gift to all
members of the Church, and that it exists for the benefit of all
mankind. The problem whether and how prophecy can also be
found outside the Church would take us too far from the subject of this lecture. But if we keep to the basic principles we
have stated above, it would appear immediately that missionary
activities all over the world would have to be reproved as useless
if we were not sure that the Spirit of God has already preceded us
in those countries, leading the way and opening the hearts of
men. As another application of a principle stated above, we see
how the disruption of human relations resulting from the aggressive quality of a post-colonial culture has rendered our missionary work more difficult and, in some countries for the time being

(until the colonial wounds have been healed), almost impossible. But we have to leave this very illuminating implementation of our theology for another occasion. Yet, even if we have to limit the subject of this paper to the fact of prophecy inside the Church, we should never forget that prophecy is never given for the benefit of the Church alone, but for that of the whole world. This true catholic dimension of the Church was happily restored by Vatican II in its "open" theology of the Church.

III

We have still a task to perform, that is, to inquire into and to describe the various functions of true prophecy in the life of the Church. This description can by no means be exhaustive, for then we should have to study all the aspects of the life of the Church.

There is one function which comes to mind quite easily. I am thinking of the critical role of prophecy. But no criticism can be accepted as valid and sensible if it is not formulated in the name of an at least implicit acceptance of and commitment to definite values and truths which support and motivate our criticisms. We shall therefore in this part of the paper analyze first the critical attitude of prophecy, and secondly its positive role.

We have first to warn of an extreme simplification which originated in Germany in the nineteenth century and lasted up to the very middle of the twentieth. In part it was caused by an emotional and romantic reaction against a culture and way of life in which institutional and authoritarian traditions were too strict. At the same time it showed too a strong anti-Roman bias and prejudice, especially in university circles where ecumenism was still to be born.

The learned and very influential tradition of liberal Protestantism, especially in the great universities of Germany, introduced in their interpretation of the history of the Old Testament a sharp distinction, or quite an opposition, between prophecy and institution, between prophets and priests. The priests were the defenders of the sacred hierarchy. As members of the priestly caste they were congenitally, as it were, fated to entrench themselves behind the ritualistic or legalistic structures of a man-made "religion." It is, as a matter of fact, in those circles that the now famous meaning of the German word "Religion" was born: any form of manipulating and submitting the divine powers to human initiative and interference. The prophets, on the contrary, were the true representatives of pure faith in God. They spontaneously abhorred any form of established religion. The priest defended religious conformism and obscurantism; the prophet espoused freedom and enlightenment.

This picture in black and white is no longer accepted by modern biblical scholars, such as Gerhard von Rad or Theodoor de Vries, both of whom have written a theology of the Old Testament, though some relics of those prejudices can still be found in the works of Wilhelm Eichrodt. One may say that even Hans Küng in his book, *The Church*, has not freed himself completely from this emotional prejudice.

In Old Testament prophecy and priesthood, charism and authority are not necessarily exclusive of one another. Normally they should function together in mutual dependency and interaction. It is not that we would think that this mutual relationship functions without tensions and frictions, which is too evident from daily experience. But prophecy without the sober and controlling authority of the priesthood easily degenerates into religious enthusiasm and anarchy. Priesthood, on the contrary, which refuses to listen to the warnings and to the protests of prophets may easily turn into ritualistic, legalistic, authoritarian religion. This happened in our Church during the last century. On the other hand we have to waive the opposite solution —dear to certain French theologians and bishops—which would identify Christian priesthood and prophetism. Especially with bishops this identification shows a tendency to identify further with charismatic inspiration the official doctrine any bishop is normally called upon to defend. Doctrinaire orthodoxy becomes prophecy, which is a contradiction, and not only a logical one.

Let us investigate this point more deeply. Man is, we have already said, a relational being. He realizes himself in and through society, in the encounter with others. He needs society as the believer needs the Church. As soon as we deny this—and there is in some places a strong tendency to do so—we are falling back into the centuries-old illusion of spiritualism or angelism. Whenever the Church passed through a crisis in history there were always men who tried to avoid the confrontation with the real problems of the visible Church and to run away from them into a vague and vaporous dream of a spiritual, purely charismatic community. In this they were ignoring the sober reality of our body and our human condition and of all that goes with it, that is, man's need for a minimum of structure and institution to live and to work together. Prophecy does not mean chaos.

Human society—any community of men—means something very real. On the base of language and common patterns of behavior inherited from the very distant past, men have elaborated various social and cultural structures which keep them together, which support and channel their common efforts, guiding and defending their meeting with one another, and in due course determining a particular way of life. Man has been doing this from the very beginning of his existence. The appearance of the "homo sapiens" is precisely linked with the discovery of such signs of social organization and behavior. It is the same with the Church, though theologians are rather slow to study the sociological implications of the Church's life as a human community. One of the best books published on those lines has been written by James F. Gustafson, *Treasure in Earthen Vessels*. The well-known sociologist, Peter Berger, has also written many helpful books in the same spirit. It is true that the Church, because of its divine origin, is readily tempted by the easy solution of a vague spiritualism.

160 PIET FRANSEN, S.J.

In this process of socialization something terrible is happening, endangering the whole process. The words and language we use, those patterns of behavior we have taken over from our parents and friends, those cultural and sociological structures, the inheritance of such a long and age-old struggle toward a deeper and broader humanization, are becoming a source of inauthenticity and bad faith. Sociologists call this negative process "alienation." The reality we are confronted with is being identified with the institutions we use to manage it; and even worse, we are identifying ourselves with the sociological roles and images we acquired in the process of socialization. The stream of life is curdled and frozen.

Now it is true that the priesthood, being the representative and almost the symbol of institutional establishment (because it has among its offices the mission to defend the Church's order), often shows a dangerous tendency to hasten this process of alienation, along the three best known ways of institutionalization: ritualism, legalism or extreme juridicism in the form of a hierarchical conception of the Church. It is a real danger, but not a necessity. The Christian minister, at least, should retain this minimum of charismatic inspiration which keeps him free of this almost natural movement of gravity. Yet experience tells us he nevertheless needs prophets to keep him in balance.

The prophet is precisely the man, priest or layman, who is being forced by God's gracious inner motion and attraction to see through all those lies and illusions in a courageous protest against inauthenticity and every form of bad faith.

Peter Berger shows how the human possibility of dreaming and of imagining other ways and forms of life enables any human society to avoid alienation and living death. Even in our days we see how "orthodox" authoritarian governments hate and persecute poets and writers, because their "dreams" infect people with the strong desire for change and reform. Their "dreams" restore the necessary "open-mindness" without which any society is dead. The "dreamers" in the Church are the prophets.

The prophet denounces the senseless and sometimes stupid

platitudes of our religious and pious language, the falsehood of our devout truisms. In doing this he is indeed renewing our religious language, just as poets do, bringing it back to a new authenticity and truth.

The prophet rips off the masks of bigotry, of hate and pride, hidden under the glorious words of racism, patriotism and class-egoism, especially in the Church where some tend to justify themselves by invoking a divine consecration and order. He unmasks the many remaining and continuously re-emerging forms of superstition in our religious and sacramental practices and devotions. He exposes the futility, the uselessness, or even the unconscious injustice of so many antiquated and hardened structures of the Church. He even challenges the smugness of our learned theologians who in the course of time have lost any relation to reality and to life. In so doing, he creates new patterns of behavior, integrating them in new ways of life, more authentic and real than before.

Most of all, the prophet unmasks whatever lies behind our cowardice, our many petty anxieties, our laziness and conformism, our childish need for security and our fear of risks and new ways of life—that deep craving of every human heart for its own man-made security and comfort, afraid as we are of the infinite and never-ending newness of God's ways with men. This fear and this need for security are the most common threats to any religion, as history shows us.

In one word, the prophet unmasks every form of "religion" —in the German sense of that word (which is nowadays becoming more and more common and accepted because of the discussions about secularization and the God-is-dead theology). He restores the newness, the directness and the authenticity of living under God's presence and love. That presence and love can never become enclosed or manipulated by our techniques and clever tricks and anxious measures of security and defense.

That is one of the reasons why men in authority frequently feel uneasy when confronted with prophecy. It is an occupational disease of sorts. The first, almost spontaneous reaction is refusal—again quite a common fact of experience. Men in authority have in fact been commissioned for the service of authority, and they are doubtless responsible before God for the people entrusted to them. But they are not God. As human beings they urgently need some safe and fixed rules to go on, some structures of law to back their policy, some simple and definite body of truths to guide them. They need it the more in that courage and endurance do not seem to be clerical virtues. At least, that is what one is forced to conclude from the many reactions of fear and anxiety one daily meets in higher clerical circles. We can, however, understand this need for more or less fixed and accepted forms of thought and government. Biologists, sociologists and psychologists have repeatedly demonstrated how the human animal needs them, since he alone among all the higher mammals is born without any "program," we would say (thinking of computers). We have to build our own patterns of thought and behavior, simply to live and to go on living. In the Church we believe that those accepted forms of thought we call doctrine and the accepted forms of activity we call morals and spiritual life do have a certain relation to God's reality.

This need for an institutional structure of life is by no means questioned here. The danger is that a too great confidence in them leads to immobility and stagnation. Especially in religious matters, living very near to the absoluteness of God, men in authority easily transfer this quality to human thoughts, principles and rules which are not endowed with the same quality of absoluteness which is the unique privilege of God. It is, as I have said already, an occupational disease. We need doubtless in the Church, too, some amount of order, organization and unity in doctrine, so as not to fall into chaos. This is today not a redundant statement! But this order, this discipline, those morals and that doctrinal body, since they remain in great part manmade, are never to take the place of God himself. It is precisely the role of the prophet to avoid this form of alienation and religious corruption, restoring the direct awareness of God's presence beyond all doctrines, customs and rules. It is, on the other side, the proper role of authority—normally exercised by priests, though not necessarily always and at every level—to see that the freedom of prophecy does not lead to anarchy and to that uncontrolled use and abuse of freedom which charisms may produce. So both have their role and mission in the Church. But the prophet's role is the more important.

Therefore one must even say, as the last Council did, that there is in Christianity no true use of authority where prophecy has no part, even among men in authority. This is the truth within a certain French theological school of thought about the nature of the priesthood, which tends to equate priesthood and prophecy. There is no true exercise of Christian and ecclesial authority where there is no awareness of the twofold fact that the concrete will of God transcends the limitations of authority's initiative and decision, and that every human decision has to respect the presence of the Spirit in the men authority is sent to guide and to serve. That is the only meaning of the new word in fashion: that the priesthood is a "diakonia," a real ministry and service. The exercise of authority in the Church is only possible where the man in authority is himself listening to the stirring of God's grace in his own heart and to the similar motions in the hearts of the people he has to lead. And that is indeed a charism, a prophetic aspect within authority itself.

We know from recent experience that in the Church only a prophetically inspired authority is capable of real guidance and influence. A religious community, essentially based upon a freely accepted faith and charity, is not efficaciously held together by laws and coercion. I have always maintained that this illusion was a form of Pelagianism in the West, where frequently we have had more confidence in canon law and Church order to bring about and to establish the Kingdom of God than in the guidance of the Spirit.

One of the most striking examples of a modern Christian prophet, who was at the same time at the summit of the institutional hierarchy, was Pope John. Probably none of the latest Popes was so widely respected as a man in authority, and nevertheless no Pope of the last century had such an insight into his own limitations, as well as the weaknesses and the powerlessness of his own ecclesiastical position and mission. His moral authority was based more upon his prophetic inspiration and view than upon the institutional rights attached to his position in the Roman Catholic Church.

The secret of prophetic power is conviction about one's own limitations and even sinfulness, together with a full confidence in the power of the truth, or better, in the final victory of God's living presence of grace. For this reason the true prophetic spirit might well flourish and thrive in a climate where there is a sense of humor. Prophecy may indeed sometimes become a tragic venture. But even then the true prophet does not take himself too seriously (though he takes his own mission and the scope of this mission the more seriously for that). There is indeed a seriousness and a sense of ego-centered tragedy which destroys every manifestation of prophecy.

IV

We may now conclude with a final question: What does prophecy have to do with hope?

We know why and how the theological virtue of hope is nowadays coming before the limelight of theological research and reflection. Our time is almost completely indifferent toward the past—in a certain sense too much so—certainly among the younger people. But at the same time we are profoundly concerned with the future of the world, and of the Church in this world. The rhythm of time is accelerating in a terrific way. We are now aware that some aspects of the future are in our hands. At least on the human level we feel that we are going to be able to manipulate and prepare effectively some aspects of the future. We are all looking spontaneously forward, and one of our most tragic problems is that precisely this power we feel in our hands regarding the future makes the future at the same time darker and more confused. How are we going to use those powers? Sometimes, we should say, we feel nearer to despair than to hope.

The virtue of hope, of hoping against and beyond all hope, has therefore a real role to play. We are indeed hoping against all hope, because we confide in God's promises and living presence in the world. The special perspective of our modern hope is that we refuse to confine it to the mere acquisition of heaven. We feel nowadays in many Christian Churches that our hope cannot be divine, if it is at the same time not truly human. We are not expecting only our individual remuneration with God. Our hope is also a corporate attitude. We hope with all our fellow men. But the rediscovery of the meaning of our body and of the earth wherein we live has brought us to the further insight that the object of our Christian hope cannot leave out our common condition here on earth. Again, in our modern Christian hope we want to waive energetically every form of angelism and bloodless spiritualism through which we finally are distracted from our real responsibilities with our contemporaries who live on this earth. Our hope in Christ should include them all, and already now, here, in their human condition. For Christ has saved the whole of man, soul and body, person and community, heaven and earth.

To restrict our hope to heaven, remaining at the same time "supernaturally" indifferent, if we may say so, toward the presence of injustice, of hunger and war in this world, seems to us, and rightly so, a betrayal of our human solidarity—but more so, a betrayal of God's love for all men as he created them. By any such indifference we are then—we feel it acutely—no more the followers of Christ, who lived for the sinners, the publicans and the prostitutes, who helped the poor, the derelict and the sick. One of the oldest signs of the coming of the Kingdom is that the sick are healed, the hungry are fed, men in prison are freed, the blind see and the deaf hear.

We are convinced that there is no true Christian hope today

where there is no strong and courageous hope for all men, a true hope against hope.

It is precisely the mission of true Christian prophecy to proclaim this hope, to strengthen it, to reinvigorate it wherever it is falling into despondency and despair.

But here again we discover the true nature of prophecy. To imagine Christian prophecy as a new way of recovering the security we have lost, as a new way of getting new comfort and safety in the prediction of sure solutions for all our problems, would be to return to a man-made religion. The comfort we lost in our present situation we would be attempting to assure for the future, our future and that of our children. It would be as if we were returning from a hard and dangerous journey, and somebody would tell us: do not fear, home is near. It would be another flight into a false illusion.

We don't know what the future is preparing ahead of us. The prophets don't know either. It remains our fate and human condition to find our way through history groping painfully and hesitantly in the dark for more truth, more justice, more freedom, more love, ignorant of what the future has in store for us. Prophecy will never restore the false security of our old Roman Catholic ways. For this would be false prophecy: not the word of God, but the silent desire of our own lonely and anxious hearts. We meet this kind of prophecy in our days too. They tell us when we complain about the crisis in the Church: this will be over soon. It is only a temporary madness. Soon the old and safe Catholic security of our little ghetto will be restored. We forget that the Church has always been in a state of crisis, but that in our days the mass media brings every happening to the limelight of world attention. The world became in a few decades very small: whatever happens in Vietnam or in South America appears the same night on our T.V. screen.

The prophet, however, has to tell us something very important. He has indeed to help us toward the decisive solution, but one which does not do away with the incertitudes and the qualms of our common human existence. It was an illusion of our former Catholic education and mentality to think that we, of all men, were freed from this common fate. The true prophet witnesses to the intensity, the livingness, the radicality of God's loving presence amid the darknesses and the incertitudes and tensions of human history, especially now when we have a more direct view upon human history than ever before.

It is now that we see how this prophetical testimony may influence the future. God left us the world to live and work in. *We* have to solve our problems here. We are still responsible for all our brothers and sisters. No solution shall descend from heaven as a miraculous gift. That was the meaning of Bonhoeffer when he wrote that we should live "ac si Deus non esset," as if God did not exist.

But only the man and the woman who takes seriously this world and his responsibility in it, and at the same time who takes God's presence still more seriously than anything else, shall be capable of preparing this human future, which at the same time shall be a gift from God.

Living with God, for God and through God we are finally, radically, living in the present, and not amid false illusions and dreams. But living thoroughly in the present we are indeed already living in the future, for only people concerned with real facts and with real people are people of the future. Our future can only be guaranteed by the intensity of our present commitment in faith and charity.

That is the reason why prophetism is nowadays so important for the life of the Church and of the whole world. If this is true, we baptized and confirmed members of the Holy Church must try to listen again to the motions of the Spirit, and to act accordingly—not forgetting, however, that the prophet, even if he stands temporarily alone, is always witnessing for the whole People of God.

For, as St. Paul says: the charisms are many, but the Spirit is one.

Daniel Day Williams

Knowing and Hoping in the Christian Faith

In his book *Eros and Civilization* Herbert Marcuse indicts religion and contemporary philosophy for their affinity with death which is the symbol of unfreedom and defeat. He says:

Theology and philosophy today compete with each other in celebrating death as an existential category: perverting a biological fact into an ontological essence, they bestow transcendental blessing on the guilt of mankind which they help to perpetuate—they betray the promise of utopia.[1]

My concern in this essay is with the meaning of hope in the Christian faith and the relation of hoping to knowing. Hope has become the central theme of much contemporary theology and has arisen with surprising power throughout our culture. I have begun with this quotation from one of the leading philosophers of the revolutionary spirit for three reasons. First, Marcuse states the familiar Marxist thesis that the forms of religious hope are ideological projections whose real function is to distract attention from the divisions in present society and therefore to block action toward the good society. Second, Marcuse links theology and philosophy together as betrayers of utopia. Presumably he is thinking of the Existentialist doctrine of authentic existence as the recognition that we run toward death, and the Stoic attitude which has no real hope but only courage in the face of the ultimate negation.

But it is what Marcuse goes on to say about death to which I call particular attention. He asserts, "Men can die without anxiety if they know that what they love is protected from misery and oblivion." [2] "If they know. . . ." Here he binds hoping and knowing together. To know something which gives hope for the future is in some way to grasp that future.

What I propose to do is to explore the relation of knowing to hoping, first as it appears in the Christian faith. But I also want to show that there is a remarkable convergence of theology, revolutionary philosophy, and the impact of modern science on our present experience, so that the present concern with hope is appearing in different contexts but with a measure of shared understanding. The possibility of a deeper reconciliation between religious, political, and scientific traditions appears when we tackle the subtle problems involved in the relation of knowing and hoping. The prospect of a greater mutuality between theology, philosophy, politics and science is so great that it may justify the risk of exploring our thesis on a very broad scale.

We begin with knowing and hoping in the Christian faith. Of course this comes directly to the heart of the biblical perspective. Human existence has a beginning and an end. The life of faith is lived in history before and with God who is working out his purpose. Hence the theme of promise and of hope is fundamental in the Bible.

Certainly the expectation of salvation and the Kingdom is essential to the structure of the Christian faith. There are the words of Jesus. "He who endures to the end shall be saved." "Blessed are the meek for they shall inherit the earth." Paul says we are "saved by hope." "Now we see in a mirror dimly but then face to face. Now I know in part, then I shall understand fully even as I have been fully understood." The words of 1 Corinthians 13 about faith, hope and love abiding are so familiar we easily miss the powerful paradox involved in the affirmation that hope *abides*. It is no temporary expectation to be immediately fulfilled, but a dimension of all life before God until the last enemy has been put down, and the last enemy is death.

The relation of hope to knowledge contains a powerful inner tension which lies at the roots of the Christian faith. What we hope for is bound up with our knowledge of who God is and what our existence means. The word of the Fourth Gospel has been a major motif of all Western civilization. "You shall know the truth and the truth will make you free." The promise is for a future fulfillment. The reference in the Fourth Gospel is quite clearly to the sending of the Spirit, the Comforter, who will lead us into all truth. But that promise is meaningless apart from the belief that Christ who is the Truth has already come to us, and we have beheld his glory "full of grace and truth." Thus hope in the Christian perspective is rooted in *the faithfulness of God,* as the Old Testament continually asserts, and in the personal Word of God who is Jesus Christ, the Truth. In the New Testament to know God in his Word is to hope. We live in a dimension of expectation which stretches into the future and beyond death, but we hope on the basis of a knowledge of our real situation before and with God. "Brothers, now are we the sons of God; it does not yet appear what we shall be." There is of course in human life a kind of hope which is sheer unknowing leap into the future; but that is not the hope of the Gospel which is founded on what we can now know.

If we consider the *content* of the hope the New Testament holds we encounter the same inner tension between knowing and the not-yet. For we do not fully know what we hope for; yet our hope is meaningless apart from what we have already seen in Jesus Christ of life on the other side of the estrangement of sin.

The relation of knowing and hoping for Christian faith is brought to its clearest focus when we consider the meaning of Christ for *forgiveness.* It is clear that Paul's theology, whatever its dimension of futurity, unequivocally rests on a present reality: God's acceptance of us now while we are yet sinners. The Gospel message is not, "God *will* forgive," but "God *does* forgive"; not that we will one day be free of condemnation but that we are now free; not that we will at some time enter into a new relationship to God through Christ, but that God has now made us a new creation in him. "Now there is no condemnation to those who are in Christ Jesus."

The content of the new life is freedom to love, to grow in grace, and it is freedom to hope; but it is freedom given to us now. So Paul pleads with the Galatians: "For freedom Christ has set us free, stand fast therefore, and do not submit to a yoke of slavery" (Gal 4:1). This life in the new freedom has one of its dimensions in the future. It is bearing about in the body the dying of Jesus that his life also might be manifest; but both the dying and the manifestation have a present reality, as well as a future expectation—for "we shall be like him."

The foundation in Christian faith of our knowledge of the new life and its hope is the story of Jesus with its climax in the crucifixion and resurrection. Here knowledge and hope are indissolubly together; for while Christ's resurrection has taken place and therefore we are no longer dead in our sins, we are yet waiting for fulfillment. Paul says, "For if we have been united with him in a death like his, we shall certainly be united with him in a resurrection like his" (Rom 6:5). The tenses become strangely mixed here. Paul thinks of the new life in Christ as partaking in the resurrection; yet he also speaks of the resurrection in future terms: "We shall all be changed." As Paul says:

Therefore since we are justified by faith we have peace with God through our Lord Jesus Christ. Through him we have obtained access to this grace in which we stand, and we rejoice in our hope of sharing the glory of God.

Peace now, glory later. What holds these together is the Spirit. It is the new life in the Spirit which both knows the power of the resurrection, that is what it means to die to sin; and which also hopes for what is not now consummated, that which we cannot now see. But the peace and the glory are mutual implicates. Without the peace of reconciliation there is no meaning to the hope for communion; and without the hope there can be no real peace in the present experience, for it is filled with suffering, with the not-yet.

If this be in barest outline the relation of knowing and hoping, in the New Testament we find three central questions which are insistently asked today, and which have led to an increasing emphasis on the importance of hope in Christian faith.

First, there is an increasing recognition that the forms of our knowledge and the language of its expression have their limitations which come from finitude, and from diverse cultural perspectives. The symbols of our knowledge and our hope point beyond themselves. We are reluctant to claim for the forms of our knowing an absoluteness and finality; there is an aspect of incompleteness, an expectation of correction. The language of the Kingdom is not yet our language except in expectation. But notice this also means that the specific forms of hope are subject to the same limitation. The eschatological concepts are notoriously "symbolic." They reach for that which is beyond our present grasp: resurrection; apocalyptic visions; heavenly expectations which lie beyond anything we can imagine. I shall not dwell on this new sensitivity about the forms of knowing and hoping, but it is important for our present situation in the expression of the Christian faith, and for the relationship between theology, philosophy, and science.

The second question arises from an honest confession of what we are doing when we claim a present knowledge of God's saving power. What kind of knowledge do we really have? When we say we know we have been set free from sin and death our statements invite an immediate disclaimer of authenticity. Do we really experience freedom from the law when we see ourselves contending for our small righteousness? Have we really been set free from the bondage of guilt into the glorious liberty of the sons of God? Ask the psychotherapists what they find in us professed believers. We believe Christ has openly triumphed over the principalities and powers and authorities; but history moves on with the principalities and powers wielding enormous force, and making a strong bid to bring the whole to a catastrophic end.

The problem here is a very old one—Is faith knowledge, or is it essentially hope? John Calvin defined faith as

. . . a steady and certain knowledge of the Divine benevolence towards us, which, being founded on the truth of the gratuitous promise in Christ, is both revealed to our minds, and confirmed to our hearts, by the Holy Spirit.[3]

This phrase, "the truth of the promise," embraces the mystery of hoping and knowing in the Christian faith. Without the truth we cannot believe the promise, but we can have the truth only with a dimension of promise.

It might be proposed here that we will be on safer ground if we always understand knowing in the Christian faith as believing. We hope that what we believe is true, even if we cannot know it to be true. And we can hope that what we believe we shall know in the end. But hope wins out now, for believing is subject to all the risk of our finitude, our uncertainty, and our sin. Believing always bears an inner counterpoint of disbelief. Luther says:

For this is the nature of faith, that it dares trust in God's grace. . . . Faith does not require information, knowledge or security, but a free surrender and a joyful daring upon an unfelt, untried, unknown goodness.[4]

Yet the dialectic of knowing and hoping cannot be overcome by believing, for belief without any basis in experience is purely arbitrary and therefore any hope founded upon it is arbitrary. We hope in the Christian faith because we have already seen a reality which makes life whole; the incarnate mercy of God and therefore a new possibility for ourselves. We are touching here upon the meaning of assurance in faith, a perennial theological topic. I am appealing to the authority of Christian experience: not for the absoluteness of the forms of expression of our knowledge, but for that real knowledge which is essential to the very hope which we hold. Unless we experience the leading and creativity of God there is no ground of hope. We can believe the promises of God only if we believe in the Promiser. What we know in Christian experience is a grace, a power, and a life which is beginning to be opened to us, and which leads us toward a future disclosure. This knowledge should prevent us from absolutizing our present state of understanding or practice. "It does not yet appear what we shall be."

The third issue is that between our ultimate hope and proximate hopes for this world and its life, the hopes for justice, for a peaceful and creative world civilization in history. Has theology here betrayed Utopia? The answer so far has to be, in part, yes. We have yet to find an adequate view of the relation of hope in time and history to the ultimate promises of the Gospel. It is surely not the case, as Marcuse and Marx and others charge, that the Church has not wrestled with this issue, or that it has always turned attention away from earthly causes. One can easily refute that from the beginning of Church history, but our concern is with the issue today. We have to solve concrete problems of social control, international war, human justice, and technological adjustment to our environment; otherwise the whole human enterprise faces catastrophe. We can understand those who say it is not ultimate reconciliation but drastic change which is required. We need not ultimate assurance but the release of human energies for survival. We need hope for present human effort.

We turn therefore to the new revolutionary philosophies. But in anticipation of our conclusion, there are two major affirmations about the relation of ultimate to proximate hopes which grow out of our analysis of the relation of knowing and hoping in Christian faith that can be stated here.

The first has to do with the new openness concerning the precise forms of hope. The future is not determined according to a pattern which has been revealed to us. All literalizing of eschatological symbols, all prediction of the future course of events, all enclosing of the Christian view of the future in optimistic or pessimistic modes must yield to a proper sense of the limitations of our sight as we learn what it means to live in hope before God. The Christian faith has always had as its deepest note the call to entrust life to God in all things in life, and in death. Our times and all times are in his hands. Providence means that God goes before us wherever we are to go. There is therefore an existential courage and commitment to serve God in present history as we have light on his purposes, even when the outcome of his working is by no means fully known to us. Against Marcuse and Camus, I am arguing that one of the contributions of Christian faith to civilization has been its ability to sustain hope in an undefined future, and to nourish a trusting expectancy for new good in history. There is a link between present action for justice and humanity and the final purposes of God.

The second observation has to do with the specific content of Christian hope. The central theme is the Kingdom of God, and that means God's reign over all things. The Kingdom is therefore a social reality. It involves the fulfillment of the kinds of relationships between man and man and man and God which show forth the divine image in human affairs. There have been, to be sure, forms of Christianity which have so individualized the meaning of the Gospel that it has been drained of its social relevance; but these are aberrations, and there is almost universal recognition in our century that the social gospel with its drive toward a new social order has its warrant in the deepest understanding of the biblical message.

The humanity for which we hope is defined by the humanity we know in Jesus Christ. It is the humanity of the servant, the man free to serve other man, and to give life for the meeting of other men in love. We have no blueprint for a Christian civilization. We have to find our way in the imitation of Christ in our time and with our problems. Christ is the Type; but the type leaves us open to the creativity of freedom itself when that freedom is exercised in love.[5]

It is this concrete human and social content of the hope for the Kingdom that gives us the basis for translating our ultimate hopes into concrete decision in history. There are principles and requirements of human justice which are the historical and present forms of what God's righteousness requires. The new theologies of hope have been asserting this but sometimes they give the impression that we have to derive all our guidance for present action from the eschatological Kingdom alone.[6] But the hope we have now is grounded in what we know about God's action, although even as we say this we recognize that our ways are not his ways and that therefore while we seek the justice we believe God requires we cannot simply identify our plans and programs with his will. Secular justice is ultimately worthful even if it does not have the absolute worth of perfection.

We turn now to the contemporary alternatives to Christian faith in the hopeful new revolutionary philosophies.

In *Man's Nature and His Communities* Reinhold Niebuhr speaks of that "wonderful combination of hope and despair which has been the motive power of all rebellions against injustice." [7] All revolution lives from some kind of hope. There must be a conviction that a new order is possible, and there must be some idea of what that new order could be in contrast to the present. It is in this sense that Marcuse uses the term *utopian*. It does not mean dreaming a glorious picture of the future with all the evils rubbed out; it means the hope for a new order which is based on a new principle, achieves a new justice, and promises human fulfillment.

Every revolutionary philosophy therefore relates knowing and hoping. What I shall try to show is that now there is a shift in this relationship in revolutionary philosophy which is akin to what we have seen in theology.

First let us look at the revolutionary philosophical stance in its own terms. I am focusing on the movement from Marx to Marcuse. The revolutionary is in the following situation with respect to knowledge and hope: As a revolutionary he must break with the present structure of knowledge which characterizes the mind-set of the established order. This mind-set is illusory, ideological, and untrustworthy. The content of the revolutionary hope is the new order, but it is just that which we do not have in our experience. How can we move from our present distorted vision to what we can hope for tomorrow?

There is a way of making this move. If not wholly discovered it was at least systematized by Hegel, and that is why most revolutionary philosophy since Hegel has directly or indirectly drawn upon him. It is the dialectical way. We can go from present knowledge to future hope when we discover that history moves according to a pattern in which the new order arises as an opposition to the old, and the new content will be that which both negates and fulfills the present order. The dialectical key to hope is that history exhibits its own structure which guarantees the shattering of the present order to make way for the new.

As we know, Hegel's version of the dialectic reaches its consummation in the Prussian State, and Hegel is the philosopher who understands the whole process. As he says magisterially in the preface to his lectures on the philosophy of history: "In the World nothing else is revealed but the True, the Eternal, the absolutely powerful essence of reason—a result which happens to be known to me, because I have traversed the entire field." [8]

Emil Fackenheim in his recent book on Hegel reminds us that in his last lectures on philosophy of religion, after Hegel has demonstrated the power of philosophy to express the absolute truth, which is for him the truth of the Christian revelation, he looks about him and finds very few people who understand the absolute Idea. Philosophers remain an isolated order of priests who cannot mix with the world. [9]

Not so with Marx. For him the point is to change the world. His view of the relation of knowing and hoping has its clue in Hegel but it has the structure of a dialectical, economically determined process. That structure can be known, because it is objectively embedded in reality, and the observer who is not confused by ideology can know it. Here is Lenin's claim for objective knowledge:

Materialism in general recognizes objectively real being (matter) as independent of the mind, sensation, experience, etc. of humanity. . . . From this Marxian philosophy, which is cast from a single piece of steel, you cannot eliminate one basic premise, one essential part, without departing from objective truth, without falling a prey to a bourgeois-reactionary falsehood.[10]

Once the nature of alienation is understood man's true essence becomes intelligible. All the oppositions in man which frustrate his full humanity are to be overcome. So the content of revolutionary hope is derived from this dialectical affirmation of the overcoming of what is at present disrupted. Marx says in his economic and philosophical manuscripts:

Communism is the positive abolition of private property, of human self-alienation, and thus the real appropriation of human nature through and for man. It is, therefore, the return of man himself as a social, i.e. really human being. . . . Communism . . . is the *definitive* resolution of the antagonism between man and nature, and between man and man. It is the true solution of the conflict between existence and essence, between objectification and self-affirmation, between freedom and necessity, between individual and species. It is the solution of the riddle of history and knows itself to be this solution.[11]

We need not dwell on the often repeated observation that Marx is giving us a secularized version of prophetic eschatology. If we substitute a completely this-worldly vision of the future society for a transcendent kingdom of God, and see the primary agency not as God but as the dialectical structure of history, the agreement with the biblical hope for the overcoming of alienation is patent. Objective scientific knowing has replaced the traditional revelation. Hope is grounded in knowledge, and the content of the hope is man's fulfillment of his essence objectified in a new order of life.

It is the fate of this Marxist confidence to be giving way in

the twentieth century to a reassessment of the relation of knowing and hoping not unlike what we have seen in theology. If we
can penetrate this phenomenon we may get some light on the
movement toward a new stage in the form of man's hope.

The confidence which Marx had in grasping absolutely the
structure of history and predicting the complete overcoming of
alienation has given way to a more open, less deterministic
conception of hope. Much contemporary revolutionary philosophy (not the doctrinaire kind of party propaganda) shows a
kinship with the theological interpretation of hope in which
there is a present insight into the reality of redemption and yet
an acknowledgment that the mystery of the future remains. In
place of a claim for absolute knowledge of the future, there is
more readiness to wrestle with the present, and move into the
future as an exploration of possibility rather than the realization of a pre-arranged plan. Put in another way: utopia seems
to be taking on a new function. It is not the complete determination of hope and the pattern of the future; but it is the assertion
of judgment on the present in order to win freedom from the
present, and to draw upon the power of hope to create a new
reality. One of the chief complaints of the critics of the new
youth revolution is that it is vague in its objective. "Precisely
what do you want?" the moderate elders ask. I am pointing out
that it is just the unwillingness to answer that question which
characterizes some of the new revolutionary stance. While this
may produce a considerable confusion so far as a sense of direction is concerned, it also shows an openness which may be more
flexible and revisable than the dogmatic secular eschatologies of
the past. Here is a characteristic statement from a student of the
new left:

The present day stranger hung-up on every cross in town
may be that so-called hippie, who is unself-consciously developing
a revolutionary style in technological America through his *ad hoc*
participation in all of life, creating a "bottom-up" revolution
with a new style (a highly individualized style learned largely
from the black movement, where oppression has preserved black

men from white contamination, wherein they created their man-
hood out of suffering, as Fanon has said), a new style that makes
leaders unthinkable and exploitation impossible for each man
now becomes his own leader. The new style is directed toward
a shared community of quality in which each man's genius is recognized, an infinitely humorous situation in which the Kingdom of
God is seen as present. Jesus the revolutionary is Jesus the
hippie, disguised in four parts as the Beatles. "Heaven sneaks
in in unsuspecting ways" as John of the Cross might say.[12]

The utopian note here is unmistakable as it finds theological
expression, yet there is no plan for the future, and no prescription for its attainment.

Two main issues have led to this new openness in revolutionary philosophy, and therefore to a new assessment of the relation of knowing and hoping.

The first point concerns the determinism in the traditional
Marxist solution. The criticism of this comes out clearly in the
Polish Marxist philosopher, Kolakowski. I must here rely on
Professor George Kline for my knowledge of Kolakowski's
thought, and I have implicit confidence in Professor Kline. The
Polish Marxist finds that absolute determinism takes all the sense
out of moral obligation. He draws upon Kant and the Existen-
tialists to recover the element of subjectivity which is essential
to authentic humanity. He sees both Marx and Hegel as caught in
historiosophy in which there are no more individuals:

. . . they appear only as instances of general ideas, bearing the
mark of their species upon their foreheads. In that world, we do
not eat bread and butter; we restore our labor power, which is
consciously organized for purposes of socialist construction. We
do not sleep, we regenerate cerebral tissue for creative work in
realizing the *Weltgeist*. We talk not to men but to carriers of
ideas, which are themselves only representatives of certain
conflicting social forces in the gigantic march of history.[13]

Within this dehumanization there is a failure of ethical judgment; for in a completely determined history we will judge
right and wrong by the success of particular movements. Moral

sensitivity is dulled by the "opiate of the Weltgeist." Hence, "between obedience to history and obedience to the moral imperative yawns an abyss on whose brink the great historical tragedies have been played." [14]

Here the relation of knowledge and hope is being redefined through the grasp of a moral imperative which transcends historical success or failure. What we know leads to a judgment on immediate history and its forms of hope. The hope which guides action will be redefined in the light of this moral dimension, for now all values have to be re-examined in the light of a moral absolute which transcends any predictable realization. Kolakowski has opened up what may be a new form of revolutionary doctrine based on a new anthropology; for if there are depths in man's self-knowledge which disclose his relation to something beyond historical actualization, then the relation of knowledge to hope must be restated.

In Ernst Bloch this new openness in the structure of revolutionary hope becomes the dominant theme. For Bloch, Marx is the prophet of liberation; but Bloch sees in both man and nature a creative becoming, which is the context of man's self-understanding. Man has to live into his future in order to know who he is, and Bloch's thought here is indebted to the biblical structure of knowledge and hope.[15]

Bloch retains much of the classic Greek view of nature. With Aristotle he sees nature as the scene of processes with potencies to be realized, primordial matter to be shaped, natural powers achieving ends. Transposed into modern evolutionary thought this means that man is the creature of an unfinished nature. His hope then is bound up with his expectation of a future which is not wholly predictable. Nature has her own mysteries.

But the greatest mystery to be explored is in man himself. For Bloch, man lives by hope, because he has unexplored depths within himself. He is the self-discoverer through his grasp of the future, a grasp secured not only by rational thought but by imagination, dreams, fantasies, constructions of what is not yet actuality. Asked to sum up his philosophy in one sentence,

Bloch is reported to have said: "S is not yet P." [16] Predicates of man the subject have not yet been actualized. To live by hope is to know existence as bearing a depth and possibility which we cannot fathom through present knowledge.

This theme of man as *homo absconditus* living toward his future reality, not possessing it, is reinforced by Bloch, in spite of his atheism, with an affirmation that we must preserve the affirmation of the *deus absconditus,* the ultimate mystery of being, else the human mystery will be robbed of its full depth. Here again the philosopher is drawing upon a theological theme for the sake of a revolutionary anthropology. It is some evidence of the move toward internal communion between radically different modes of thought.

As we assess the relation of knowledge and hope today we have to introduce a third approach, that of Science. Whitehead points out that modes of thought which have characterized modern science are now spread throughout the civilized world.[17] These include empiricism, the search for the stubborn and irreducible facts; the relation of facts to general theories which give intelligibility to the facts; and the spirit of tentativeness concerning all conclusions. There are always more data. Science must be revisionist in its attitude toward theory, for the method is the practice of critical reflection moving toward new exploration. It is science above all which has caused the revision of our world-views, and it has had much to do with modifying the relation of knowing and hoping in both theology and philosophy. From Bergson to Whitehead and Teilhard de Chardin the story of metaphysics is the struggle to get time into being. Now the relation of knowledge and hope has a new metaphysical context.

It is instructive to ask about the specific relation of knowing and hoping in science, for here it appears to have a somewhat different structure and in some measure a distinctive outcome. After all, in science we really *do know*.

All science implies a relation between present inquiry and the possibility of future truthful resolution of inquiry. The structure of past, present, and future is inescapable. Present knowledge leads to new hypotheses, and we learn by predicting future consequences and testing them. Notice the hope in science is *not* that a particular hypothesis will be confirmed, but that out of experiment and confirmation or disconfirmation more fruitful hypotheses will emerge.

What becomes then of the truth which makes us free when the absolute truth can only be spoken about as a limit? Charles Peirce defined truth in the following way:

The opinion which is fated to be ultimately agreed to by all who investigate, is what we mean by the truth, and the object represented in this opinion is the real. That is the way I would define reality.[18]

Thus the hope of future agreement becomes the very meaning of the scientific process. William James continually declares the significance of truth as the end of inquiry. It does not negate the past, but it must weld the past to new experience:

New truth is always a go-between, a smoother over of transitions.[19]

The absolute truth, meaning what no further experience will ever alter, is that ideal vanishing point towards which we imagine that all our temporary truths will some day converge. . . . Meanwhile we have to live today by what truth we can get today, and be ready tomorrow to call it falsehood.[20]

James' word falsehood might be too strong, for a fragmentary truth corrected is not necessarily a falsehood. But he says the absolute truth will have to be *made*, made as a relation incidental to the growth of a mass of verification-experience, to which the half-true ideas are all along contributing their quota.[21]

Now this conception of truth as being made in history, startling as it appears, converges with the theological and philosophical standpoints we have been examining. Truth in history rests upon the present reality of a community of shared experience and of inquiry, but that community can grasp truth only as having a dimension of hope.

We seem to have come upon a guiding conception of the relation of knowledge and hope as inhering in communities which bind time with hope. Our communal theory of truth would hold together present knowledge born out of communal experience and mutual criticism, with an expectation of correction and fulfillment in the future. As Josiah Royce said, to live within a community in history is to experience a sharing of memory and hope.[22] Here James' and Peirce's pragmatism and Royce's idealism tend to converge. They all claim to be giving an interpretation of truth which conforms to the scientific mode of knowing.

There has been a considerable reinforcement of this view of science as the function of communities of inquiry in Thomas Kuhn's book *The Structure of Scientific Revolutions*. Kuhn comes close to denying for example that there is such a thing as linear progression toward truth in science. Rather, there is a series of revolutions in which new statements of problems appear, and new questions are asked. No scientific theory ever fits the facts completely, and the choice between competing paradigms "proves to be a choice between incompatible modes of community life." [23]

Kuhn may not give sufficient weight to the cumulative achievement of science, especially in the more precise realms such as physics; but he shows that science lives in communities which move into the future armed with theories which have attained verification yet which are subject to radical revision in the light of new problems, new data, and new shifts of interest. This is not to deny the reliability of science in the ordinary sense of that term but it is to deny the finality of any particular stage of scientific theory. Kuhn feels constrained to ask whether we may not have to surrender the view that "there is some one full, objective true account of nature and that the proper measure of scientific achievement is the extent to which it brings us closer to that ultimate goal." [24] The real mystery, Kuhn says, lies in the question of what kind of world we must be living in so that science is possible at all, and that question remains unanswered.[25] There begins to appear in science a structure of hope for a future truth which cannot be clearly defined in the present, a hope whose fulfillment is eschatological.

Scientific knowing then has its own internal dialectic between knowing and hoping. It appeals to a radically open future into which the scientific community moves, along with the rest of the human community, as an essential dimension of science itself.

Beginning with the question of knowledge of God and salvation and its relation to hope in the Christian faith we have been led to a reconsideration of the general theme of the relation of knowledge and hope. As we draw the threads of this discussion together certain conclusions emerge. We see a convergence of perspective on knowledge and its relation to hope in theology, in philosophy, and in science. Our age is certainly not conspicuous for its tendency to achieve agreement on major articles of faith, yet it may be that there is a deeper current of common searching and outlook in our time than the outward appearance shows. If so our exploration of knowing and hoping might lead to a reinforcement of hope for mutual understanding and relevant criticism among these different perspectives. I do not believe we are grasping at straws when we detect in the analysis we have made a basis for these conclusions:

1. Man's existence has a thrust into the future so that the dimension of hope is an essential constituent of humanity. The meaning of the present is not derived from the past or present alone; it is derived from its linkage with a future toward which we move.

2. The future is the unfathomed realm of possibility. Our relation to it, while grounded in present knowing, is a relationship to an as yet unencompassed, and unobjectified reality. Man bears a depth within his own being which is not only the

abyss of negation and death—*pace* Heidegger—but the depth of openness to possibility beyond what he now is, and in that sense beyond death itself.

3. Hoping is meaningless apart from knowing. The grounds of hope and the content of our hopes are always rooted in what the past and present of experience give us by way of values, goals, frustrations, and expectations. We clash about what we hope for indeed; but the remarkable fact today is a tempering of the forms of the hope by a sense of our limitation, a recognition that hope lies deeper than its particular forms.

4. The truth which makes us free is a truth which is both present and future. It must be grasped as we live into it. It is that which is the ground of our humanity, yet its promise looks toward what we may become.

This discovery that what we know includes a dimension of hope beyond what we can fully know could open the way to a mutual interchange between Christian theology and revolutionary hope, between humanists, scientists, and theologians. The Christian affirmation of the Kingdom of God at the "end" of history is not a restriction on hopes for this world, but rather a release of hopefulness without dogmatic prediction. Whatever man does in history he lives in the light of the Kingdom which fulfills life in freedom. The biblical eschatology so understood ought to release human energies for the most strenuous action toward the reconstruction of existence.

I have argued that theology has been helped to understand more profoundly the relation of knowing and hoping by what revolutionary thought and science have given it in criticism. But does the Christian faith with its view of the relation of knowing and hoping have any distinctive truth to speak to our culture?

I return to Professor Marcuse's statement: "Men can die without anxiety if they know that what they love is protected from misery and oblivion."

The theological question could not be put more sharply; and woe to theology if it offers a glib answer. The Christian faith does claim a knowledge that what we love as God loves it is protected from misery and oblivion. This would be faith's testimony to a time wracked with agony, death, and frustration; not the avoidance of effort but the release of it, knowing creative action is worthwhile.

But here theology does speak a strange language, of death and resurrection; of the earthly passage as a pilgrimage to eternity, of knowledge of God who ventures into the future preserving what "in the world is mere wreckage," as Whitehead says. [26] That knowledge has never been a simple objective knowledge which can be spread out for everyone to see. It is the knowledge shared in a community of living and dying people whose faith has been transformed by the experience of Israel and the life of Jesus seen in the light of his death and resurrection.

Do we leave this world of real things and "betray utopia" when we talk of knowing the power of the resurrection and the hope it brings? I do not believe so. The resurrection is the sign of the hope which gives life in the midst of death. We do not know fully what it means, but in its light we have begun to know that there is a God who does not leave us in despair or death.

Marcuse closes his book *One Dimensional Man* with the statement that his critical theory of society cannot bridge the gap between present and future. It remains negative, and yet must not refuse to stand by those who are without hope yet refuse to submit to present inhumanity. He quotes Walter Benjamin at the beginning of the Nazi era:

It is only for the sake of those who are without hope that hope is given.

But surely all men at some time are without hope, or tempted to be without hope. That is why the theological question about the sources of hope, and its witness to the reality of God who gives hope, remains relevant to every age and every time, including our own.

NOTES

1. Herbert Marcuse, *Eros and Civilization,* Boston, 1955, p. 236.
2. *Ibid.*
3. John Calvin, *Institutes of the Christian Religion,* Bk. III, chap. 2, 7.
4. Martin Luther, wks. Weiman ed., 10, III: 3, 329. Quoted in Wilhelm Pauck, *The Heritage of the Reformation,* Boston, 1950, p. 20.
5. Cf. James Gustafson, *Christ and the Moral Life,* New York, 1968.
6. It seems to me that the connection between eschatological hope and present social action is insufficiently made in Jürgen Moltmann's *The Theology of Hope,* New York, 1967.
7. Reinhold Niebuhr, *Man's Nature and His Communities,* New York, 1965, p. 102.
8. G. W. F. Hegel, Preface to the *Philosophy of History,* trans. by J. Sibree, *Modern Student's Library,* New York, 1929, p. 350.
9. Emil Fackenheim, *The Religious Dimension of Hegel's Thought,* Bloomington, Indiana, 1967, p. 235. Cf. G. W. F. Hegel, *Lectures on the Philosophy of Religion,* Eng. tr., 3 vols., London, 1895, Vol. 3, pp. 149-51.
10. V. I. Lenin, *Materialism and Empirio-criticism* (Selected Works, Vol. XI), New York, p. 377.
11. Karl Marx, *Economic and Political Manuscripts* in Erich Fromm, *Marx's Concept of Man,* New York, 1961, p. 127. Italics omitted.
12. Robert Hundley, an unpublished manuscript "Revolutionary Youth Movements." Quoted by permission.
13. Quoted in George L. Kline, "Leszek Kolakowski and the Revision of Marxism," in Kline ed., *European Philosophy Today,* Chicago, 1965, p. 146.
14. *Ibid.,* p. 149.
15. Ernst Bloch, *Das Prinzip Hoffnung,* Frankfurt, 1959.
16. Harvey Cox, "Ernst Bloch and the Pull of the Future," in *New Theology* No. 5, edited by Marty and Peerman, New York, 1968, pp. 193-94.
17. Alfred North Whitehead, *Science and the Modern World,* New York, 1931, p. 3.
18. Charles Peirce, *How To Make Our Ideas Clear.* This and the following quotations from William James will be conveniently found in Konvitz and Kennedy, eds., *The American Pragmatists,* New York, 1960. Peirce quotation, p. 38.
19. William James, *What Pragmatism Means,* p. 36.
20. William James, *Pragmatism's Conception of Truth,* p. 55.
21. *Ibid.,* pp. 55-56.
22. Josiah Royce, *The Problem of Christianity,* New York, 1914. One volume ed., Univ. of Chicago Press, 1968.
23. Thomas S. Kuhn, *The Structure of Scientific Revolutions,* Chicago, 1962, p. 93.

24. *Ibid.*, p. 170.
25. *Ibid.*, p. 172.
26. Alfred North Whitehead, *Process and Reality,* New York, 1936, p. 525.
27. Herbert Marcuse, *One Dimensional Man,* Boston, 1964, **PB** 1966, p. 257.

David Stanley, S.J.

The New Testament Concept of the Future

When men look to the future, they turn their attention to what does not yet exist, but is certain to come into existence in history.[1] When the men who wrote the New Testament think of the future, they contemplate either the historical future, or the reality which lies beyond history, but which as such has not yet fallen within personal experience. They may *represent* this second reality as future to the whole course of history, as "the age to come" (and then they tend to speak of it after the manner of the historical future), or they may represent it as already existent "above." To generalize for the moment, the first mode of thinking of the "beyond history" as future appears more congenial to Paul; the second conception of it as a reality which is contemporaneous, but "above" human existence, is characteristic of the Johannine literature.

The scope of our present inquiry is orientated chiefly to the attitude evinced by New Testament writers with respect to the future of history. And surely, if any one of us were asked to characterize that attitude, he would unhesitatingly indicate it as Christian hope. "Faith and Hope in the Future" is in fact the general title of this lecture series. The Christian hope in the future of history, then, is the topic which concerns us here. What does Christian hope expect from the historical future? How does Christian hope confront the future of history? How does Christian hope move into the future?

Almost as soon as we begin our investigation, we meet a curious phenomenon. The letters of Paul provide the major source of references to Christian hope, while the only other writings in which the term occurs are those exhibiting Pauline influence: the Pastorals,[2] Hebrews,[3] 1 Peter.[4] Christian hope is mentioned in Acts solely in speeches credited to Paul. The Synoptic evangelists never employ the word to designate Christian hope. More surprising still, perhaps, Christian hope is not expressly named in any of the books ascribed to John—neither in the Apocalypse, nor in the Fourth Gospel. The single exception to this remarkable fact is the appearance of the word in the Christian sense at 1 Jn 3:5. I have described this state of affairs as surprising, because the Gospels in particular, as well as other New Testament writings, are undoubtedly redolent with the reality of Christian hope. Each of these books, in its own way, as A. M. Hunter has rightly noted,[5] exhibits some relationship to the kerygma, the oral gospel, which was essentially a message of hope to a world in despair of salvation. While indeed the hope of which these writers speak is focused ultimately upon the future as the "beyond history," they do reflect an authentic hope in the historical future. The conviction of the evangelists that Jesus had revealed his intentions regarding the future existence of the Church by his institution of the Twelve and of the Eucharist is an indication of this hope in history. One thinks also of the Christian hope in the historical future expressed by the concluding line of Matthew: "Remember, I am with you always, until the end of time" (Mt 28:20).

Such considerations enable us to clarify and specify the course of our present investigation into the Christian hope in the future. If we assume that Paul is rightly regarded as the theologian of hope, two questions immediately arise: what is Paul's attitude to the future of history, and what reasons can be discovered in the nature of Paul's approach to the Christian mystery, which led him to reflect, more consciously than other New Testament writers, upon the nature of Christian hope? These questions will form the first part of our study. In a second part, we shall attempt to discern how the Johannine writings represent the Christian hope in the future of history, even though they do not give it that name. As W. Grossouw observes in an article on "Hope in the New Testament" in *Revue Biblique,* "it is helpful to take into account the nuances which the Johannine writings bring (to the subject) and thus avoid exclusive preoccupation with the doctrine of the Apostle of the Gentiles." [6] In fact, as you are no doubt aware, such a criticism has been leveled against the current theology of hope created by Jürgen Moltmann [7] and his colleagues, as Gerald O'Collins notes in his little book *Theology and Revelation:* "Those biblical elements which either do not fit into the scheme, or would fit only with difficulty are left out. Thus the Epistle to the Hebrews with its stress on the future is highlighted in Moltmann's *Theology of Hope,* but there is not a single reference to St. John's Gospel." [8]

I

Before we begin our examination of the views taken toward the future of history in the theologies of Paul and of John, it will prove helpful to consider some general attitudes, shared by many if not all New Testament writers, with regard to the future.[9] There are four such general positions, implicitly or explicitly adopted by the inspired authors, which deserve mention here.

In the first place, it is to be noted that the very existence of this body of sacred literature is the result of a concern for the future in the men who composed it. These writers set forth the facts and evidence relative to Jesus' earthly life and the experiences of the earliest churches, together with their interpretation of these data, because they realized, at least vaguely, the significance of what they wrote for the Christians who would come after them. The Church itself in succeeding centuries, by collecting these books as well as "the Scriptures" of Israel into a "canon" or authoritative rule for Christian living, simply confirmed this original, forward-looking view of the sacred authors. Paul voices his assurance on this point with regard to the Old Testament. "For what was written was written for our instruction, that through endurance and the consolation of the Scriptures, we might have hope" (Rom 15:4). The author of the Fourth Gospel addresses his future readers in stating the purpose of his work. "These things have been written that you may deepen your faith that Jesus is the Messiah, the Son of God, and through faith you may obtain life in his Name" (Jn 20:21). The seer of Patmos is no less aware of his readers. "Happy the man who reads this prophecy, and those who hear it read, and treasure what has been written in it" (Apoc 1:3). As he ends his book, he issues a stern warning against adding or deleting anything "of what is written in this book" (Apoc 22:18-19). The possession of this collection of sacred books is one of the distinguishing marks of the Church by the end of the first century, contrasting it with the various pagan religions of the ancient Mediterranean world, which created no similar sacred literature. It is one of the qualities which give Christianity, like the religion of Israel, its character as an historical religion.

The second observation particularly concerns a salient feature of the four Gospels, but it applies also to the rest of the New Testament. The insight I owe to Professor Krister Stendahl, who once pointed out to me that the Gospels display no nostalgia for the early life of Jesus. Nowhere do the evangelists betray any desire to return to this privileged period in the life of the Twelve during Jesus' public ministry as a kind of vanished golden age. In fact, the fourth evangelist places upon the lips of Jesus a beatitude pronounced upon future generations of Christians. "Happy those who have accepted the faith without having seen" (Jn 20:29). This forward-looking posture of those who composed the Gospels has been noted and exploited by the Form Critics, who point out that these books were not intended to be biographies of Jesus. In fact, the original context of the narratives and sayings which they contain is to be located in the life of the primitive Church, *not* in the historical setting of Jesus' own life. This updating tendency on the part of the evangelists shows that they had set their sights upon Christian existence in the future, and not upon the past as past. Their very application of Jesus' words and actions to the situations in which the young Church of their day found herself may be considered an implicit invitation to later believers to reformulate and adjust their doctrinal conclusions to future contingencies.

In the third place, the New Testament authors amply demonstrate their conviction that the advent of the *eschaton* in the death and resurrection of Jesus did not deprive subsequent, future history of all significance for Christian faith. The proclamation of the kergyma, that God has definitively reconciled the world to himself (2 Cor 5:18) in the death and resurrection of Jesus Christ, did not mean that history has been swallowed up by eschatology. That God had fulfilled his promise of redemption in Christ signified a turning point in sacred history; it did not signify the consummation of that history. The serious manner in which these authors address themselves to the task of discovering the meaning of the time between the first and second comings of Jesus Christ is striking proof of this viewpoint. Hebrew's nostalgic comment on the line from Psalm 8, "You have set everything beneath his feet," is relevant here. "But we do not as yet see everything made subject to him" (Heb 2:8). One thinks also of the indignant rejection by the author of 2 Peter of the despairing insinuation of "the mockers," who complain, "Where is the promise of his parousia?—For from the time our fathers fell asleep, everything remains the same as from the beginning of creation" (2 Pt 3:4). This writer's rebuttal of such cynicism reveals his insight into the purpose of history prior to the second coming. "The Lord of the promise is not procrastinating, in the sense that some think. He is simply displaying patience toward you, since he does not intend that some perish, but rather that all be brought to repentance" (2 Pt 3:9). The inclusion of the missionary mandate "to make disciples of all the nations" (Mt 28:19; cf. Lk 24-49; Jn 20:21-23; Acts 1:7-8) in the post-resurrection narratives attests the evangelists' understanding of the future of history in terms of the mission of the Church. The dawn of "the last times" with Jesus' death and exaltation has in truth meant a new beginning, a new future for history.

The fourth and final attitude we wish to mention with regard to the future of history characteristic of the New Testament is a thoroughgoing Christian realism in the face of suffering and frustration, which man's existence upon earth entails. The consciousness that Christianity (unlike Gnosticism) is not religious escapism is attested by the position of prominence which the evangelists accord to the Passion narrative. As Albert Vanhoye has remarked,[10] one might perhaps have expected this sorrowful, humiliating sector of Jesus' earthly existence to have been glossed over in favor of emphasis upon his resurrection. That the story of the Passion occupies, on the contrary, a proportionately large section in all the written Gospels is proof of the confidence and lack of disillusionment with respect to the future on the part of these Christian writers. They knew full well that it was not the Father's intention to intervene miraculously and save Jesus from his sufferings by any display of divine power (Mt 27:35). Rather, it was through these painful episodes of his Passion that he was already gaining the victory. As Jesus' followers, they too could count upon God's help in confronting the harsh realities of their future existence; they could not expect to escape the carrying of their own cross (Mt 8:34). Indeed, this Christian hope in the historical future, on the testimony of the Fourth Gospel, was created by Jesus himself. "In the world you will have tribulation; but take heart, I have overcome the world" (Jn 16:33).

These five salient characteristics of the positive view adopted toward the future of history reveal the paramount importance of Christian hope in the outlook shared by the writers of the New Testament.[11] We must now turn to the letters of Paul, who devotes so much attention and reflection to hope, in an effort to comprehend his preoccupation with it. Why is it that Paul names this virtue more frequently than any other inspired author, when the reality of Christian hope is taken for granted everywhere in the New Testament?

II

One valuable clue to Paul's special interest in hope lies in his distinctively personal comprehension of the primitive formula of faith, "Jesus is Lord," which runs like a refrain through his correspondence (Phil 2:11; 1 Cor 8: 5-6; 12:3; 2 Cor 4:5; Rom 10:9; Col 2:6). For Paul is at once aware that this ancient *credo* acknowledges Jesus' divinity, revealed by his exaltation as *Kyrios,* before whom "every knee . . . must bend in adoration" (Phil 2:10), and that it also implies, by the belief that Jesus has been constituted Lord of history, that his lordship is very much a piece of unfinished business. If Christ is "constituted Son of God in power" (Rom 1:4), it is that this divine power is to be deployed in the ongoing process of history. "There is but one Lord, Jesus Christ, through whom all [comes into being], and through whom we all [return to the Father]" (1 Cor 8:6).[12] This commitment of faith to Jesus as Lord is summoned to transcend itself, because of the promise for the future of history implicit in Jesus' exaltation. "For he must reign as king, until he has put all his enemies beneath his feet" (1 Cor 15:25). Christian hope in the future of history is born from Christian faith in a lordship that will only be completed at the term of history by the parousia, when "death will be destroyed as the last enemy" (1 Cor 15:26). By his very vocation the Christian is invited to share in this campaign, which gives meaning (hence, hope) to his life. The spiritual accoutrement for this eschatological warfare is enumerated in 1 Thessalonians. "We who belong to the day must remain sober, armed with the breastplate of faith and love, and with the hope of salvation as a helmet" (1 Thes 5:8). The future of history is not, in Paul's view, an anticlimax to Jesus' exaltation. His elevation as Lord has imparted to history a new, divinely ordained teleology, the full realization *in fact* of the promise contained in that lordship. The hymn cited by Paul to the Philippians, to which we have already referred, presents this grandiose enterprise as a cosmic liturgy, in which all creatures participate in order to assist in the realization of their redemption, by voicing the cry "Jesus is Lord" (Phil 2:11).

There is however, I venture to suggest now, a more basic reason which led Paul to dwell more than other New Testament theologians upon the special function of hope in Christian living. It is the fact that Paul appears to have been impressed most forcibly, more so perhaps than other inspired writers, with the quality of Christian existence as a new beginning. One perceives this in the analogy he considers most apt to denote it, the divine act of creation. As a consequence, his theology, in my opinion, may be properly denominated as a theology of *discontinuity*. As we shall presently point out, it is this aspect of his thought which presents such a striking contrast to the conception of the Christian mystery discernible in Johannine thought (both in the Fourth Gospel and in the Apocalypse), where emphasis is placed rather upon *continuity*. I should like to amplify and illustrate what I mean by suggesting that in Paul we have a theology of discontinuity before reviewing the various aspects of his theology of Christian hope.

It may not be out of place to point out that we are dealing with a question of emphasis in speaking of such discontinuity, without any wish to deny to Paul a real sense of the continuous character of Christian existence. At the same time, because this emphasis has, I believe, a bearing upon his attention to the role of hope, it will be necessary to take into account the perspective from which the members of the Johannine school consider hope and the future of history, in order to acquire a balanced view of the place accorded this virtue in the New Testament.

Paul, as is well known, has been led, through his theological reflection, to view the death and resurrection of Christ as the radical dialectic which governs his understanding of history. This two-faced event by which man is redeemed involves a radical discontinuity and a totally new beginning. Of this the efficacious symbol is "the cross of our Lord Jesus Christ" on which the Christian "boast" securely reposes. "God forbid that I should boast, except in the cross of our Lord Jesus Christ, on which the world has been crucified once for all to me, and I to the world. For neither circumcision, nor the lack of it counts for anything, but only a new creation" (Gal 6:14-15). "So that," as Paul writes to the Corinthians, "if anyone is in union with Christ, it is a new creation. The old order has passed away; lo! it has become new" (2 Cor 5:17).

It would seem that this peculiarly Pauline optic derives from the unique character of his own conversion, as the sequel in the passage just quoted indicates. "All this comes from God who reconciled us to himself and gave us the ministry of reconciliation" (v. 18). A few paragraphs earlier in this letter Paul actually refers to his own initial Christian experience in terms of the creation of light. "The God who said, 'Light, shine out of darkness,' is he who shone his light in our hearts to effect the illumination of the knowledge of the glory of God upon the face of Christ" (2 Cor 4:6). Paul regards his own conversion as the great source of discontinuity in his own religious life, forcing him, as he tells the Philippians, to reject "as loss" and "garbage" all he had previously esteemed as "profit" (Phil 3:7-11).

A similar radical discontinuity is discernible at the origin of every Christian life. "For we consider that a man is made upright by faith, apart from works of the law" (Rom 3:28). Paul had personally rejected "any uprightness of my own making from the law," accepting instead "that through faith in Christ, an uprightness from God springing from faith" (Phil 3:9).

The accent on discontinuity operates in Paul's Christology, where it explains the strange attitude he adopts toward Jesus' earthly history, that is, the infrequency with which Paul alludes to the words of Jesus [13] and his all but total omission of any narrative concerning him. "For even if we had known Christ according to the flesh, we now no longer know him thus" (2 Cor 5:16). This view is simply a corollary from Paul's consideration of the Incarnation as the coming of the Son of God, "born of woman, made subject to the law" (Gal 4:4) "in the likeness of sinful flesh" (Rom 8:3). By a "death once for all to sin" (Rom 6:10), Jesus broke definitively with the old sinful solidarity which bound himself and the whole human race to Adam. Raised by the Father to a totally new "life with God" (Rom 6:10), Christ stands at the head of the new family of grace as "the last Adam" (1 Cor 15:45). "He was handed over for our sins: he was raised for our justifying" (Rom 4:25).

The same pattern of discontinuity is discernible in the lifestyle of the Christian. "Just as surely as we have borne the image of the earthly man, so too shall we bear the image of the heavenly man" (1 Cor 15:49). This process, to be consummated only by the glorious resurrection of the body, is seen to be in progress within our present life. "Now all of us, as with unveiled faces we behold in a mirror [14] the glory of the Lord, are being transformed into the same image with ever increasing glory" (2 Cor 4:18). This conformation to Christ, "the image of God" (2 Cor 5:4), is effected in this life by a continuing participation in his death and resurrection. "[We are] continually bearing the dying of Jesus in our person, in order that the life of Jesus also may be manifested in our person. For always we, the living, are being handed over to death for Jesus' sake, that Jesus' life be also manifested in our mortal flesh" (2 Cor 4:10-11).

This somewhat lengthy review of the theme of discontinuity in Paul's thought will perform a twofold service for our inquiry into the prominence in his letters of Christian hope. First, it recalls how different is Paul's outlook on the future of history from the evolutionary view, which the modern mind, since the middle of the nineteenth century, is inclined to adopt. History, for Paul, proceeds by crisis; the redemptive pattern death-resurrection has imposed itself upon his attitude to the future of history, as for instance in that of the Chosen People discussed in Romans. To Israel's rejection of the gospel will correspond her future acceptance of it, as the conversion of the Gentiles "to stir Israel to emulation" indicates (Rom 11:11). "For if their rejection [signified] the reconciliation of the world, what will their admission [mean] but life from death?" (Rom 11:15). The element of discontinuity enters into Paul's attitude to his own future life. He tells the Philippians: "Brothers, I do not consider that I have reached [the goal] as yet. There is one thought in my mind: forgetting what lies behind and reaching out to what lies ahead, I race intently toward the goal for the prize, God's election in Christ Jesus to the life above" (Phil 4:13-14). The text suggests how vitally necessary to this forward-looking view of the future is Paul's hope.

A reference to his terrifying experience at Ephesus when he came face to face with death, recounted at the beginning of 2 Corinthians, indicates how hope is conceived to operate within the context of the dialectic of death-resurrection, which governs history. "Indeed, we felt in our hearts that we had received a death sentence, in order that we might not put our reliance on ourselves, but on God who raises the dead. He it was who rescued us from such deadly peril; and he will save us again! He on whom our hope is fixed will continue to save us, if you will cooperate through your prayers for us . . ." (2 Cor 1:9-11). Paul's hope is anchored, as he states earlier in the same paragraph, upon God "the all merciful Father, the God of every consolation, who consoles us in all our tribulations" (vv. 3-4). For he recognizes that the alternation of suffering and consolation he experiences is his participation in Christ's death and resurrection. "As Christ's sufferings overflow upon us, so also through Christ our consolation overflows" (v. 5). Paul is far from conceiving hope as a means of escape from life's realities. Its effectiveness issues from his belief that he must "fill up what is lacking in Christ's tribulations in my human flesh for the sake of his body, the Church," and in this he rejoices (Phil 1:24). In fact, the two qualities most frequently associated with hope in Paul's letters are endurance and joy.

William Lynch, S.J. in his *Images of Hope* remarks that "we are too much inclined to think of hope as an emergency virtue that saves itself for crisis (one that is really meant for use in moments when there is not much or any hope at all). The truth is that it is present in each moment as it looks to the next." [15] This faculty of transcending the present in its outlook on the future characterizes Pauline hope. Abraham stands out as the great exemplar of Christian hope, since his indestructible hope in the divine promise that he would be "father of many nations" survived the supreme trial of God's demand that he sacrifice Isaac, his sole natural hope of seeing the promise fulfilled. "Contrary to [natural] hope he believed with hope that he would become 'father of many nations' according to the promise" (Rom 4:18). For Abraham's unwavering confidence was fixed upon "the God who gives life to the dead, and summons to existence what does not yet exist" (Rom 4:17). [16]

As we have remarked, Paul associates hope with joy, as well as with endurance. "For what hope or joy, or crown of pride is ours, if it is not yourselves, when we stand before our Lord Jesus Christ at his coming?" (1 Thes 2:19). Hope, as this text shows, is not individualistic, but reaches out to include the Thessalonian community which Paul founded. [17] He associates hope with joy as he writes from prison to the Philippians. "Yes! rejoice I will, since I know that this will result in salvation for me through your prayers and the support of the Spirit of Jesus Christ. Such is my expectation and my hope that I shall have no cause to be ashamed, but the greatness of Christ will shine out in my person through life or death" (Phil 1:18-20). [18] Paul exhorts the Romans to "rejoice in hope" (Rom 12:12). He asks in his prayer for them, "May the God of hope fill you with all joy and peace by faith in him, until by the power of the Holy Spirit you overflow with hope" (Rom 15:13). The absence of hope, which for Paul characterizes pagan existence, means the absence of such joy. "We do not wish you to remain in ignorance, brothers, concerning those who have fallen asleep, so that you may not grieve as do the rest of men who have no hope" (1 Thes 4:13). The former pagan life of the Ephesians is similarly described. "At that time you were cut off from Christ:

you were aliens to the commonwealth of Israel and strangers to the covenants expressing the promise, in a world without hope and without God" (Eph 2:12).

We shall conclude our consideration of Paul's hope in the future of history by noting the relation of hope to faith and love in three of the passages where this characteristically Pauline triad appears (cf. also 1 Thes 5:8; 1 Cor 13:7, 13; Gal 5:5-6; Rom 12:6-12). Each of these describes the Christian accept-ance of the gospel. It is instructive to note that, despite Paul's reputation as the theologian of justification by faith, he can provide an adequate description of conversion only by com-bining faith with love and hope. The "election" by God of the Thessalonians involves "the effectiveness of your faith, the labor of your love, and the endurance of your hope in our Lord Jesus Christ" (1 Thes 1:3-4). The endurance of their hope is proven by their "reception of the word, despite grave tribulation with joy in the Holy Spirit" (v. 6) and by their "waiting for [God's] Son from heaven, whom he raised from the dead, Jesus our rescuer from the wrath that is coming" (v. 10).

A similar description is given of the Colossians' acceptance of the gospel. "We thank God, the Father of our Lord Jesus Christ . . . because we have heard of your faith in Christ Jesus, and the love you bear toward all the saints, on account of the hope, stored up for you in heaven, of which you originally learned in the word of truth, the gospel" (Col 1:3-5). Paul appears to suggest how hope assists and sustains belief in Jesus' death and resurrection and also aids the practice of love in the community. A few paragraphs later Paul identifies the source of this phenomenon as "Christ in you: the hope of glory" (Col 1:27). Like faith and love, Christian hope implies a personal relationship with the divine persons: to Christ (as here), to the Father, "on whom I have set my hope" (in 2 Cor 1:13), and to the Holy Spirit in the next passage we must consider.

In Romans Paul gives what might be termed a brief psy-chology of hope when describing the Christian response to the gospel. "Therefore, since we are made upright by faith, we are at peace with God through our Lord Jesus Christ, through whom we have acquired an entry to the sphere of God's grace, where we now stand; and we exult in the hope of the glory of God" (Rom 5:1-2). "Peace with God" sums up the Christian acceptance of God's offer of reconciliation through the gospel, as Paul makes clear a few lines later. "God has put together a proof of his love by the fact that while we were still sinners, Christ died on our behalf. Therefore, how much more certainly, now that we are justified by his blood, shall we be saved through him from wrath. For if, while we were his enemies, we were reconciled to God through the death of his Son, how much more surely, now that we have been reconciled, shall we be saved through his life" (vv. 8-11). The past act of divine reconciliation founds the Christian "hope of the glory of God."

Yet, Paul knows, it is *in history* and in function of the future of this life that Christian hope develops. Thus God's love has provided a living basis of that hope, which falls within Christian experience: the gift of the Spirit.[19] It is Paul's inclusion of this experience in his analysis of the genesis of hope, which prevents his being misunderstood in a Pelagian sense. "We exult in present tribulations, since we know that tribulation effects endurance: endurance produces virtue that has stood the test; tested virtue is the ground of hope. Such a hope is not illusory, because God's love has been poured forth in our hearts by the Holy Spirit he has given to us—if indeed when we were weak, Christ died at the decisive moment on behalf of the wicked" (Rom 5:3-6).[20]

The Christian faces the future of history with joy and confidence by reason of his faith in Christ's act of reconciliation and by the experience of God's love through the indwelling Spirit. Paul returns to this experience later in this letter to the Romans. "We, who possess the first fruits of the Spirit, groan inwardly as we await the fulfillment of our adoptive sonship, the redemption of our bodies. For by hope we are saved. Yet a hope when it is seen ceases to be hope. For who hopes for what he already sees? But if we have hope for what we do not see, we wait with endurance" (Rom 8:23-25).

Paul understands the ability to transcend the present moment, to move toward the future, as a chief constituent of Christian hope. The ultimate goal, "the redemption of our bodies," lies in the consummation: salvation in Paul is consistently viewed as a totally eschatological reality beyond history. It is hope that moves us toward that salvation, even though it is something which remains outside our present capacity of perception. Vision belongs to the state beyond history. Meanwhile, it is hope that prevents us from confusing time with eternity, from absolutizing the present moment. Hope provides the *élan* empowering us to move into the future, to wait out the period of non-vision with fortitude and confidence.[21] This is what Paul means by "endurance."

In the paragraph immediately preceding these verses, Paul sees this endurance reflected in some mysterious way in the irrational creation, which like man himself he knows to be the object of Christ's redemptive work. The world of things will not be destroyed. That tenet of Stoicism is rejected by Christian faith in favor of their transformation, at Christ's parousia.[22] "For the expectation of the [irrational] creation awaits the revelation of the sons of God. Creation was subject to frustration, not by its own choice, but by him who made it so—yet with the hope that the creation itself would be freed from the slavery of corruption and enter upon the freedom of the glory of the children of God. All creation, we know, groans in unison and suffers the pangs of childbirth until the present" (Rom 8:19-22). On this profound view, the *capacity for risk* in the face of the future of history, which is hope, is implanted deep in the entire creation. To the eyes of Christian faith the contingency of things is perceived as a "hope," teaching man himself the relative nature of everything created, including time. Thus this very contingency, ingrained in all that is seen, becomes a promise of future transformation which is unseen.

III

What view of the future of history is taken by the writers who belong to the "school of John," the authors of the Apocalypse, 1 John, and the Fourth Gospel? To answer this question it will be necessary to explain what we meant by characterizing their thought as a theology of continuity. This will provide the context in which to perceive the reality of Christian hope, which is present without being so denominated in these books.

The Fourth Gospel stands in marked contrast with the other three inasmuch as it is from his own present Christian situation that its author has deliberately and self-consciously chosen to present Jesus, his actions and words. The point may be most easily grasped by means of a simple question. John speaks of Jesus' acts as "signs," when Jesus himself refers to them in this Gospel as "works." For whom are they considered "signs"? Since their sign-value is perceptible only to the eyes of Christian faith, they are intended by the evangelist as signs for the Christian reader. John tells us that while "Jesus performed many other signs, which have not been written in this book, these have been written that you may deepen your faith . . ." (Jn 20:30-31).

Faith in this Gospel is characteristically contemplative: it beholds the divine reality latent in history. It sees "the Son" in Jesus (Jn 6:40); it has "beheld his glory" (Jn 1:14), and so has in fact "seen the Father" (Jn 14:9), the "God no man has ever seen" (Jn 1:18). This entails a foreshortening of perspective in John's presentation of Jesus, and he tends to think of him, even in his earthly condition, as the glorified, contemporary Christ. This is what differentiates the Johannine Son of Man sayings from those in the Synoptics, where they are related to three distinct phases of Jesus' existence (his ministry, Passion, and eschatological role). John's Son of Man is the glorified, contemporary Christ whether as mediator (Jn 1:51), as source of Christian faith and eternal life (Jn 3:13-14), as already exercising judgment (Jn 5:27), as Eucharistic food (Jn 6:27, 53, 62), as revealer of his own divinity (Jn 8:28). As the Passion begins (Jn 12:23), he is glorified (Jn 13:32). When Jesus asks the blind man, "Do you believe in the Son of Man?", John discloses to the Christian reader the mystery of Jesus' true identity (Jn 9:35-36). Yet Jesus refuses to identify himself as Son of Man to the crowd, who ask the same question (Jn 12:24), since this secret is only comprehensible to Christian faith.

The seven "I am" sayings indicate the same telescoping of perspective. "I am the bread of life" (Jn 6:35, 51); "I am the light of the world" (Jn 7:12); "I am the sheep-gate" (Jn 10:7, 9); "I am the genuine shepherd" (Jn 10:11, 14); "I am the resurrection and the life" (Jn 11:25); "I am the way, the truth, and the life" (Jn 14:6); "I am the true vine" (Jn 15:1, 5). By means of these various symbols, the relationship of the glorified Christ to the Christian life is clarified.

This foreshortening effect of John's theological perspective operates also on what lies beyond history. John never tires of repeating that the Christian has eternal life *now* (Jn 3:15, 16, 36; 5:24; 6:40, 47, 54; 10:28; 20:31). Similarly, the man with faith has avoided the judgment (Jn 5:24): he is not judged (Jn 3:18). John is aware of the evangelical tradition regarding a judgment "on the last day" (Jn 12:48) and the resurrection "on the last day" (Jn 6:39, 40, 44, 54), yet he shows no concern that these eschatological realities cannot be brought within his theological optic.

Despite the difference of literary genre (apocalyptic), in which the last book of the New Testament is written, its author likewise seeks to center attention upon the contemporary Christ as Master of history. This is the central purpose of his symbolic presentation of Christ as "the Lamb that has been slain" (Apoc 5:6), to whom the opening of the scroll, containing the meaning of history, is confided (v. 7). Christ appears also as Judge in the Apocalypse, yet while the seer does not neglect the eschatological aspect of this function (Apoc 12:5; 19:11, 15; 14:14-16), he prefers to direct attention to the continuing exercise of that judgment through history. It is as "one like a Son of Man" (Apoc 1:13), who passes judgment in the present upon the existent Christian communities, that Christ is described in the first three chapters of this work. Indeed it is precisely because of the writer's repeated insistence upon Christ's involvement with the ongoing process of history, whereby he guarantees ultimate victory without snatching his suffering Church from tribulation, that the Apocalypse achieves its purpose as a message of hope and consolation.

Yet it would be misleading to suggest that the seer of Patmos has been able to resist completely the eschatological pull of the apocalyptic genre upon his Christology. Christ is presented as "he who comes," not only throughout history to judge and support his Church, to do battle against "the inhabitants of the earth," but also at the end of history. The concluding lines of the Apocalypse depict the daily life of the Christian people as a kind of liturgy of the parousia, in which the Church by the prompting of the Spirit cries out daily, "Come! Lord Jesus" (Apoc 22:17-20).

Enough has been said perhaps to illustrate the proclivity of the writers of the Johannine school to favor the continuity which they perceive to exist between the past, the present and the future activity in history of the Word become flesh. The prologue to the Gospel presents the Word as revealer of God already operative in the creation (Jn 1:2, 9-10), in Torah (Jn 1:11), before the Incarnation. Thus the reader is alerted to the continuity that obtains between this definitive self-revelation of God and the Old Testament. The disparagement of the Mosaic institutions, so prominent in Paul, rarely (cf. Jn 8:17; 10:34; 15:25) appears in John. "The law was a gift (of God) through Moses" (Jn 1:17). This law is the manifestation of God's will, addressed to man and soliciting his obedience in faith (Jn 7:19, 22-23). It is simply the initial, imperfect communication of that "graciousness and truth" imparted fully from the "plenitude" proper to "the only Son" (Jn 1:14, 16) through his gift of the Spirit (Jn 7:37-39). There is not the sharp division between the old and the new so characteristic of Paul. In fact, the word "old" occurs nowhere in the Fourth Gospel. If Jesus' command to love one another is termed "new" (Jn 13:34), it can as aptly be designated "the old commandment" in 1 Jn 2:7-8 and 2 Jn 5.

The Pauline conception of Christian existence as a "new creation," of Christ as "the last Adam," is not echoed by the school of John. By contrast it is described as a rebirth "from above" (Jn 3:3, 5), an image suggesting continuity with its antecedent causes. The chief argument of 1 John, "to assure you that you possess eternal life" (Jn 5:13), derives its cogency from the truth that the Christian is "begotten by God" (1 Jn 2:29; 3:9; 4:7; 5:1, 4, 18). The metaphor of generation indicates a mode of conceiving the divine action distinctively different from the Pauline view of it as a new creation. The seer of Patmos indeed speaks of "a new sky and a new earth" (Apoc 21:1; cf. 2 Pt 3:13), but this only serves to exemplify the distinction between the eschatology of Paul and that of the school of John. Paul habitually represents eschatological reality within a horizontal framework, as future to the future of history. The Johannine schema exhibits a vertical orientation: the eschatological reality is "above," co-existent with the historical process. It is from above that Jesus has come (Jn 3:13) and whither he has returned through death and resurrection (Jn 13:1; 3:14, 28; 16:10, 17).

John's Christology accentuates the continuity between Jesus' earthly history, his present status as the glorified Christ, and his future function as eschatological judge. In addition to what has been already remarked about certain of the sayings of Jesus in the Fourth Gospel, we draw attention to the peculiar character of the Johannine post-resurrection narratives as *recognition scenes*. Although the risen Lord is perceptible only to the eyes of faith, [23] the reader is made aware of the continuity between the glorified Christ and the Jesus who was nailed to the cross, performed his "signs" in the presence of the disciples, and earned the devotion of Mary Magdalene. The awesome Master of history, who appears as Son of Man to the seer of Patmos in his opening vision, provides the clue to his own identity with the phrase, so familiar upon the lips of the earthly Jesus, "Stop being afraid!" (Apoc 1:17).

John's conception of Christian existence as "eternal life" already possessed in this world is the last aspect of this theology of continuity to be noted. The believer has now "passed over from death to life" (Jn 5:24; 1 Jn 3:14). Faith's knowledge of the "genuine God," its recognition of his emissary in Jesus Christ, *"is* eternal life" (Jn 17:3). For the author of the Apocalypse, the Christian believer is not to be considered as one of "the inhabitants of the earth." [24] The purpose for which the first epistle of John was written was to help the Christian recognize that eternal life is now present through fraternal love (1 Jn 2:3-8) and the orthodox profession of Christian faith (1 Jn 4:13-14).

If we have not misrepresented Johannine theology by our discernment in it of a consistent emphasis upon continuity, the lack of any formal reference to Christian hope appears easily comprehensible. What may not be so readily apparent, however, in such a viewpoint is the expectation of these writers with respect to the future of history.

In the Apocalypse the Christian attitude toward the future is inculcated in those under stress of persecution by the assurance that the risen Christ as Master of history actually directs the course of events in this world. It is not despite, but because of their suffering, that he accomplishes his own designs for his people. This purpose is manifest in "the men who have passed through the great tribulation" (Apoc 7:14), for "the Lamb . . . will be their shepherd, and will guide them to the source of the water of life; and God will wipe all tears from their eyes" (v. 17). Hope of victory has been already held out to the Christian in John's message to the seven churches (Apoc 2:7, 11, 17, 26-28; 3:5, 12, 21). The principal images of hope in the future of history are discernible in the protective measuring of the temple (Apoc 11:1-2), the assimilation of the two witnesses to the paschal mystery (Apoc 11:3-13), the woman clothed with the sun (Apoc 12:1-17), and the marriage of the bride with the lamb (Apoc 19:6-9). Yet it is the vision of the risen Christ himself, like "a lamb standing that has been slain" (Apoc 5:6), which best images forth the Christian hope in history. By means of this powerful symbolism John reminds his reader that the exalted Lord Jesus is what he now is in glory by reason of his sacred Passion. As a consequence, the experience of the future for God's people is intended to prepare them for the wedding with the lamb, for the "fine linen, clean and shining" with which the bride is adorned signifies nothing less than "the just deeds of the saints" (Apoc 19:8).

The single mention of the term hope in 1 Jn 3:3, unique in the Johannine literature, denotes the manifestation at the parousia of the Christian's status as a child of God. "Beloved, we are now God's children, though what we shall be has not yet appeared. We know that when he appears, we shall be like him, because we shall see him as he is. And everyone who possesses this hope in him purifies himself as he is pure" (1 Jn 3:2-3). The author mysteriously indicates the source of Christian hope during this life as "anointing" (1 Jn 2:20, 27), *chrisma,* in a context where mention is made of Antichrist, and also as "seed" (1 Jn 3:9) in a context where the Christian is said to have been begotten from God. These metaphors probably refer to the abiding gift of the Holy Spirit. "By this we know that we remain in him, and he remains in us, because he has given us his Spirit" (1 Jn 4:13). This verse contains the hint of two themes which will be developed in the Fourth Gospel, where they constitute the main motifs of the Johannine theology of hope: the role of the Spirit and the concept of "abiding in." Before we turn to this development, mention must be made of the most moving expression of hope in the entire New Testament. "By this we shall know that we belong to the sphere of the truth, and in God's sight we shall persuade our heart, even if that heart condemns us, that God is greater than our heart, and he knows all" (Jn 3:19-20).

The author of the Fourth Gospel is led, paradoxically, to express his hope in the future of history as a consequence of Jesus' departure from this world to return to the Father. This theme, as is well known, constitutes John's most characteristic presentation of Christ's work for man's redemption. It forms the introduction to the narrative of the Last Supper (Jn 13:1, 3) and dominates the discourse which follows it. Jesus announces his departure from his dismayed and bewildered followers (Jn 13:33), bidding them not to be troubled at heart, since he goes to prepare a dwelling for them in his Father's house, where he promises to be reunited with them (Jn 14:1-3). Meanwhile he leaves them his peace, which the world cannot impart (Jn 14:27); yet he also predicts their sufferings in the world when they are bereft of himself (Jn 16:2-3). His departure is essential for their well-being, since only thus can he send the Holy Spirit (Jn 16:7), the "advocate" which will replace himself (Jn 14:16).

The Spirit of Truth, "the other Advocate," is the source of the Christian hope in the future, since he is the personal fulfillment of the promise of Jesus, "I am coming back to you" (Jn 14:19). In the Fourth Gospel, the Spirit *takes the place of Jesus* in history. "He will teach you everything and recall to your minds everything I have told you. I leave you my peace; I give you my own peace" (Jn 14:26-27). That peace is the Holy Spirit, since it is through his presence that the disciples will recognize, Jesus says, that "I am in the Father, and you in me and I in you" (Jn 14:20).

This theme of the mutual remaining in one another is illustrated at length by the allegory of the vine and the branches (Jn 15:1-10). It is another expression of the Johannine hope in history. The recognition by the disciples of this vital relationship will imbue them with that aspect of hope which Paul has called endurance, the dynamic staying power to wait out the present in favor of the future.

The Spirit as Advocate has another office to perform for Christian hope. Before the bar of history he will convict the world of the sin of disbelief, prove the case for uprightness, and convince men that judgment has been passed upon evil (Jn 16:8-11). And because bearing testimony is his business, the Spirit will make witnesses of the disciples (Jn 15:26-27).

Prominent among the images of hope in the Fourth Gospel stand two tiny parables. "Unless a grain of wheat dies when it is cast into the earth, it remains isolated. But if it dies, it bears much fruit" (Jn 12:24). The example illustrates primarily the paschal mystery as it unfolds in the death and resurrection of Jesus. Yet as his comments on it show, it establishes the pattern for "anyone who serves me" to follow. "Where I am, there also will my servant be. If anyone serves me my Father will honor him" (v. 26). Here there is implied an aspect of hope which is also dear to Paul (Phil 3:10-11). The Christian hope in history involves the prospect of participating personally in the paschal mystery.

The other small parable also concerns birth. "When a woman is in labor, she grieves because her hour has come. But when she gives birth to a child, she no longer remembers her tribulation for joy that a human being has been born into the world" (Jn 16:21). Hope enables the Christian to see things in perspective, by providing a context from experience in which the pain of the present may be evaluated in the light of future joy.

The Christian hope in the future reflected in the Johannine writings is no less virile or vigorous than in the letters of Paul. Like Pauline hope it too springs from the exaltation of Christ as Lord and from the inner promptings of the Holy Spirit. Yet, while not devoid of expectation, hope for John appears to be less a virtue-for-crisis, more a dynamic transcending of the present moment, an ever recurring resiliency surging up from the assured possession *in the now* of "eternal life."

NOTES

1. The small book by Josef Pieper, *Hope in History,* London, 1969, will be found to contain some discerning philosophical reflections upon this problem. One might also consult the series of articles in *Lumière et Vie,* no. 41 (1959), both scriptural and theological, on the subject of hope.

2. Space does not permit us to treat the interesting evidence for Christian hope in the future, which these epistles contain. Such a hope is implicit in the precious testimony they evince to the awareness of the Church at the close of the apostolic age that it faced a crisis with the passing of the apostles. The author warns against the dangers of future heresy, draws attention to those offices in the Church, created by the gift of the Spirit through the "laying on of hands," upon which reliance is placed for the safeguarding of "the deposit" (1 Tm 6:20) of orthodoxy, which the dying Apostle hands on to Timothy for preservation by the help of the Holy Spirit (2 Tm 1:14). After Paul's death it is hope "in the living God" (1 Tm 4:10) that will sustain Timothy and the other delegates of the Apostle. This hope is presented as the only solid basis of the Christian life in the future (1 Tm 5:5), even for "the rich of this world" (1 Tm 6:17). Its authentic character will be revealed by the persevering endurance of trials (2 Tm 2:10-12; Ti 2:2; 1 Tm 6:11). Yet it is upon the hope beyond history that the author's eyes are chiefly fixed: "Jesus Christ our hope" (1 Tm 1:1), "the hope of eternal life" (Ti 1:2; 2:13; 3:7).

3. The Christian hope in the future of history is only an incidental and subalternate interest to the author of Hebrews. This writer "is rather seeking to say something positive to the people of God of the new Covenant by means of Old Testament typology and through a special ('Alexandrian') kind of scriptural exegesis, in order to stimulate it on its way to the heavenly future world" (Rudolf Schnackenburg, *The Church in the New Testament,* New York, 1965, p. 89). The Christian religion, by contrast with Judaism, is qualified as "a better hope" (Heb 7:19) because it offers more effective aids, through Christ, to the heavenly goal (cf. C. Spicq, *L'Épitre aux Hébreux,* Vol. 2, Paris, 1953, p. 194). The Christian life in this world is best characterized, after the example of Abraham, by patient waiting (Heb 6:15; 9:28) and by endurance of difficulties (Heb 10:32; 12:2-3); cf. C. Spicq, *op. cit.,* Vol. 1, p. 128). It is peculiar to Hebrews' theological viewpoint that faith tends to be fused with hope. Faith, as "the guarantee of what we hope for" (Heb 11:1), presents hope as its dominant aspect (C. Spicq, *op. cit.,* Vol. 2, pp. 102, 371). And this hope is related, more explicitly and frequently than with Paul, to God's promise (Heb 6:11; 10:23) and oath (Heb 6:17-19).

4. F. W. Beare (*The First Epistle of Peter,* 2d ed., Oxford, 1958, p. 37),

is probably correct in rejecting the notion, "once widely held, that the writer is pre-eminently the 'Apostle of Hope.'" Yet hope is presented as a dominant characteristic of the present Christian existence. The most striking phrase, relevant to our present concern in this little treatise (God "has caused us to be born anew to a living hope through the resurrection of Jesus Christ from the dead"—1:3) is, in Dr. Beare's words, truly "a pregnant paraphrase of the new life itself" (Beare, *op. cit.*, p. 56). And the virtue of faith in this epistle is considered simply as the foundation of hope (cf. R. Leconte, *Les Épitres catholiques de saint Jacques, saint Jude, et saint Pierre*, Paris, 1953, p. 61; also F. W. Beare, *op. cit.*, p. 82). Still our author is scarcely preoccupied with the future of history. In his view, it is the time given for the practice of Christian endurance (2:20), the defense and profession of the Christian way of life, whose content is summarized as "the hope that you have" (3:15; cf. F. W. Beare, *op. cit.*, p. 139). E. G. Selwyn (*The First Epistle of St. Peter*, 2d ed., London, 1949, p. 70) makes the interesting suggestion that the phrase "living hope" (1:3) would seem to imply "that the readers had known other hopes that were dead. . . . And with those hopes lay buried all other ideas of a political theocracy, an earthly Paradise, as the goal of human life, which men had then conceived or might conceive in the future."

5. A. M. Hunter, *The Unity of the New Testament*, London, 1943, p. 30: "Through the variegated fabric of the New Testament now clear and conspicuous, now veiled and hidden, runs the golden thread of the *kerygma*." Cf. C. H. Dodd, *History and the Gospel*, London, 1947, pp. 72f.

6. W. Grossouw, "L'Espérance dans le Nouveau Testament," *Revue Biblique* 61 (1954), pp. 508-532. The article however, being devoted to a study of the term "hope" and its cognates, does not attempt to discern the *reality*, which is Christian hope, in the Johannine literature.

7. Jürgen Moltmann, *Theology of Hope*, New York & Evanston, 1965, whose thesis is that "Christianity is eschatology, is hope, forward looking and forward moving. . . . The eschatological is not one element of Christianity, but it is the medium of Christian faith as such, the key in which everything in it is set" (p. 16). For this distinguished German thinker, in fact, there is admittedly "only one real problem in Christian theology, which its own object forces upon it and which it in turn forces on mankind and on human thought: the problem of the future" (p. 16). This may sound as if Moltmann is embarked upon the same project which interests us here. He is not. Indeed, he rejects any comprehension of the object of the eschatological hope in terms of an historical future. Still, it is difficult to resist the impression that, in Moltmann's thought, there is a tendency to conceive what is beyond history as an historical future. Thus, for example, he speaks of "the future of Christ" as "what he will be" (*op. cit.*, p. 203); he talks, in the language of Ernst Bloch, of "a God with 'future as his essential nature'" (p. 16).

8. Gerald O'Collins, *Theology and Revelation*, Cork, 1968, p. 84.

9. Actually there is no proper term for the "historical future" in the New Testament. The authors frequently adopt the rabbinical distinction be-

tween "this age" and "the age to come" (Mk 10:30; Mt. 12:32; Lk 18:30; 20:35; Eph 1:21). Paul's expression, "the things present and the things to come" (Rom 8:38), is probably to be taken in this sense also, as is "the promise of the present life and of the life to come" in 1 Tm 4:8 (cf. Heb 2:5; 6:5; 13:14). The author of the Apocalypse may have the historical future in mind, when he represents the risen Christ as saying, "Write down what you have seen: what now exists and what will come to pass after these things" (Apoc 1:19). Yet any biblical student ought to know what pitfalls lie in wait for the unwary investigator who seeks to identify actors or events in this eschatological drama with historical personalities or happenings.

10. A. Vanhoye, S. J., "Structure et théologie des récits de la Passion dans les évangiles synoptiques," *Nouvelle Revue Théologique* 89 (1967), p. 135. This valuable article is available in English translation from the Liturgical Press, Collegeville, Minnesota: *Structure and Theology of the Accounts of the Passion in the Synoptic Gospels* (translated by C. H. Giblin, S. J.).

11. As Hans Conzelmann has rightly noted, "a definition of the formal structure of time" will not help us discover "the relationship between past, present and future" in the minds of the New Testament authors (cf. *An Outline of the Theology of the New Testament,* New York & Evanston, 1969, p. 184).

12. For the reasons behind this translation and interpretation, cf. A. Feuillet, *Le Christ Sagesse de Dieu d'après les Épitres Pauliniennes,* Paris, 1966, pp. 59-85.

13. Cf. "Pauline Allusions to the Sayings of Jesus," *Catholic Biblical Quarterly* 23 (1961), pp. 26-39.

14. Cf. A. Feuillet, *op. cit.,* pp. 137f.

15. William F. Lynch, *Images of Hope,* New York & Toronto, 1966, p. 25.

16. Heb 6:13-19 also uses Abraham as an example of hope, but insists rather upon his patience in waiting for the fulfillment of the promise (Gen 22:16-18), confirmed by the divine oath, which was made only after the "sacrifice" of Isaac. In Heb 11:8-10, Abraham provides still another illustration of the faith-hope demanded of Christians by leaving his home in Ur "without knowing where he was going" and by "looking forward to that city upon solid foundations, whose architect and builder is God."

17. William F. Lynch insists on this social aspect of hope: cf. *op. cit.,* pp. 19f. "Hope cannot be achieved alone. It must in some way or other be an act of a community. . . . Hope is an act of the city of man . . . in the sense that it must occur between persons, whether they be man or God."

18. This is but one instance of Paul's hopeful attitude toward the future of history, which recurs like a refrain in his letters: cf. Phil 2:19; 4:13; 2 Cor 1:7; 3:12; 5:11; 8:5; 10:15; Rom 15:24; Phlm 22. As W. Grossouw (*art. cit.,* pp. 527f.) points out, this hope in the historical future, not directed to eschatology properly so called, is, in the New Testament, peculiar to Paul. 1 Tm 3:14 is probably the only extra-Pauline instance of what Grossouw terms "apostolic hope."

19. This significant Pauline attribute of Christian hope is not mentioned in

the Pastorals, Hebrews, or 1 Peter. On the other hand, the function of the Spirit in history as the "other Paraclete" (Jn 14:16) replacing Jesus is an important feature of Johannine hope.

20. William F. Lynch, *op. cit.*, p. 28, describes this growth of hope in modern terms. "In fact, one of the principal ways in which hope becomes steadier and more mature . . . is that it develops precisely this quality for being able to live contextually. It comes to know that things have contexts and are not absolute, atomic units."

21. Cf. Lynch, *op. cit.*, p. 24: "What we are already saying is that hope is, in its most general terms, a sense of *the possible*. . . . Hope therefore involves three basic ideas that could not be simpler: what I hope for I do not yet have or see; it may be difficult; but I *can* have it—it is possible." Cf. also Pieper, *op. cit.*, p. 91: "Thus what marks the true hoper is that he holds himself in readiness for a fulfillment which goes beyond every imaginable human postulate."

22. Josef Pieper makes this "Point One" (of two) in his summation on the nature of Christian hope: cf. *op. cit.*, p. 81. ". . . the Christian expects this present Creation, the reality we see before our eyes, to pass through death and disaster in order to achieve perfection. That is the 'salvation' we hope for. The 'Kingdom of God' will be realized nowhere but in the midst of this historical world."

23. This truth, of paramount importance for an understanding of the post-resurrection narratives in the Gospels, was clearly grasped and articulated by St. Thomas Aquinas; cf. *Summa Theologica*, III, 55, 2 ad 1. "Christum post resurrectionem viventem oculata fide viderunt, quem mortuum sciverant."

24. The identification of "the inhabitants of the earth" as "false Christians" has recently been made in a fascinating, new commentary on the Apocalypse by Paul S. Minear, *I Saw a New Earth*, Washington & Cleveland, 1969, p. 80.

Louis Dupré

Hope and Transcendence

One of the most durable myths of the West is the story of Pandora. According to Hesiod's version, Zeus, dissatisfied about Prometheus' stealing of the fire, decided to give man a gift in which he would embrace his own destruction. So he ordered the celestial mechanic Hephaestus to fabricate a woman with sweet voice, lovely maiden shape and deceitful nature. Athene girded and clothed her, the divine Graces put necklaces of gold upon her and the Hours crowned her head with spring flowers. He called her Pandora, gift of all, because all the Olympians had contributed something. Then he sent her to Epimetheus, Prometheus' brother, accompanied by a huge vase containing all possible ills to man as well as the hope which would enable him to sustain them. Epimetheus, unmindful of his brother's advice never to accept gifts from Zeus, took the woman but soon realized that he had brought an evil thing into the world. In Hesiod's words:

The woman took off the great lid of the jar with her hands and scattered all these [ills, toils and sickness] and her thought caused sorrow and mischief to men. Only Hope remained there in an unbreakable home within under the rim of the great jar and did not fly out at the door; for ere that, the lid of the jar stopped her, by the will of the Aegis-holding Zeus who gathers the clouds. But the rest, countless plagues, wander amongst men; for earth is full of evils and the sea is full.[1]

Pandora's successful mythical career partly results from the persistent Christian urge to compare her to the Biblical Eve— *Eva prima Pandora*.[2] Most fascinating to the successive generations of graphic and literary artists proved the enigmatic hope in the vase. In some cases she eclipsed Pandora altogether. Thus, in the painting of Giulio Bonasone an unknown man slams the lid on a vase out of which a diminutive hope is busily attempting to escape.[3] In a sixteenth-century book of emblems hope apparently has crawled out and lounges defiantly on top of a cask (a Northern permutation of Hesiod's vase) which presumably contained her before. Most instructive about her true nature is the poem accompanying the woodcut:

Why do you lazily sit on the cover of a vat?
Because I alone stayed home while all the evils fluttered about everywhere,
As the hallowed Muse of the Ascraean sage has told us.
Which bird is accompanying you? The crow, most faithful of augurs.
When he cannot say, 'All is well', he says, 'All will be well'.[4]

The last verse alludes to the crow's cry: *cras, cras*—the Latin for *tomorrow*.

One cannot but admire the mixture of grief and hope which this myth so beautifully balances. A blind Fate will often be cruel but there is no reason why it should not be equally promising. Modern man might still profit from its ethical wisdom, for a cautious optimism that things will somehow work out in the end contains more truth than blind despair. For him who is able to maintain sufficient distance, all oppositions blend. I can at least *accept* the inevitable and thereby surpass my Fate.[5]

Yet the hope in Pandora's vase is not the one in modern man's mind. He is no longer interested in the unpredictable turns of a wheel handled by blind Fortune. Instead he bases his hopes upon powers which he *knows* he possesses or which he *believes* he may invoke. His hero in the story is no longer Pandora or the imprisoned hope. It is Prometheus who challenged Zeus' will and the wiles of Fate, and singlehanded stole the fire from heaven by which he would forge his own destiny. Similarly modern man relinquishes his earth basis to explore the depths of space and of the ocean, he enriches the land and bans toil, he cures disease and is only halted by death itself. Yet he also destroys, pollutes and kills. But hopeful or threatening, the future resides within himself. Still man's Promethean power remains an object of hope insofar as he will never fathom the mysterious depth of its creativity. Freedom manifests this strange paradox: it holds its own future, yet can never predict it. That is why it still speaks in the language of myth (perhaps in the form of science fiction) rather than in the logic of deduction.

Beside this terrestrial hope—and often inhabiting the same mind—another hope exists for what is unattainable by human effort. It is not blind as Pandora's, since it knows what to hope for even though it does not *know* what it hopes. It is the hope of which faith is the substance (Heb 11:1). Christianity did not invent it; it inherited it from a long Messianic tradition which Israel itself shares with others. Yet how deeply Christianity transformed it appears upon comparing the meaning of the words of 1 Cor 2:9 with their original sense in Is 64:4: "Things beyond our seeing, things beyond our hearing, things beyond our imagining, all prepared by God for those who love him." In this hope of faith the future rests no longer in man's hands as the fruit of his own work. Nor can misfortune in this life undo its promise. "For I reckon that the sufferings we now endure bear no comparison with the splendor, as yet unrevealed, which is in store for us" (Rom 8:18). Christian hope is not based upon moral wisdom or confidence in human power but upon an eschatological intervention of the transcendent.

Now, one might argue, all true hope is based upon some faith and, indeed, Promethean hope itself is an offspring of that unique Judaeo-Christian directedness toward a self-transcending future. Although I agree with this line of reasoning I do not intend to pursue it here, for the thesis of my essay is precisely that, regardless of their origins, the two forms of self-transcendence as well as the hopes which accompany them fundamentally differ and cannot be reduced to each other. However, Promethean hope and the hope of faith share one common character which I cannot ignore. The future envisaged in hope always overcomes the alienation of the present. Man builds up his hopes according to what he considers to be the estrangement of the present. In the inspiring words of Gabriel Marcel: " 'I hope' in its full strength is directed towards salvation. It really is a matter of my coming out of a darkness in which I am at present plunged." [6] This is true even for the confident Promethean anticipation of the future: man creates in order to liberate himself from existing servitudes. We anticipate our self-made utopias in the same images as the coming of the divine kingdom. This remarkable fact has led Ernst Bloch and some theologians of hope to identify one with the other.

Yet religious salvation cannot be reduced to a hope for this world even though it also responds to the demands of the negative situation expressed in the various social-economic, psychological and ontological forms of alienation. Salvation to be meaningful requires that man first become aware of the full wretchedness of his condition; it implies that life is not good enough to be accepted as it is. To awaken a feeling of insufficiency, then, is the first task of faith. Nor can the religious consciousness ever build its own categories in a vacuum. It must rely on the negative experiences of life under certain physical, social and psychological conditions as well as of existence itself. Yet faith is not satisfied with these experiences which in themselves are neither religious nor, as Camus and Kafka witness, *per se* conducive to the adoption of a religious attitude. What religious man regards as the situation from which he must be "saved" refers to all alienating experiences with which man is acquainted. Indeed it amplifies and universalizes them. But it also adds an important facet which is not part of the original experiences: religious man considers himself estranged from himself *because he is estranged from the sacred,* that is, from an ultimate principle of Being which lies beyond existence.

The added dimension to the concept of alienation accounts for the fundamental difference between religious hope and Promethean anticipation of man's self-made future. For the secular philosopher Ernst Bloch and the Christian theologians Wolfhart Pannenberg and Johannes B. Metz the two lines of hope seem to converge in an infinitely distant future. Thus Bloch predicts the coming of a new era in which the kingdom of the Son of Man will occur "not merely as something 'above' but also as something before us." [7] Bloch's position is by no means to be equated with the somewhat simplistic social Messianism of Karl Marx. It rather marks a return to Feuerbach's anthropological attempt to incorporate God into man. But in Bloch's eyes even Feuerbach did not give its due to the transcendent aspects of faith. God is not simply man as he was for Feuerbach; he is the future of man, that is, man insofar as he *transcends* his present self. Bloch agrees with Feuerbach that all transcendence is self-transcendence. But, he claims, man cannot conceive of this transcendent potential in any other than religious terms. "The *res infinita* of the religious ideal cannot be reduced to the *res finita* as conceived by Feuerbach. Religion may feel perfectly at home with ignorance, even stupidity, but never with triviality: mysteries are the anti-trivial *par excellence*." [8] The utopian space which religion opened up is the form of man's self-transcendence. The gods who fill this space are mythical projections of the *homo absconditus*. The content of religion is the totality of all-comprehensive hope, the Messianic Kingdom in which man's now hidden potential will be revealed. [9] Not God but the kingdom is the true object of man's hope. Only a religious conception could sound its depth and its height. Yet to retain the utopian character of his vision man must exorcize the sacred space and time from the gods who now inhabit them. The kingdom can remain messianic, that is future-oriented, only by becoming atheistic. The gods anticipate the future ideal in a mythical present. To adore them is to presume that the future is already with us and thus to neglect the task of making it. "Far from being the enemy of religious utopia, atheism is its presupposition: without atheism there is no room for Messianism." [10] For Bloch Messianism is the core of the religious attitude which has no other function than to manifest man's potential to himself. The ideals in which the religious dream expresses itself are mythical (and as such unacceptable to modern man) insofar as they posit as present *above us* what must remain a transcendent projection *before us*.

Such a concept of hope as *ideal* of the future needs an *ontological* basis if it is to be more than wishful thinking. Bloch fully realizes this and therefore posits what he calls an ontological priority of the future. Yet such a priority presupposes an over-arching unity which connects the future with the present and with the past. Horizontal transcendence can be established with certainty only if there is a *prior* (in the ontological sense) *vertical* transcendence which launches man on his journey into the future. Undoubtedly, freedom is possible only as long as man is future-oriented, that is, as long as he hopes. But hope itself degenerates into facile optimism if no transcendent reality in the present supports it. Such a reality is not restricted to *what is,* but unless it is also present in the *now, what will be* becomes a mere *what may be.* The difficulty with Bloch is that he seems to interpret religious transcendence (in the traditional sense) as *merely* present or, even stranger, as entirely past. The religious consciousness does not confine God to either present or past. One does scant justice to the religious notion of transcendence by conceiving it in terms of a once-for-all act of creation. Neither Jews nor Christians ever understood God— or, for that matter, his creative activity—as a reality in the past. Nor was he ever religiously conceived to be, as Pannenberg maintains, "an absolute thing in the mode of presentness." [11] God's "present," if we use that anthropomorphic expression to describe the eternal, is not opposed to the future and the past. Consequently it is just as meaningless to consider his mode of being as future (Pannenberg, Metz), as it is to relegate him, after the fashion of a Cartesian Creator, to the past. A God who is only future is inevitably finite and therefore not God.[12] The kingdom as Bloch and his theological followers conceive it must remain human, transcendently human but nevertheless human.

This brings me to another inaccuracy in Bloch's interpretation of the religious idea of God which the theologians of hope fail to point out. God is never primarily an ideal to man but a *reality* and as such first and foremost related to the present. He constitutes the other dimension of the real—the super-real. It is only because this super-reality cannot be compressed in the present that man projects his God into the past (the beginning of the creative event) and into the future (the coming of the eschatological Kingdom). Judaism and Christianity are unusually future-oriented. This has led to a great emphasis on hope and has produced a civilization which regards itself as an unlimited ascent. But the exposed over-simplifications of the eschatological school of exegesis (Weiss and Schweitzer were its main representatives) should caution us against absolutizing a distinctive aspect of the Christian faith to the point where it ceases to be a *religious* faith at all.

On the other hand, the traditional metaphor of God "above us" has led to a number of misconceptions against which the theologians of hope rightly protest. For to assert that God is our beginning and our end does not mean that he is an immutable instant conceived after man's experience of the present. Divine eternity cannot be the same *with* the development of history as it would have been *without* it. History must mean more to God than an enormous parenthesis within an unchanging eternity. If anything comes out of God it must necessarily exist in God. Which means that God cannot remain indifferent to a development in which he is immanent. Since the immanence of God in all that is, is as essential as his transcendence, it must be true in some very real sense that *God becomes* and that history does make a difference to him. Yet, and here lies my disagreement with the theologians of hope, the development takes place *within* the all-comprehensive unity of God. Once history exists it cannot leave God unaffected, since it takes place *in* God. Yet it does not make him more divine. God becomes, but he does not become God (which would be a contradiction since a being which starts from *intrinsic* imperfection can never become all-perfect). He is immanent in history to the extent that its development occurs in his very heart or, more correctly, that he is its very heart. But its effect is that *man* becomes more man, not that God becomes more God. It may be true that historical development reveals God more fully, for it gradually manifests all reality, but God transcends even his revelation. More revelation is not more God, as a strange combination of biblical fundamentalism and speculative unorthodoxy leads Pannenberg to believe. This also implies that the development of history is not *determined* by its divine immanence. No one but man directs the course of history. God is immanent in history-making man, but he is also *transcendent* to the process. In plain language this means that man alone remains responsible for its course. The transcendence of God *is* the autonomy of the creature. God "needs" history only to let man become man; none of its events can ever contribute to his divinity. The autonomy of man is what makes the real difference to God, and to preserve this autonomy he must remain transcendent.

If there is no other transcendence than that of the future (even the indefinite future), there is no transcendence at all. The future holds the key to man; it does not hold the key to God. Theologians of hope rightly emphasize the immanence of God in human development; they fail to point out that God transcends the future as much as the present and the past. The *before* is yet another expression of negative theology; it circumscribes divine transcendence as little as the *above* did. *Immer weiter Gott* says no more than Goethe's *Immer höher Gott*.

NOTES

1. *Works and Days*, H. G. Evelyn-White, Loeb Classical Library, Cambridge, 1950, p. 7.
2. On this equation in the graphic arts, one may consult Erwin and Dora Panofsky, *Pandora's Box*, New York, 1965, pp. 12-13, 62-66.
3. *Ibid.*, pp. 82-84.
4. *Ibid.*, p. 28.
5. Gabriel Marcel, *Homo Viator*, trans. by Emma Craufurd, New York, 1962, p. 34.
6. *Ibid.*, p. 30.
7. "Der Mensch als Moglichkeit" in *Forum. Oesterreichische Monatsblatter für Kulturelle Freiheit*, 13 (1965), p. 361. Trans. in *Cross Currents*, 18 (1968), p. 283. The qualifiers "not merely" and "also" seem to be of later vintage. They do not appear in *Das Prinzip Hoffnung*.
8. *Das Prinzip Hoffnung*, Frankfurt, 1967, p. 1518.
9. *Ibid.*, p. 1410.
10. *Ibid.*, p. 1413.
11. "The God of Hope," in *Ernst Bloch zu Ehren*, Frankfurt, 1965, pp. 209-25, trans. in *Cross Currents*, 18 (1968), p. 289.
12. Pannenberg seems to hedge on this issue. In an article "Was Ist der Mensch" in *Disputation zwischen Christen und Marxisten* (München, 1966), p. 186, he writes: "Such a reality [which transcends what is present] must in some sense already pre-exist (*vorgegeben sein*)." Two pages further: "On the other side of the present (*jenseits des Vorhandenen*) is only the future. This may be an indication that God, to quote Ernst Bloch, must be thought with the future as mode of being."

George A. Lindbeck

The Sectarian Future
of the Church

However pretentious attempts to discern the shape of the future may be, they are becoming unavoidable. The mantle of Elijah is descending upon all of us, and we are forced to prophesy whether we will or no.

The reason for this is that we are in a period of transition, of rapid change. As a result, proposals come to us in the guise of predictions. We are told that disaster confronts us, and we must act to avoid it or, alternatively, something or other—whether science and technology or revolutionary, psychedelic Freudianism—will inevitably triumph, and the churches must accommodate to the victory.

Such proposals have theological import, and so theologians, if they are to carry out their responsibility of "testing the spirits," must examine them. This, however, we are ill-equipped to do, for contemporary forecasts make no claim to preternatural origin, but rather are clothed in the language of the empirical sciences. If we are to do our job, there is nothing for it but to plunge into the arcane depths of history and sociology, and make our own estimates of where current trends are leading us. This then is my excuse for venturing a theologian's version of a sociological scenario for the future of the Church.

Against avant-garde visions of the Church as an open and

226

theologically relativistic movement of revolutionary or counter-cultural type, I anticipate a sociologically sectarian future in which the exclusivist claims of the orthodox mainstream of the Christian tradition are maintained, even if reinterpreted. This does not mean, however, that I agree with more conservative projections, such as those of Andrew Greeley,[1] for example. A sectarian future, while not anti-institutional, implies a de-institutionalization of old structures and a re-institutionalization in new forms which are perhaps even more radical than what the avant-garde envisions.

Even if you find my forecasts unconvincing, I hope they will serve one purpose. I hope they will help persuade you, assuming that persuasion is necessary, that the future may well be quite different from what you now consider probable. This might help to free us from undue preoccupation with forecasting. Ulti-mately the grounds for the Church's choices should not be guesses about "inevitable trends" or "waves of the future." Rather it should be convictions about what is good and right, about what should be, rather than must be. In the words of Daniel Bell, the dean of the American sub-species of the new breed of scientific prognosticators, of futurologists, "the func-tion of prediction is not, as often stated, to aid social control, but to widen the spheres of moral choice." [2]

The "sectarianism" about which we shall be talking is rather like the "diaspora" which Karl Rahner in particular has so eloquently described.[3] It is a sociological, not an ecclesiological, concept. The mainstream of early Christianity was sectarian in the sense in which we use the term. It consisted of a small, strongly deviant minority, unsupported by cultural convention and prestige, within the larger society. This was true even though it was also "catholic" in the ecclesiological sense of em-bracing a wide variety of classes, races, theologies, liturgies and styles of life, and of being unified, rather than splintered into competing groups. In later centuries, however, when the ma-jority of people became Christian, sociological and theological sectarianism necessarily coincided, rather than doing so only occasionally as in the first centuries (e.g., in the case of the Montanists). Once a deviant minority within the larger society became one which also fragmented the *corpus christianum,* it naturally tended to insist on a particular and narrow interpretation of Christianity and to recruit its adherents from a single racial, social or cultural group. In other words, it almost inevitably added to its sociological sectarianism the theological and ecclesiological aspects as well. Conversely, when what a Roman Catholic might regard as theological sects were not sociological ones, as was true of the larger Protestant bodies, they tended toward some degree of comprehensiveness or catholicity. Our question, then, is about what will happen if this connection between sociological and theological sectarianism is broken. What will happen if we move into a period when once again catholic or ecumenical Christianity which emphasizes a comprehensive and internally diversified unity will itself be sociologically sectarian?

For obvious reasons, we shall refer frequently to the first centuries of our era in trying to answer this question. It is the only period up until now when the Church has been both catholic and sociologically sectarian.

The first thesis which I shall advance is that the Christianity which survives into a hypothetical radically de-Christianized future will be sociologically sectarian, sharply distinguished from the society at large, and continuing to make the traditional Christian claims regarding the unsurpassable finality of revelation in Jesus Christ.

The second thesis is that, in such a situation, "Catholic" or "ecumenical" sociologically sectarian Christianity could have a competitive advantage over what I shall call the "divisive" or "schismatic" varieties.

Third, I shall discuss what would need to be done to actualize this advantage.

We need not pause long over the hypothesis of a radically de-Christianized future. Clearly the churches have lost greatly in status and influence even among those who remain practicing members. Clearly also there is a great deal of residual Christianity in traditionally Christian countries, even in those which are under Communist rule. We could discuss at length how soon, if at all, present trends would produce a fundamental de-Christianization of Western culture so that, in all strata of society, explicit profession of the faith would be socially odd. There is no need, however, to settle this question. We are simply envisaging the possibility of a world in which the majority of the people everywhere are indifferent or hostile, for either secular or religious reasons, to anything which could claim to be distinctively Christian. Our concern is with what this would mean for the churches if it were to occur.

We have already mentioned that some writers propose that in these circumstances Christianity could and should become the very opposite of an exclusivist sect. It should become, they argue, an open movement,[4] forswearing clear-cut creeds, confessions or standards of conduct, composed of people who, while they have some kind of preference for Christian symbols over the symbolic systems of other religions or ideologies, associate and cooperate as freely with others as with their own co-religionists. If this happens, Christians will have a chance of becoming a kind of elite, the vanguard of humanity, distinguishable chiefly by their openness to the future and by the courage and love with which they risk themselves in the service of humanity.

Many Christians and virtually all non-Christians react to this as impossibly romantic. The reason for their negative response is perhaps best formulated in terms of the sociology of knowledge.[5] For the vast majority of human beings, the only way in which a distinctive belief, value and action system can be acquired or maintained is through frequent interaction with significant others. As long as society is widely permeated by Christian ideas and behavioral patterns, it is not necessary for those who consider themselves Christians to form close-knit fellowships in order to develop or preserve their religious identity. They can be either cultural Christians or even personally

committed in a rather individualistic way. But to the degree
generalized social support disappears, it becomes necessary for
Christians or members of any other deviant minority to gather
together in small, cohesive, mutually supportive groups. They
must become, sociologically speaking, sectarian.

A second part of our first thesis is that Christian sectarianism
would continue to be "orthodox" in the sense of maintaining
recognizable continuity with the absolute and exclusive claims
of the mainstream Christian tradition. It would persist in affirming that Jesus is the Lord of lords, the unsurpassably significant
event in the space-time world of human life and history, the
norm of norms and the criterion of all criteria for evaluating
whatever purports to be knowledge or experience of the mystery
which surrounds our beginnings and our end.

The formulation and interpretation of this claim has changed
often in the course of Church history and will no doubt change
again. This is not the place to discuss the detailed possibilities.
One point must be noted, however, in order to avoid misunderstanding. The orthodox Christian absolutism and exclusivism of
which we are speaking does not necessarily conflict with a
certain kind of universalism. This has been shown in our day
by theologians such as Karl Rahner as well as by Vatican II,
on the Roman Catholic side and, in a very different way, by
Karl Barth on the Protestant. Views analogous to theirs were
widespread implicitly—and occasionally explicitly (Origen)—
in the early Church. The Bible itself, as becomes clear when it
is interpreted historically, holds that God works redemptively
outside the Church as well as within it, and that Christians
must therefore respect and be ready to learn from non-Christians and to adopt "dialogue" rather than "proselytism" as the
appropriate form of witness. Such attitudes in both their Jewish
and Christian form are compatible with the conviction that the
truth to which one's own community is elected to testify is the
final revelation which will endure until the end of time. It is
reasonable to expect that the absolutism of an ecumenical sectarianism would have this modified character and that only

theological sects would persist in the narrow interpretation of the *extra ecclesiam nulla salus* which became dominant throughout all of Christendom in the post-Constantinian era.

Could Christians survive without exclusivism? They might, of course, temporarily maintain themselves in ghetto-like enclosures similar to those of the Pennsylvania Amish or Hasidic Jews, but such self-segregation was not characteristic of early Catholicism and is incompatible with the Church's fundamental understanding of itself as a people sent to witness and serve in all nations. Further, as we shall have occasion to see in more detail, this kind of sociological isolation is increasingly difficult to maintain for generation after generation in the modern situation. Our argument, then, is that the kind of exclusivism which we have described is essential to a sectarian existence which is "in but not of the world."

This discussion will detain us for some time. It will at first be a purely conditional one, not arguing that Christian absolutism can in fact resist the relativizing acids of modernity, but simply that this absolutism is a necessary though not sufficient prerequisite for Christian survival in a de-Christianized world.

The first point is that in the absence of exclusivist claims, Christians would not be socially deviant enough to qualify as sects. They would be like the cults and quasi-religious philosophical schools which proliferated in the early centuries of our era. In contrast to early Christianity, these were not sociologically sectarian. They were syncretistic, making no claims to exclusive uniqueness. As A. D. Nock puts it, "One mystery cult did not exclude another"; [6] at most it would profess to be the best way of worshiping the Godhead. Men also passed easily from one philosophical school to another. Similarly the Gnostics, even those who called themselves Christian, did not refuse divine honors to the Emperor. They thought it silly of the Catholic Christians to risk martyrdom because of a pinch of incense. This kind of religious tolerance was normal, we recall, not only in the Greek and Roman world, but also in India, China and Japan. Only the peoples of the book, only those who claim Abraham for father, only Jews, Christians and Muslims, have invented this novel doctrine that their revelations are universally and exclusively true; and it is therefore chiefly they among the religions of the world, and their secular offspring such as Marxists, who have a built-in tendency toward sectarianism when they are a minority.

Thus, if Christianity does not maintain its exclusive claims, it is not likely to become sectarian, even when its numbers are drastically reduced. It would evolve in the manner of the various denominations in pluralistic Christian societies. Each of them is simply one competitor in the religious marketplace. Like all sellers who view their products as variants, even if superior ones, of what others are offering, each denomination tailors its wares to fit the changing tastes and needs of potential buyers. It loses its uniqueness and becomes only superficially distinguishable from the others. So also in a de-Christianized situation, under similar competitive circumstances, and in the absence of all absolutistic affirmations, Christianity as a whole, like the ancient mystery religions, would not diverge enough from prevailing cultural standards to be forced into sectarianism.

There is a second point which I would like to make which goes even farther and suggests that some degree of absolutism is not only a sociological, but a logical necessity for Christian survival. The affirmation of the Lordship of Christ is historically so thoroughly embedded in the very notion of Christian identity, that it is, as the psychologists would say, cognitively dissonant to maintain one without the other. We see this operating in those Unitarians and Universalists who, despite the history of their denominations, find it increasingly odd to call themselves Christian. So also, if the Christian mainstream were to abandon its historic profession on this point, it could make no rational case for not surrendering the Christian title to whatever might be the future equivalents of Fundamentalist or Old Believer fringe groups. That there would be some such groups is, I suppose, as certain as anything the future holds. If they are the only ones who can plausibly claim to affirm what has historically been essential to Christian identity, it is they alone who would inherit the name. Needless to say, names are not unimportant in such matters. Substantial continuity is not always maintained while names remain the same, but when names change, continuity is always lost. If one is concerned about the future of Christian communities in an increasingly de-Christianized world, it is only the ones which try to insist that Jesus is Lord that need be worried about.

We must now, in concluding our consideration of the first thesis, ask whether such communities could survive. So far, as already noted, we have been arguing hypothetically: if Christians everywhere become a socially deviant minority, their peculiar beliefs, values and behavior can be maintained, if at all, only by their gathering together in sect-like groups affirming unique access to absolute truth. One may grant that these are necessary conditions for survival while still doubting that they can be actualized.

Until recently, the reason generally advanced for such doubts was secularization. A reputable anthropologist writing in 1966 still regarded it as indisputable that "as a cultural trait, belief in supernatural powers is doomed to die out, all over the world, as a result of the increasing adequacy and diffusion of scientific knowledge." [7] This mood, however, is shifting with astonishing speed. New outbursts of supernaturalism, particularly among the young, have shaken the secularizers' confidence. *The Feast of Fools* has followed hard upon *The Secular City*. And yet, as far as I can see, renascent religiousness in no way decreases the scandal of Christian particularity. More and more people, including theologians, simply assume that belief in any kind of exclusive finality will disappear.

I choose at random a quotation from a seminary professor: "It is obvious in the encounter with other religious stories that the Judaeo-Christian story can no longer lay claim, as it once did in its relative isolation, to any absolute truth." [8] He is assuming, clearly enough, that one world will bring with it, perhaps not one religion, but a relativizing of all religions. No

religion is believable if it maintains that it has uniquely privileged access to the truth. To the extent that Christianity insists
on this, it is bound to disappear.

There is much to be said for this position, although I would
argue for it in a somewhat different way. Modern industrial
society is characterized by rapid and continuous change, high
mobility and mass communications. Basic associational patterns
shift swiftly, not only from generation to generation, but within
a single lifetime. This undermines the entire range of intermediate communities, whether these be familial, geographical,
occupational, cultural, educational, political or religious. More
and more we are a society of individuals passing from one
temporary friendship or acquaintance group to another within
a framework of highly rationalized, large-scale bureaucratic
structures. There is a tremendous variety of ideological and
religious options available, but it is easy to change quickly from
one to another, thus producing the phenomenon of what Robert
Lifton has called "The Protean Man." [9] Even when commitments are more enduring, they tend to be privatized and com-
partmentalized, affecting only a small part of a man's life and
the public dimension scarcely at all. Obviously this renders
problematic the long-term viability of any markedly distinctive
minority, and thus of the beliefs, especially the absolutistic
beliefs, which such a minority might possess.

These are forceful objections to the possibility of Christian
sectarian survival, and yet there are reasons for believing that
powerful countervailing tendencies may come to prevail. It can
be argued that a mass society such as we have just described
is inherently self-destructive or at least unstable.

The most faddish way of making this point is to refer to the
ecological apocalypse to which modern mass societies seem
doomed. It is precisely because they are geared to never-ending
technological development, an expanding GNP and high con-
sumption that they are also rationalized, bureaucratized and
subject to rapid change. If we are to avoid total disaster,
Robert Heilbroner has suggested, we must persuade all men

"that conservation, stability, frugality and a deep concern for the distant future must now take priority over the personal indulgence for which they have been culturally prepared." [10] The new era must be one of a "grand slowing down." [11] It must be regressive rather than progressive, in which mankind no longer tries to pack a thousand years into a single day, as has been done in recent times, but rather looks at a thousand years as if it were only a day. If humanity is forced to thus reverse its headlong rush into the future, much of the most modish theology of the present with its emphasis on constant and ever-accelerating change will shortly be archaic.

Even when one excludes such speculative projections, however, there are still good reasons for suspecting that reactions to the present relativizing trends are inevitable.[12] We often hear it said that the de-humanizing impersonality of the contemporary order undermines the very basis of society. Stated more technically, the problem is that intermediate communities— communities of face-to-face encounters—are the primary socializing agencies. It is through them that human beings develop a sense of both personal and communal identity. When such communities are weakened and pluralized, the first and most obvious effect is an upsurge of individualism. People feel and act increasingly as isolated atoms. This may be initially experienced as liberating. One now has freedom to move everywhere and do everything within the wider social structures. When the processes of socialization further deteriorate, however, the result is anomie: loss of sense of identity, not knowing who one is or where one belongs, powerlessness in the face of impersonal forces reinforcing the feeling that one is a mere cog in the machine. Ultimately reactions must set in. The search for community becomes obsessive simply because most people have so little of it. "Togetherness" becomes a primary desideratum, and this then escalates into sensitivity training and its more and more exotic offspring. Increasingly there is the realization that even more radical solutions are necessary, and so we have the formation of communes designed to be permanent or semipermanent substitutes for the traditional intermediate groupings of family, church, neighborhood, school and guild. These latter are defective and must be rejected because they have been distorted by adaptation to the needs of mass society and no longer effectively serve their traditional socializing functions of conferring a sense of communal belonging, loyalty and personal identity.

It is not necessary to adopt any particular view of the future of contemporary communalism in order to see it as a symptom that a mass society generates the need for stable intermediate communities which are important for the whole of life in a fashion not unlike that of the early Christian congregations. Such communities provide the sociological infrastructure necessary for resisting the relativizing pressures of a pluralistic society, thus making conceivable the maintenance of Christian claims to final revelation.

Indeed, the historical record suggests that exclusivism may actually be a competitive advantage under these circumstances. E. R. Dodds, who is not a Christian, says of the early Church that "its very exclusiveness, its refusal to concede any value to alternative forms of worship, which nowadays is often felt to be a weakness, was in the circumstances of the time a source of strength. The religious tolerance which was the normal Greek and Roman practice had resulted by accumulation in a bewildering mass of alternatives. There were too many cults, too many mysteries, too many philosophies of life to choose from: you could pile one religious insurance on another, yet not feel safe. Christianity made a clean sweep. . . . One choice, one irrevocable choice, and the road to salvation was clear. Pagan critics might mock at Christian intolerance, but in an age of anxiety, any 'totalist' creed exerts a powerful attraction." [13]

The pertinence of this passage to our possible future needs little elaboration. The present confusing variety of choices is likely to escalate. Most of them, including the Eastern religions, will be confessedly relativistic, and those which are not, such as classical Marxism, will be ideologies for particular periods and places, too immanental and lacking in transcendental reference to be able seriously to maintain their absolutism for any length of time. It is not impossible that the Christian exclusivism (which has seemed just as incredible to the established wisdom of the West ever since Lessing as it once did to that of the Hellenistic world) may once again in a minority situation become a strength. It would be a strength, not in persuading either conservative or revolutionary Establishments, but in attracting the socially marginal people who are in special need of community or want support in standing against the prevailing mores.

The plausibility of this projection increases in the light of the sociological thesis that every society requires some non-conformists, protesters and deviants in order to define and test its own standards of normality. How can one know that one belongs unless there are some who do not? In a predominantly relativistic culture, it is precisely those who make absolutistic counter-claims who serve this function. Needless to say, the Christians among these resisters to normlessness would have considerable advantages. Their tradition supplies them with abundant resources for protesting against the powers that be. For these reasons, then, we conclude that sectarian Christianity might not only survive but even flourish in a de-Christianized world of the future.

We come now to our second thesis. It is Catholic or ecumenical sectarianism, not narrow, divisive and schismatic varieties, which would have the competitive advantage.

One reason for thinking this is, once again, logical—or, if you prefer, theological. A Catholic position which embraces variety is internally more consistent, and in that sense plausible, than a schismatic position. It is consonant with the basic Christian sources to focus exclusivist claims, not on secondary elements, but on Jesus Christ, and thus allow for pluralism and that unity in love which includes the really diverse (as were Jewish and Gentile Christians in the first generations, and Eastern and Western Christians in later periods). Theological sectarians, whether of the radical or of the fundamentalist and traditionalist sorts, simply cannot make out as good an intellectual case for the Christian authenticity of their views as can ecumenists; and in the long run, other things being equal, intellectual considerations do carry some weight.

More immediately compelling, however, is the social-psychological superiority of Catholic sectarian communalism. It not only has the advantage of greater range, but it may also be just as intense and supportive of the individual as are schismatic movements. This is hard for us to realize, not only because the post-Constantinian Catholic or established churches have rarely favored small-group fervor, but also because these churches in our day are increasingly bureaucratized, remote and impersonal, thus leaving the schismatics as the only ones who really cultivate *koinonia*. (Of course, there are all sorts of intimate fellowships within the larger denominations, but they know little of the sectarian experience of special closeness, loyalty and responsibility to all within the Church.)

In the early centuries, however, when Catholicism was sociologically sectarian, it was precisely the sense of belonging it engendered which was one of its greatest strengths. To quote E. R. Dodds again: "Modern social studies have brought home to us the universality of 'the need to belong' and the unexpected ways in which it can influence human behaviour, particularly among the rootless inhabitants of great cities. I see no reason to suppose that it was otherwise in antiquity. . . . Such loneliness must have been felt by millions. . . . For people in that situation, membership of a Christian community might be the only way of maintaining their self-respect and giving life some semblance of meaning. Within the community there was human warmth: someone was interested in them both here and hereafter." [14]

Now this role of the ancient Church was performed in a situation which was more cosmopolitan, mobile and pluralistic than any other which existed before the twentieth century. The sense of belonging which the Church conferred was not attached exclusively to a homogeneous group, particular geo-graphical area, or single parish. It was perhaps more like the sense of belonging produced in past decades by membership in the international network of communist cells. If you were accepted in one, you were at home everywhere. Each group was small enough so that its membership, though shifting, was able to know each other well. So also, and in an even higher degree, the early Church was an association which had some of the characteristics of a primary community, a family, and yet was a worldwide and comprehensive fellowship.

Further, "Christianity was open to all. In principle, it made no social distinctions; it accepted the manual worker, the slave, the outcast, the ex-criminal; and though in the course of our period it developed a strong hierarchical structure, its hierarchy offered an open career to talent. Above all, it did not, like Neoplatonism, demand education. Clement might smile at the quaint beliefs of the *simpliciores,* Origen might declare that true knowledge of God was confined to 'a very few among the few'; but the notion of 'Pass and Honours standards in the service of God' (as Arthur Nock once phrased it) was originally foreign to the spirit of Christianity, and on the whole remained so." [15]

The need and longing for such a brotherhood and sisterhood is likely to grow immensely in the coming years as mankind becomes more and more a unified but uprooted mass. To the extent that the Church becomes a purified yet ecumenical mi-nority, composed of personally committed, not conventional Christians, purged of its present denominational, class, racial and national barriers, it would be able to supply an experience of community which many would treasure above all price. The practical importance of such a transcultural fellowship in help-ing make mankind more than an amorphous mass might be immense, even though Christians, having their fundamental unity in Christ, would consider this a by-product, a matter of fruit-bearing, rather than the primary purpose of their brother-hood. It is sensible to suppose that Catholic sectarianism, as in

the early days of the Church, would have a wider appeal than
the schismatic groups which do not emphasize universality or
embrace diversity.

There is much more that could be said about our hypothetical
future. We could discuss what would be the appropriate shape
of Christian teaching, worship and action. These are by no
means unimportant topics. The success of the early Church
depended on the effectiveness with which it adapted the biblical
good news to late Hellenistic life and thought, and an analogous
task of reinterpretation is equally indispensable for the coming
age.

This is not the place, however, to engage in such reinterpretation and this is, in any case, the stock in trade of contemporary theological discussion. Our contribution in this essay
has simply been to propose some sociological guidelines as to
what reinterpretations would be relevant to the Church in a
de-Christianized future. They would have to be usable by bands
of devout worshipers who insist that Jesus is supreme Lord,
and that the stories about him provide the best access to ultimate truth available to mankind until the consummation of
history. Any proposals unusable by such groups are *ex hypo-
thesi* irrelevant, for they will be the only Christians left. This
raises doubts regarding the long-range value of some radical
contemporary theological trends, for these assume a very different future, but it still leaves untouched the worth of much
current theological activity.

This brings us to our final topic of what should be done
to prepare for the future. How can Catholicity be maximized
and divisiveness minimized? On this I am pessimistic, for none
of the current institutional developments favor ecumenical sectarianism. It seems likely, in terms of our scenario, that it is
the schismatics who will inherit the Christian name.

The reason for thinking this is that if nothing is done to
seed the future with ecumenical bands of sectarian fervor and
"orthodoxy" (in the sense that we have defined), then the
surviving close-knit groups will come from the theological sects

of the present and from those deeply committed to divisively understood particular denominational heritages—i.e., the fundamentalists and *immobilisti*. Ecumenism would disappear either through accommodation to the general culture or by reabsorption into denominational sects. In its present forms, ecumenism is either too unstructured or too bureaucratic to long survive the cold winds of thorough de-Christianization. Only stable groups of zealous ecumenists would be able to reproduce and spread, and there is little evidence that these are coming into existence.

It is hard to see how they could emerge without deliberate action of the major churches. I am not thinking here of church unions of the conventional kind (which do nothing to promote sectarian fervency), but rather of the formation of ecumenical groupings of highly committed Christians in new types of parishes, religious orders and secular institutes. Only if such formations are officially supported can they become truly Catholic and ecumenical, creative of larger unities. Only then can they become sufficiently stable to reproduce and spread. In the absence of such approval and support, ventures of this kind are likely to be merely schismatic, composed of people who think of themselves as transcending all barriers, but who actually divide themselves from their previous communities in order to constitute their own little, socially homogeneous, separatistic, evanescent groups. Such communities need to be cooperatively sponsored by the established churches in order to actualize their ecumenical and catholic potential.

It would, however, be totally unrealistic to expect the present denominations to do this. They are not likely to commit institutional hara-kiri by establishing and nourishing forces which would eviscerate their own. Once the ecumenical sectarian option were regularized, it would attract into its ranks many of the best laity and clergy—thus seriously, perhaps mortally, damaging the ability of the present structures to operate. Even when churches formally unite, as in the case of COCU or Eastern and Western rite Catholics, they take precautionary measures against such contingencies. It is perhaps not only institutionally but also morally necessary for this to be done, because leaders who have assumed responsibility for the welfare of an organization ought not on their own initiative preside at its demise. That would be to violate the understanding, the premises, on the basis of which they were chosen.

Thus the present institutional structures of the major churches seem to preclude action. They were built to serve mass Christianity and cannot be turned to sectarian purposes. In recent times, with their progressive rationalization, bureaucratization and de-personalization they have become even more unusable, and this applies to some Protestant denominations even more fully than to the Roman Catholic Church.

I am not as entirely pessimistic as this sounds. For one thing, de-Christianization, if it comes, may well take a very long time, thus providing the opportunity of all kinds of preparatory developments. Perhaps we will not stumble into the future with only divisive sectarians to carry the Christian banner. Further, given the pressures of a hostile environment, a new and catholic ecumenism might coalesce out of schismatic fragments. The empirical grounds for these projections may be slim, but then, after all, I am not a sociologist or only a theologian, but a would-be believer, and this sometimes sparks transcendent hopes that God will unite and strip his Church for action in whatever times of trouble may lie ahead.

NOTES

1. See his *Religion in the Year 2000*, New York, 1969.
2. Quoted by J. P. Sisk in "The Future of Prediction," *Commentary*, Vol. 49 (1970), p. 68.
3. See esp. *The Christian of the Future*, New York, 1967, pp. 77-101.
4. Gregory Baum, "The New Ecclesiology," *Commonweal*, Vol. 41 (1969), pp. 123-128 develops the notion of the church as movement although he does not express it in as extreme a form as I have here done.

5. For the sociology of knowledge as it applies to religion see Peter Berger, *The Sacred Canopy*, New York, 1967.
6. *Early Gentile Christianity and Its Hellenistic Background*, New York, 1964, p. 104.
7. A. F. C. Wallace, *Religion: An Anthropological View*, New York, 1966, p. 265.
8. R. A. Underwood, "Ecological and Psychedelic Approaches to Theology," *Soundings*, Vol. 52 (1969), p. 366.
9. In an article of that title in the *Yale Alumni Magazine*, 1969.
10. *The New York Review of Books*, April 23, 1970, p. 8.
11. In the remainder of this paragraph I have drawn on Frederick Elder, "A Different 2001," *Lutheran Forum*, Vol. 4 (1970), pp. 8-11. Cf. his *Crisis in Eden*, Abingdon, 1970.
12. This analysis owes much to the writings of R. A. Nisbet, especially his *Community and Power*, New York, 1962.
13. E. R. Dodds, *The Dialogue of Paganism with Christianity*, Cambridge, 1965, pp. 133-134.
14. *Ibid.*, p. 137.
15. *Ibid.*, p. 134.

Avery Dulles, S.J.

An Apologetics
of Hope

In a frequently quoted passage from the *Pensées,* Blaise Pascal comments on man's ceaseless tendency to delve into his own future:

We do not rest satisfied with the present. We anticipate the future as too slow in coming, as if in order to hasten its course; or we recall the past, to stop its too rapid flight. So imprudent are we that we wander in the times which are not ours, and do not think of the only one which belongs to us; and so idle are we that we dream of those times which are no more, and thoughtlessly overlook that which alone exists. . . . We scarcely ever think of the present; and if we think of it, it is only to take light from it to arrange the future. . . . The past and present are our means; the future alone is our end. So we never live, but we hope to live, and, as we are always preparing to be happy, it is inevitable that we should never be so.[1]

If this preoccupation with the future is inseparable from human nature, it has greatly intensified in our time, as the literary trends bear witness. A century ago it used to be common to write books about the origins of man and of civilization. Later it became fashionable to write about the recent past. Books included in their title the word "yesterday." Then it was thought necessary to write only about the contemporary; books did not sell unless they were entitled "today." But within the past few years even to write about the present is to invite boredom and disdain. Unless an author addresses himself to the future, he feels that he has no claim to be taken seriously. The dust jackets in our book stores therefore bear titles such as these: *The Future of Man, The Future of the Church, The Future of Religion, The Future of Belief,* even *The Future of God.* One can hardly suppress a sense of envy at the endowments of those who feel able to write so voluminously about things which have yet to come into being.

This increasing preoccupation with the future is no doubt a result of the progressive acceleration and radicalization of change. Until recently it seemed possible to look upon change as a superficial phenomenon which occurred only within a stable and immutable framework of nature. But modern science and technology have called into question, and to a great extent undermined, the apparent stability of nature itself. We know now that there are no immutable particles of matter, that the earth is in rapid and constant motion, and that there are no fixed stars above us. The days, the seasons, even the movements of the heavenly bodies are subject to interference and disruption. Man can even go to work on himself, and drastically alter his own physical and mental constitution. Conscious of this, we have lost the secure feeling that what is basic and essential in reality is permanent.

It has generally been assumed, at least since the eighteenth century, that change means progress. With man's increasing mastery over himself and his environment, it began to appear that he could overcome most of the hostile forces which his ancestors had dreaded. Some God-is-dead theologians even proclaimed that God had become superfluous, now that man was in a position to do for himself the things which God had traditionally been supposed to do for him. But in the years since 1967, especially here in the United States, such optimism has all but vanished. The mounting social problems, the increase of crime and drug addiction, and the frustrations of the war in

Vietnam are but symptoms of man's inability to carve out for himself the bright future of which he was but recently dreaming. Amid threats of thermonuclear disaster, violent revolution, world starvation, and environmental pollution, some are seriously questioning whether mankind can anticipate a tolerable existence on this planet—or any planet—for more than another generation or two. If the world has no future, is not all man's toil in vain? Might not a nuclear holocaust be the best escape from the impossible muddle in which man now finds himself?

For a ray of hope, some look to the religions. As Kant maintained in his *Critique of Pure Reason,* the question "What may I hope for?" is the proper sphere of concern for religion.[2] And to this he added, in his *Critique of Practical Reason,* that the hope of happiness begins with religion only.[3] The current outburst of "theology of hope" literature reflects a serious effort on the part of Christian thinkers to meet the current wave of anxiety about what lies ahead.

The new theology of hope is not a mere fad, but the recovery of a basic theme which has not received its proper share of attention in classical theology. Judaeo-Christian faith, as set forth in the Bible, was always, most fundamentally, an acceptance of God's promise, and therefore it contained within itself an element of hope. According to the New Testament, to be a believer and to be a man of hope are practically synonymous. The Gentiles, for Paul, are "those who have no hope" (1 Thess 4:13). Abraham, in Paul's view, was the spiritual prototype of Christians inasmuch as he "against hope, believed in hope" (Rom 4:18). If Paul teaches, as he does, that we are saved by faith (Rom 3:28), he is equally ready to say that "in hope we are saved" (Rom 8:24). Faith itself, according to Heb 11:1, is "the substance of things hoped for."

In terms of the recent emphasis on hope, the nature of theology is being redefined. For the traditional concept of theology as "faith seeking understanding" (*fides quaerens intellectum*), Jürgen Moltmann proposes to substitute the definition, "hope seeking understanding" (*spes quaerens intellectum*). A question must therefore be raised about apologetics. Traditionally it has been viewed as the effort to set forth in a systematic and convincing way the reasons which tell in favor of the truth of the Christian religion, considered as a set of speculative statements about what God is and what God has done. Would it not be better today to think of apologetics as the discipline which seeks to exhibit the reasons for Christian hope? The centrality of hope to apologetics is indicated by the one text from the Bible which deals most explicitly with apologetics. 1 Pt 3:15 exhorts its readers: "Always be prepared to make a defense (*apologian*) to anyone who calls you to account for the hope that is in you." Without denying the necessity of an apologetics of faith, as traditionally understood, I should personally accept the desirability—and urgency—of an apologetics of hope.

The element of hope has not always been prominent in Christian apologetics. When Christian existence was conceived primarily as an acceptance of eternal and necessary truths, apologetics concentrated primarily on showing that the Christian, rather than the pagan sage, was the true man of wisdom. In recent centuries, when revelation was viewed primarily in the categories of history, apologetics sought to show that men were obliged to accept the Christian message, since that message was so conspicuously accredited by prophecy and miracle. Only with the Modernists and Blondel do we begin to sense a new orientation. Reinterpreting religious truth in terms of the dynamism of the human spirit, they sought to show that Christianity leads to an enrichment and intensification of life. In this perspective apologetics became concerned with the capacity of Christianity to answer questions such as those asked by Blondel with passionate intensity at the beginning of his *L'Action* (1893): "Has human life or has it not a meaning, and has man a destiny?" [4] In his *Letter on Apologetics* (1896) Blondel points out that it is not sufficient to oblige a man to assent to religious truth as something imposed by extrinsic evidences. There must be something in the message of Christianity which meets man's inner aspirations and speaks to his anxieties and concerns. "Apologetics must tend not only to make us know and believe," writes Blondel in an article on Dechamps, "but . . . also and primarily to make us be and act more and better." [5] Thus the problem of credibility, for Blondel, could never be separated from the problems of human hope and destiny. With Blondel we are already on the way to an apologetics of hope, and in this respect he must be accounted the master of Teilhard de Chardin. Part of Teilhard's enormous influence is no doubt due to the fact that he, from his own specialized point of view, developed a full-fledged theology of hope. There is perhaps no other Christian thinker of whom this can be said.

Whatever one may hold about the nature of apologetics in general, it seems clear that an apologetics for our times must take seriously the problem of hope. It must answer the question, so insistently asked by many of our contemporaries, whether man's efforts are doomed to ultimate frustration or whether the things he does in time are laden with eternal consequences. Apologetical theology must take cognizance of the exorbitant hopes and fears which alternately raise man to the heights of optimism and plunge him into the depths of despondency. An apologetics of hope might be expected to establish two propositions: first, that it is fitting and proper for man always to hope and never to despair, and second, that Christianity sustains the type of hope which it is good for man to have. Of itself this argument does not prove that Christianity is true, but it provides strong reasons for taking the Christian message seriously.

I

At the outset it will be helpful to distinguish between hope and hopes—a distinction more easily made in French, which has the two words, *espérance* and *espoir*. By hope (in the sense of *espérance*) I mean a general attitude, a subjective stance of hopefulness. Such hopefulness is not tied to any determinate object, that is, to anything we can imagine within the sphere of worldly possibilities. No amount of money, health, friends, learning, or the like can ever so satisfy a man that he does not crave for something more. On the other hand, no amount of destitution or deprivation can ever annihilate man's hope. Man's hope, therefore, exceeds his hopes. As Marcel puts it, "By a *nisus* which is peculiar to it, [hope] tends inevitably to transcend the particular objects to which it at first seems to be attached." [6]

There is an analogy here between hope and faith. Man's primordial attitude of faith, as an orientation to transcendent mystery, is incapable of being exhausted by any enumeration of truths in which we believe; faith itself is more than the beliefs by which it is articulated. So too, hope is neither essentially bound to, nor exhausted by, any of the determinate realities toward which our hopes are directed.

If one were to think of hope as essentially tied to particular objective realities, one could easily dismiss hope as fragile, if not illusory. Any one of the specifiable things for which we hope may fail to come to pass. Does this mean that our hope was excessive? Does disappointment teach us to hope less? Rather, disappointment might be described as an educative experience, which weans our hope from illusory attachments and liberates it for the transcendent. When it is truly itself, hope can be detached from everything a man can specify to himself as its object.

The Heidelberg physician, Herbert Plügge, published in 1962 a number of psychological studies on incurably ill patients.[7] He found that, at the very point when the hope of a physical cure was abandoned, there very often arose not despair or bitterness but a vague and nameless kind of hope which he called "fundamental" or "authentic" hope. It was directed toward nothing which a person might expect to receive or "have," but rather, as Pieper puts it, toward "what a person 'is,' with the selfness of the human being." [8] This inarticulate hope, transcending every kind of representation, is not destroyed by disappointments, but comes into its own through the loss of all illusions.

Despair, properly so called, is the abandonment of transcendent hope. When our particular hopes are disappointed, the possibility of despair confronts us. We are tempted to decide that there is no way out at all. But to assert this would be to anticipate our own destruction, to go to pieces under the threat of a sentence which has not yet been pronounced. The temptation to despair, by challenging the very existence of hope, enables hope to rise to its full stature. "The truth is," writes Marcel, "that there can, strictly speaking, be no hope except where the temptation to despair exists. Hope is the act by which this temptation is actively and victoriously overcome." [9]

Is hope as a transcendent attitude justifiable? In contrast to many authors, who would seek to vindicate man's transcendent hope in terms of previously ascertainable grounds, Peter Berger argues from the fact of hope itself to the reality of the transcendent. The kind of hope we have been describing would be, in Berger's vocabulary, a "signal" of the transcendent. In his own words:

Man's "no" to death—be it in the frantic fear of his own annihilation, in moral courage at the death of a loved other, or in death-defying acts of courage and self-sacrifice—appears to be an intrinsic constituent of his being. There seems to be a death-refusing hope at the very core of our *humanitas*. While empirical reason indicates that this hope is an illusion, there is something in us that, however shamefacedly in an age of triumphant rationality, goes on saying "no!" and even says "no!" to the ever so plausible explanations of empirical reason. [10]

Since transcendent hope, by its very nature, goes against the appearances, one would look in vain for external evidences establishing its validity. By its nature it is "hope against hope." But man's spontaneous tendency to hope is itself an evidence, "the evidence of things unseen." Hope bears witness to its own divine origin when it feels secure enough to dispense with the conventional calculations of human prudence, and to dispense with empirical support.

If there is any rational (or discursive) justification for this vague, implicit, transcendental hope, I should be inclined to seek it, somewhat as Kant did, in the realm of practical reason. Kant argued that without belief in God and in immortality—without acceptance of a God who knows us for what we are and who rewards our reverent fidelity—a man would not have the necessary motivation to submit, as he knows he ought to, to the demands of the moral law. Kant here substantiates, within the framework of his own systematic positions, Plato's contention that it is impossible for the good man to be harmed by doing good, even though he must pay the price of life itself. Plato goes further than Kant in maintaining that the moral argument for a future life has speculative as well as practical validity. For if it were not speculatively true, we should have to admit that the universe is ultimately amoral and absurd. Besides, a hope which it is necessary for man to have in order to live well cannot be illusory and deceptive. Otherwise man would be simultaneously obliged to believe (on practical grounds) and to disbelieve (on speculative grounds). He would be in an absurd and contradictory situation.

The pragmatic argument for the legitimacy of hope can easily be substantiated by instances from a variety of situations. I have already referred to the medical studies of Herbert Plügge on patients facing the prospect of imminent death from incurable diseases. Similar findings are offered by many studies of the behavior of prisoners in concentration camps during World War II. Viktor Frankl in his little classic, *Man's Search for Meaning,* speaks of the moral and physical degeneration of prisoners once they had lost their faith in the future. "Any attempt to restore man's inner strength in the camp [at Auschwitz] had first to succeed in showing him some future goal. . . . Woe to him who saw no more sense in his life, no aim, no purpose, and therefore no point in carrying on. He was soon lost." [11]

The ultimate meaningfulness of life, as Frankl has said in this and other works, cannot possibly depend on finite and contingent factors. He speaks of the "purgatory" which he himself endured in the concentration camp after the loss of the manuscript of his first book:

Later, when my own death seemed imminent, I asked myself what my life had been for. Nothing was left which would survive me. No child of my own. Not even a spiritual child such as the manuscript. But after wrestling with my despair for hours, shivering from typhus fever, I finally asked myself what sort of meaning could depend on whether a manuscript of mine was printed. I would not give a damn for it. But if there is a meaning, it is unconditional meaning, and neither suffering nor dying can detract from it. [12]

Frankl here comes close to repeating, in a far different theological framework, what Josef Pieper maintained in his 1951 lecture on "The Hope of the Martyrs," namely that there is no point in speaking seriously about hope unless there is hope for the martyr—that is, for one whose expectations within this world have been entirely erased. [13]

To verify the beneficial effects of a transcendent hope, we do not need to limit ourselves to boundary situations such as the death camps and religious martyrdom. Daily life puts heavy demands on men's generosity, patience, tolerance, courage, and perseverance. Transcendent hope, by placing man's true security beyond anything this world can give or take away, bestows a sovereign freedom of action. It protects a man from falling prey to a cynical nihilism which is at root bitter and rebellious. It helps to cure the weakness which undermines our best efforts. If we could really locate our hopes where the center of meaning of our lives is to be found—that is, in a transcendent fulfillment—we would not react so defensively when our position, reputation, or property is attacked. We would not become hostile, aggressive, devious and dishonest. A transcendent hope, freeing us from pessimism and anxiety, would enable us to commit ourselves generously and enthusiastically to the tasks before us and, if necessary, to accept what, in the eyes of men, appears to be defeat.

II

Presupposing now that transcendent hope is justifiable, either intuitively by reason of its own attributes or discursively by reason of its beneficial effects, and that despair is never an appropriate human attitude, I should like now to turn to my second major point, to the effect that Christianity is to be esteemed as a provider of hope. The non-Christian, as we have seen, can possess very meaningful implicit (or nameless) hope. But Christianity, I shall maintain, is a uniquely powerful thematization of hope, and as such it focuses, directs, and fortifies the fragile, existential hope which we have thus far been considering.

In the remarks that follow I shall not attempt to compare Christianity with any other religion, though such comparison would be relevant to a complete apologetics. I shall simply compare the condition of the Christian with that of the man who lacks any articulate religious faith.

First of all, it must be recognized that the Christian doctrine of God and man gives powerful motives for hope. God, according to the Bible, is both loving and powerful. If he were loving but not powerful, our hope would not be secure, because he might prove incapable of accomplishing the good things he intends. If, on the other hand, God were powerful but not loving, men would still have no solid basis for hope. Instead they would have to stand in dread of God's arbitrary cruelty or of his just punishments. The God of the Bible, however, is both powerful and forgiving. His mercy is above all his works. Since God both rewards the virtuous and holds out hope of pardon to the wicked, belief in him brings with it a lively and consoling hope.

Christian anthropology, moreover, is able to account for man's irrepressible tendency to hope, of which we have been speaking, and to show the justification for this tendency. According to the New Testament, hope is instilled in us by the Holy Spirit who has been poured forth into our hearts and who gives testimony within us that we are sons of God and fellow heirs with Christ (Rom 8:14-17). Being gifted already with the "first fruits of the Spirit" (*ibid.,* v. 23), we have already received some anticipation of the eternal blessings. This grace-experience provides the psychological basis for that capacity to "hope against hope" which is so highly praised by the biblical writers.

Theology therefore puts us in a position to account, in some degree, for the transcendent hope so admirably described by Marcel and Berger. Hope, like faith, is a grace. It is grounded not in anything that a man can point to or objectively verify, but in a deep pre-conceptual experience of the God who lovingly communicates himself in grace.

By accepting the Christian doctrine of God and man, we can solidify and thematize the implicit hope that arises, by a kind of instinct, within the human heart. The theological reasons give strength, security, clarity, and joy to a hope that would otherwise be troubled, threatened, and obscure. Revelation enables us to proclaim a hope of which we should otherwise only stammer.

If we take time to examine more closely the attributes of Christian hope, we shall be further struck by its capacity to bring out the best that is in man. Christianity offers man a hope that is invincible, comprehensive, realistic, and fruitful. Let me say a few words about each of these four attributes.

Christian hope is *invincible* because it is founded not on creatures but on God. We cannot entrust ourselves with total confidence to any created agency. The evolutionary process, not being God, might fall short of its goal. Our fellow men, even at best, are not completely reliable, and therefore we should not totally rely upon them. Of Jesus himself it is written that he did not entrust himself to those who believed in him, "for he himself knew what was in man" (Jn 2:25).

A hope totally centered in God cannot collapse because it is built upon an unshakable foundation. "Heaven and earth will pass away, but my words will not pass away" (Mt 24:35). Because it rests upon the one who alone can never prove false, our hope is well described in Hebrews (6:19) as a "sure and steadfast anchor of the soul." Expressing this sense of invincibility, Paul can conclude his great hymn to hope with the triumphant cry: "I am sure that neither death, nor life, nor angels, nor principalities, nor height, nor depth, nor anything else in all creation will be able to separate us from the love of God in Christ Jesus our Lord" (Rom 8:38-39).

The second characteristic of Christian hope is its *comprehensiveness*, its unlimited breadth. It is not simply an individual hope, a hope of each man for himself. A purely private hope might narrow men's outlook, making them selfish and inconsiderate. Theology, however, teaches that God's redemptive love, the basis of our hope, is extended to all men in Christ. There is not a single individual on earth—even the most obdurate sinner—for whom we may not and should not hope. We therefore hope not just for ourselves but for one another. We are brought together into a community of hope. "There is one body and one Spirit, just as you were called to the one hope that belongs to your call" (Eph 4:4). The corporate dimension of our hope is expressed in various biblical images, such as that of the "Kingdom of God." In the final Kingdom our common hope will be fulfilled in such a way that we will be sharers in one another's joy.

To speak of the Kingdom of God in terms of human solidarity is still too narrow. In its full meaning, hope embraces even the inanimate world. Paul tells us that the whole of creation "waits with eager longing for the revealing of the sons of God";

all creation is "groaning in travail together" until such time as it will be "set free from its bondage to decay" (Rom 8:19-22). Man's hope, therefore, extends to the material world about him. With the apocalyptic writers of the Old and New Testaments, we can eagerly anticipate "a new heaven and a new earth" (Is 65:17, 66:22, 2 Pt 3:13, Apoc 21:1). In these days of ecological consciousness it is well to reflect on the cosmic dimensions of our Christian hope.

Third, Christian hope is *realistic*. It can look at the world with sober realism, and is not obliged to take refuge in illusions. The Christian has no need to shrink in fear from the prospect of poverty, disgrace, captivity, physical pain, apparent failure, even death. None of these eventualities dejects him because he has been taught that to share in Christ's sufferings is the normal way to prepare oneself to share in his glory. He does not feel compelled to look upon man's future, in some pollyannaish way, as an endless progress. He soberly recognizes that no Utopia will ever be constructed through human planning.

The Christian has little enthusiasm for what Ernst Bloch holds forth as the ideal of a "Kingdom of God—without God." [14] Such a dream bears all the marks of an illusion concocted by an alienated mind. Like a mirage, it recedes further and further into the distance as we march toward it. And even if attainable, it would not satisfy the deepest cravings of the human spirit. If man could be so domesticated that he ceased to yearn for the transcendent, he would have forfeited his greatest claim to dignity. In reply to Nietzsche, Père de Lubac acutely observed: " 'Nothing but the earth' is the cruelest of all illusions." [15]

Lastly, Christian hope is *fruitful*. Rightly understood, it is not a sterile aspiration for eternity which divests the things of time of all interest and importance. The believer knows well that his own redemption and that of his fellow men will not be accomplished without human cooperation. Like the Incarnate Christ, the Christian is turned in compassion toward the earth and its children. Only by seeking to realize on earth some anticipation of the Kingdom of God can we hope to have a part in the final Kingdom in eternity. Christian hope therefore impels us to follow Christ in his life of obedience and service. In view of the biblical teaching, "As a man sows, so shall he reap," we dare not be idle.

It is often objected that because Christian hope is concentrated on what happens beyond historical time, it deprives man's activity on earth of any real significance. This charge, at its most extreme, includes the accusation that religion is the "opium of the people" and that it seeks to quiet men's legitimate aspirations by promising them "a pie in the sky." This charge is difficult to answer, because Christians are not totally agreed as to the relationship between man's toil on earth and the final consummation of history. Some world-renouncing eschatologists profess an almost Plotinian contempt for the world, and concentrate almost exclusively on the blessings of the life to come. Other socially involved Christians stress the importance of human activity almost to the point of seeming to hold that man has a commission to build the Kingdom of God here on earth.

A balanced view, in my opinion, would avoid both these extremes. God does not dispose of man without regard for what man makes of himself. But the final Kingdom, according to the Christian sources, is not something that man can achieve by his own planning and resourcefulness. Just as the resurrection of Jesus presupposes that Jesus lived and died in total fidelity to God, so the final transfiguration of the cosmos presupposes that men have labored and suffered in selfless love. In this sense, man's fidelity to the moral demands of the gospel is a pre-condition for the full realization of the Kingdom. It is not necessary, however, that man's efforts should always be attended by what the world can recognize as success. It is quite possible that Christ's faithful followers, like their master, may have to suffer rejection and humiliation. This they can willingly accept because their hope is transcendent.

The most celebrated apologist of Christian hope, Teilhard de Chardin, seems to express a more terrestrial hope. At one point he suggests as the hypothesis most congenial to his system that the final maturation of mankind will consist in a gradual recession of evil. "Disease and hunger," he writes, "will be conquered by science and we will no longer need to fear them in any acute form. And, conquered by the sense of the earth and human sense, hatred and internecine struggles will have disappeared in the ever-warmer radiance of Omega. Some sort of unanimity will reign over the entire mass of the noö-sphere. The final convergence will take place in *peace*." [16] This, however, is only one of several possibilities envisaged by Teilhard. In various texts he admits darker eventualities as also likely: on the material plane, the exhaustion of the physical resources of the planet, and, on the human plane, a profound schism leading to a paroxysm of evil, an ecstasy of discord, a strike in the noösphere.[17]

Authentic Christian hope, I submit, is not tied to any particular speculation about the manner in which history will close. We should not imitate those sects which seem to specialize in esoteric interpretations of apocalyptic texts so as to excite the imaginations and emotions of the faithful. The Bible, having no intention of supplying detailed predictions, is content to speak in figurative or hyperbolic language about the events of the end-time. The trustful believer, secure in the faith that God is Lord of history, is content to leave to him not only the times and the moments but also the circumstances of the *parousia*.

The only point I should wish to underscore, in the present context, is that man's activity is not futile. Every thought and word as well as every deed makes an eternal difference. The time and characteristics of the final Kingdom will depend, to some extent, upon man's fidelity to his mission. In a certain sense, man has a hope because he has a mission. Because God has committed a task to man, man can be sure that God will be with those who faithfully perform their mission and that he will crown their efforts in the end.

Before concluding I should like to say a word about the special urgency of Christian hope today. On this point, too, Teilhard de Chardin can be our guide. He was essentially correct, I believe, in his analysis of the historical juncture in which we find ourselves. All over the world, he noted, men are being forced together into closer union thanks to new media of communications, expanding governmental and business networks, and burgeoning associations for purposes of every kind. It is becoming increasingly difficult to exist, act, or even think alone. In fact it appears almost as though mankind were turning into a huge superorganism; and this situation is fraught with immense dangers as well as immense opportunities for good. Many, repelled by the threat of depersonalization and enslavement, seek to resist this process of planetary collectivization. Hence the necessity for hope:

The modern world, with its prodigious growth of complexity, weighs incomparably more heavily upon the shoulders of our generation than did the ancient world upon the shoulders of our forbears. Have you never felt that this added load needs to be compensated for by an added passion, a new sense of purpose? To my mind, this is what is "providentially" arising to sustain our courage—the hope, the belief that some immense fulfilment lies ahead of us.[18]

Elsewhere Teilhard lays down as the essential prerequisite for man's further advance "a great hope held in common." Hope alone, he maintained, can arouse a passionate longing to grow, and can overcome all enervating skepticism, pessimism, weakness of spirit, and heaviness of heart. A hope proportioned to our times, moreover, must make for greater synthesis and unity. "Our hope can only be realized if it finds its expression in greater cohesion and greater human solidarity."[19]

As an apologist to the world of science, Teilhard sought to foster "this great hope held in common" by a retrospective view of the evolutionary process as it has taken place thus far. In virtue of the triumphs of biological evolution against almost incredible odds, he thought it necessary to postulate as an explanation a powerful force of attraction drawing the whole process forward toward itself as the point of ultimate convergence. This hypothesis of an "Omega Center," as Teilhard called it, converged remarkably, in his opinion, with the biblical doctrine of the universal Christ. For the Christian, therefore, Teilhard reasoned, Omega was not merely a scientific hypothesis but a fact to be accepted in faith. The cosmic Christ in Teilhard's system provides the believer with unshakable confidence in the future success of the evolutionary process.

Some have criticized Teilhard's "apologetic of hope" on the ground that it relies too much on merely empirical reasoning regarding the process of biological evolution.[20] There is some basis for this charge, but it should be recognized that biological evolution, as a scientific datum, is not the central feature of Teilhard's apologetic of hope. Instead he is at pains to insist that revelation is needed to set man's hope on a secure basis. The death and resurrection of Christ, as Mooney points out, were for Teilhard "the sole guarantee that God's designs for his universe must inexorably succeed in spite of all opposition."[21]

As presently informed, I should be inclined to quarrel with Teilhard's apparent view that the occurrence of the *parousia* must depend upon the prior success of man's biological and technological evolution on earth. If he had said only that the generous dedication of men animated by selfless love is a necessary prerequisite, I should have no difficulty in agreeing. By inspiring and demanding such selfless love, Christianity has a mission of eschatological moment. By setting forth before mankind the figure of the crucified and risen Lord, the Church can inspire the type of hope most needed by mankind, especially in this crucial period of planetization. Christianity is uniquely adapted to arouse that "great hope held in common" which Teilhard correctly identified as a demand of our times. Thus I believe that there is great value in Teilhard's apologetic of hope.

I do not propose an apologetics of hope as self-sufficient, still less as a substitute for all other forms of apologetics. To show the full credibility of the Christian message it is necessary, today as always, to appeal to the data of history. The story of Jesus of Nazareth cannot be bypassed, for Jesus himself is the most striking sign of the truth of his own message. The resurrection of Jesus stands as the most powerful expression of God's omnipotent redemptive love. But the resurrection remains largely inaccessible to the historian, if he follows the conventional methods of scientific research. He has no way of dealing with such a unique phenomenon, in which the barriers between time and eternity dissolve, and the end of all history is anticipated. To accept the reality of this event one must already be, or at least one must be disposed to become, a man of transcendental hope. Only he who is prepared to believe in a God who finally triumphs over every enemy, not excepting death, can credit the testimonies.

The estimate which one makes of the credibility of the accounts, therefore, depends in great measure on how one hopes. As Moltmann has well said, "the point of the historical debate on the resurrection of Christ was never merely historical." [22] The real question at issue is "a struggle for the future of history and for the right way of recognizing, hoping, and working for that future." [23] Thus the apologetics of history, as it deals with the resurrection, interlocks with the apologetics of hope. What one makes of the narratives depends in great part on how one answers the question, "What may I hope for?"

To be generally effective in persuading men to accept the gospel, an apologetics of hope would have to be something more than a theory about what Christians ought to be. It would have to be a convincing description of what they actually are. In the world today, the church-going public does not always appear as a radiant sign of hope. Christians, like other men, seem to be primarily concerned for those things which, in the words of Jesus, the Gentiles seek. They are worried about material possessions, honors, and the like. For this reason, more than any other, they are often anxious and disturbed, gloomy and dejected. They do not really put their trust in God. Thus they become, in some measure, a countersign of hope.

Apologetics can at least point out that these attitudes are obstacles to Christian proclamation. Before addressing itself to unbelievers, apologetics has a task with regard to Christians, many of whom are greatly in need of conversion to the gospel. If it can persuade the Christian faithful to accept wholeheartedly the hope which is their rightful heritage, apologetics may perhaps make an important contribution to the future of the Church. An apologetics of hope, therefore, is in my opinion much to be desired.

NOTES

1. B. Pascal, *Pensées* (ed. Brunschvicg, fr. 172), trans. by W. F. Trotter, New York, 1941, pp. 60-61.
2. *Critique of Pure Reason*, trans. by N. K. Smith, New York, 1961, pp. 635-44. See also C. C. J. Webb, *Kant's Philosophy of Religion*, Oxford, 1926, pp. 1-2.
3. *Critique of Practical Reason*, trans. by T. K. Abbott, London, 1909, p. 227.
4. *L'Action*, Paris, 1893, p. vii.
5. Article by F. Mallet (pseudonym for Blondel) in *Annales de philosophie chrétienne*, March, 1907, pp. 573-74.
6. "Sketch of a Phenomenology and a Metaphysic of Hope," *Homo Viator*, trans. by Emma Craufurd, Chicago, Regnery, 1951, p. 32.
7. Herbert Plügge, *Wohlbefinden und Missbefinden. Beiträge zu einer medizinischen Anthropologie*, Tübingen, 1962. Josef Pieper, to whose work I am indebted for this reference, points out the particular interest of the two sections "On Suicidal Patients" and "On Hope." See J. Pieper, *Hope and History*, trans. by R. and C. Winston, New York, 1969, pp. 24-26. See also the discussion of Plügge's findings in Wolfhart Pannenberg, *Jesus: God and Man*, trans. by Lewis L. Wilkins and Duane Prisbe, Philadelphia, 1968, p. 85, note 78.
8. Pieper, *op cit.*, p. 26.
9. *Homo Viator*, *op. cit.*, p. 36.
10. Peter L. Berger, *A Rumor of Angels*, Garden City, 1970, p. 80.
11. Viktor E. Frankl, *Man's Search for Meaning*, trans. by Ilse Lasch, New York, 1963, p. 121.

12. Viktor E. Frankl, *The Will to Meaning,* Cleveland, 1969, p. 156.
13. "Sur l'espérance des martyrs," in *Espoir humain et espérance chrétienne* (Semaíne des Intellectuels catholiques), Paris, 1951, pp. 76-84.
14. Ernst Bloch, *Das Prinzip Hoffnung,* Frankfurt am Main, 1959, p. 1413; as cited by Pieper, *Hope and History, op. cit.,* p. 64.
15. *The Discovery of God,* trans. by Alexander Dru, Chicago, 1967, p. 179.
16. Pierre Teilhard de Chardin, *The Phenomenon of Man,* trans. by Bernard Wall, New York, 1959, pp. 287-88.
17. *Ibid.,* pp. 288-89. See also his *The Future of Man,* trans. by Norman Denny, New York, 1964, pp. 306-308.
18. *The Future of Man, op. cit.,* p. 117.
19. *Ibid.,* p. 72.
20. Pieter Smulders, *The Design of Teilhard de Chardin,* trans. by Arthur Gibson, Westminster, 1967. pp. 151-61.
21. Christopher F. Mooney, *Teilhard de Chardin and the Mystery of Christ,* New York, 1966, p. 143; cf. Mooney's comment on Smulders, p. 246, note 95.
22. Jürgen Moltman, *Theology of Hope,* trans, by J. W. Leitch, London, 1967, p. 182.
23. *Ibid.*